I0469898

Arguing *Marbury v. Madison*

Arguing
Marbury v. Madison

Edited by

MARK TUSHNET

STANFORD LAW AND POLITICS

An imprint of Stanford University Press • *Stanford, California* 2005

Stanford University Press
Stanford, California
© 2005 by the Board of Trustees of the
Leland Stanford Junior University

No part of this book may be reproduced or transmitted in any form
or by any means, electronic or mechanical, including photocopying
and recording, or in any information storage or retrieval system
without the prior written permission of Stanford University Press.

Library of Congress Cataloging-in-Publication Data

Arguing *Marbury v. Madison* / edited by Mark Tushnet.
      p. cm.
   Includes bibliographical references and index.
   ISBN 0-8047-5226-5 (cloth : alk. paper) —
   ISBN 0-8047-5227-3 (pbk. : alk. paper)
      1. Judicial review—United States—History. 2. Separation of
powers—United States—History. 3. Marbury, William, 1761 or 2–
1835—Trials, litigation, etc. 4. Madison, James, 1751–1836—Trials,
litigation, etc. I. Title: Arguing Marbury versus Madison.
II. Tushnet, Mark.
KF4575.A965 2005
347.73'12—dc22

                                          2005015408

Original Printing 2005
Last figure below indicates year of this printing:
14 13 12 11 10 09 08 07 06 05

Typeset at Stanford University Press in 10/14.5 Minion

To the memory of Gerald Gunther

Contents

Contributors

MARK TUSHNET is Carmack Waterhouse Professor of Constitutional Law, Georgetown University Law Center.

DAVID A. STRAUSS is Harry N. Wyatt Professor of Law, University of Chicago.

SUZANNA SHERRY is Cal Turner Professor in Law and Leadership, Vanderbilt University.

SUSAN LOW BLOCH is Professor of Law, Georgetown University Law Center.

BARRY FRIEDMAN is Jacob Fuchsberg Professor of Law, New York University.

DOUGLAS REED is Associate Professor of Government, Georgetown University.

STEPHEN M. GRIFFIN is Rutledge C. Clement, Jr., Professor of Public and Constitutional Law, Tulane University.

VICKI C. JACKSON is Professor of Law, Georgetown University Law Center.

LOUIS MICHAEL SEIDMAN is Professor of Law, Georgetown University Law Center.

The judges participating in the oral argument are HARRY EDWARDS and DAVID SENTELLE, U.S. Court of Appeals for the District of Columbia Circuit, and SONIA SOTOMAYOR and ROBERT KATZMANN, U.S. Court of Appeals for the Second Circuit.

Arguing *Marbury v. Madison*

Introduction

Marbury v. Madison, decided in February 1803, is conventionally taken as the origin of judicial review in the United States. As Suzanna Sherry's chapter here shows, scholars have known for years that this understanding is wrong. The Constitution's framers assumed that the national courts would have the power to overturn laws that the judges found were inconsistent with the limitations the Constitution placed on government power. In the decades before *Marbury* state courts around the country exercised the power of judicial review as well.

The arguments—that is, the reasons—for judicial review were well-established by the time Chief Justice John Marshall wrote the Court's opinion in *Marbury*. The argument—that is, the presentation to the Supreme Court of their positions by advocates for both sides—in *Marbury*, in contrast, did not even take place. As David Strauss's reflections on presenting the executive's position indicate, President Thomas Jefferson ensured that no one showed up to offer the Court Madison's side of the case.

On the two hundredth anniversary of *Marbury v. Madison* four prominent federal judges sat as a bench to hear oral arguments in the case—although, as Judge Harry Edwards indicated at the argument's conclusion—not to render judgment. The transcript of that argument opens this book. Professor Strauss and I attempted to present arguments, based on the materials available in 1803, that made sense to lawyers in 2003. We could not forget, of course, what judicial review had become over the succeeding two hundred years. Still, we attempted to rely only on ideas about the U.S. Constitution and about constitutionalism more generally that were common currency in 1803. At the least, the argument shows how far we have traveled from the origins of judicial review.

The facts of *Marbury* are familiar, so only a summary is necessary here. The case arose out of the confluence of policy and politics. Members of the first Congress knew that federal courts were needed, but they did not have a firm grasp on the details of good institutional design—not surprisingly, as they were designing a system from scratch. They also worried that there might not be enough judges with a sufficiently national orientation to staff a full court system, and they wanted to save money. Finally, they faced some political constraints arising out of the nervousness about national power that had led the Constitutional Convention to propose, not a constitutionally entrenched system of national courts, but only that Congress would have the power to create such courts.

The first Judiciary Act of 1789 tried to accommodate all these concerns. It set up a system with three levels. At the bottom were federal district judges, at least one in each state. The district judges handled minor matters on their own. At the top was the Supreme Court. In the middle were circuit courts. The circuit courts were not conventional appeals courts of the sort we know today. They were the trial courts in which some major cases were to be heard first. Among these were so-called diversity cases, suits between citizens of different states, and between citizens and noncitizens. These lawsuits frequently were the continuation of disputes arising out of the Revolutionary War and the economic turmoil of its aftermath. The circuit courts were staffed by a district judge and two Supreme Court justices, later reduced to one. The justices therefore had to "ride circuit" to sit in the circuit courts, in addition to their duties as Supreme Court justices.

The next decade showed that this design was an administrative nightmare. Supreme Court justices would have to hear appeals from their own decisions in the circuit courts. More important were the physical burdens that circuit riding placed on the justices. Distances were long and roads were bad. The justices grumbled about how hard it was to go from the nation's capital out on circuit, then return for the Supreme Court's own work. Pressures for reforming the structure of the nation's judiciary built up over the 1790s.

Congress eventually responded with the Judiciary Act of 1801. It expanded the jurisdiction of the lower federal courts, for the first time giving them the power to hear cases raising issues of national law. The Act abolished the existing circuit courts, thereby eliminating circuit riding. It created in their place six new circuit courts, to be staffed by sixteen new federal judges.

Considered as a reform aimed at improving the administration of justice in the national courts, the 1801 Judiciary Act was a sensible response to problems that had arisen over the prior decade. But in 1801 and 1802 it could not be considered only in those terms. The Act was also a major episode in the transformation of national politics. The political setting gave *Marbury* its importance.

The Constitution's framers imagined that the system they designed would lead to the selection of the best national leaders from all over the country, who would combine representation of their localities with a national perspective. They did not expect that nationally organized political parties would emerge rapidly, but they were wrong. Such parties began to develop in conflicts between Thomas Jefferson and Alexander Hamilton in the first years of the 1790s, and crystallized into real organized parties by the end of the decade.

The creation of a party system transformed the constitutional order. The election of 1800 demonstrated how a national crisis could arise when parties were inserted into a Constitution that did not expect them to exist. In that election Thomas Jefferson and his running mate Aaron Burr clearly prevailed over John Adams and his running mate Charles Cotesworth Pinckney. "Prevailing" meant that electors pledged to Jefferson and Burr outnumbered electors pledged to Adams and Pinckney. The 1789 Constitution provided that each elector would cast two votes, without distinguishing between votes for the presidential and vice-presidential candidates. The electors cast their votes and, because of poor planning, Jefferson and Burr received the same number of votes. This sent the election to the House of Representatives, which went through more than thirty votes before some of Adams's supporters resolved the crisis by letting Jefferson become president.

Jefferson and the Democratic Party he headed swept the elections in late 1800, gaining control not only of the presidency but of the Senate and the House of Representatives as well. But, once again, a flaw in the 1789 Constitution emerged. Jefferson would not take office until March 4, 1801, leaving Adams and his Federalist Party allies in control of the government from November 1800 through the end of February 1801. The Judiciary Act of 1801 was adopted on February 13, 1801. Understandably, Jefferson and the Democrats saw it as a politically motivated statute, not an administrative reform. The Act would give the outgoing and repudiated president the opportunity to entrench sixteen of his political allies in the new circuit courts. Even more, in what Jeffersonians took to be dramatic evidence of the Act's political motivation, the

Act reduced the size of the Supreme Court from six to five as soon as a sitting justice left the Court, which meant that Jefferson would not have the chance to fill the first vacancy that occurred during his term.

Jefferson and his allies immediately moved to repeal the Judiciary Act of 1801. Members of Congress engaged in an extended debate over the constitutionality of the repeal, with Federalists contending that repealing the 1801 Act would violate the Constitution's requirement that federal judges have life tenure by eliminating the sixteen new judgeships. The question of judicial review recurrently arose during these debates, with Federalists asserting that, were the repeal to be enacted, the Supreme Court would hold it unconstitutional. Fearing that the Federalists were right, the Democratic Congress included a provision in the repeal, eventually adopted as the Judiciary Act of 1802, postponing the next sitting of the Supreme Court, apparently hoping that a cooling-off period might lead the justices to accept what Congress had done.

Marbury raised questions about the power of the courts to declare national legislation unconstitutional, and so implicated the repeal of the Judiciary Act of 1801. Marbury himself, though, was not one of the sixteen judges who lost their jobs as a result of the repeal. He got his job (or seemed to) from *another* statute enacted by the lame-duck Congress in 1801. That statute created a new circuit court of the District of Columbia, the significance of which is discussed in Susan Low Bloch's essay here. This second statute also authorized the president to appoint forty-five new justices of the peace in the District. Adams rushed to fill the new posts, but—as every student of *Marbury* knows—the paperwork was incomplete when Jefferson took office. Four commissions signed by Adams were sitting on the desk of his Secretary of State, awaiting delivery to the new justices of the peace, on March 4. As the oral argument indicates, the Secretary of State was John Marshall himself, serving for a few weeks as both Chief Justice of the United States and Secretary of State (another indication of the underdeveloped character of the national government at the time). Jefferson directed his Secretary of State James Madison to withhold delivery, whereupon Marbury sued.

Readers of this collection will already know the complexities of the questions Marshall found in Marbury's case, and I do not plan to address them in detail here. But it is worth noting that some receive less attention than they should. Marshall's opinion for the Supreme Court conceals some of the problems with establishing the merits of Marbury's claim. Was Marbury entitled to his commission? The oral argument suggests not: All federal judges have to have life tenure, but Marbury's term was limited by statute to five years. Perhaps, then, Marbury was not a "judge" in a constitutional sense. What then might he have been? Perhaps an employee of the executive branch, something like today's administrative law judges. But, then, the designation of a specific term of office might be an unconstitutional intrusion on the president's power to discharge executive branch employees, a matter that received some attention in the first half of the nineteenth century—in contrast to the inattention paid during those years to *Marbury*'s holding on judicial review. And, further, even if, as Marshall eventually concluded, Marbury's appointment as a justice of the peace was complete when Adams signed his commission, perhaps Jefferson's refusal to deliver the document should be treated as firing Marbury, an act, on this view, within the president's complete discretion.

Beyond this are the questions, at the heart of Marshall's opinion, about whether Marshall offered a defensible (or even plausible) interpretation of the jurisdictional statute on which Marbury relied, or a defensible (or even plausible) interpretation of the provisions of Article III of the Constitution on which Marshall relied in holding unconstitutional Congress's attempt—as Marshall saw it—to give the Supreme Court jurisdiction over cases like Marbury's. Generations of law students have worried over these questions, and I can add nothing to the well-developed discussions of them.

Addressing the constitutional questions did give Marshall a chance to establish that the national courts had the power to declare acts of Congress unconstitutional—not, in itself, a controversial proposition. What would have been controversial was a more direct confrontation with Jefferson's administration and the Jeffersonian Congress. That confrontation would have occurred had the Supreme Court agreed with the Federalists' objections to the repeal of the 1801 Judiciary Act.

A week after *Marbury* was announced, the Court again avoided that confrontation, in *Stuart v. Laird*. John Laird won a judgment against Hugh Stuart from one of the circuit courts created by the 1801 Act. He then had to get hold of Stuart's property to satisfy the judgment. Doing so required that he go back to court. But, by the time Laird returned to court, the 1801 Act had been repealed and the circuit judge who had heard Laird's case was gone. Instead, Congress told litigants like Laird that they could go to the revived old circuit courts, the ones with a district judge and Supreme Court justices riding circuit. Laird did so, and got what he wanted. Stuart then appealed to the Supreme Court, arguing that only the court that issued the judgment in the first place could enforce it and that the Constitution did not allow Supreme Court justices to ride circuit. In three paragraphs the Court unanimously rejected Stuart's arguments. On circuit riding, the Court said that the practice had been in place from the beginning of the national court system, and that this practice was a "contemporary interpretation of the most forcible nature." The Court treated Congress's decision to direct the second case into the old circuit court as a mere administrative question, involving the "transfer" of a case from one court to another. Nowhere did the Court discuss the reason the transfer was necessary, that the judge who had heard the case the first time had had his court kicked out from under him. Perhaps, though, the Court's decision implicitly upheld the elimination of the circuit courts created in 1801. A contrary decision would almost certainly have led to efforts in Congress to retaliate against the Supreme Court, perhaps through an aggressive use of the impeachment process.

Marbury confirmed that the national courts had the power of judicial review. *Stuart v. Laird* confirmed that the justices were likely to be prudent in exercising that power—at least for a while. What was the power's reach? I think it helpful to distinguish between what some scholars call "departmentalist" judicial review, itself with two variants, and judicial review as judicial supremacy.

The examples of judicial review that preceded *Marbury*, and most of the theoretical discussions of judicial review in the early Republic, adopted what might be called a self-defensive departmentalist view, a position that Professor Strauss supports (modestly) in his argument. According to this view, courts had the power to declare unconstitutional those statutes that interfered with their proper functioning. *Marbury* itself could be seen as exercising self-defensive departmentalist review, with the Court saying that Congress had tried to thrust on the Supreme Court tasks that it could not constitutionally be asked to carry out. Depending on what precisely would count as an intrusion on the courts, self-defensive departmentalist review could have quite a broad scope. Expansive departmentalist review of this sort might allow the courts to refuse to enforce criminal statutes they believed to be unconstitutional, on the theory that Congress in enacting the statute and the executive branch in enforcing it were attempting to dragoon the courts into helping them make effective an unconstitutional law. Marshall's example in *Marbury* of a statute that unconstitutionally allowing conviction of treason on the basis of only one witness might be an example of expansive self-defensive review.

Some aspects of statutory law might lie outside the scope of self-defensive departmentalist review, as when the national government administers an entitlement program through agencies rather than through the courts. Yet, the courts provide valuable resources to the other branches, and in the real world self-defensive departmentalist review might cover an enormous amount of what the government does. For example, another of Marshall's examples involves an unconstitutional tax on the export of cotton. Tax collectors usually find it helpful to use the courts, suing tax delinquents, at which point the courts could declare the tax unconstitutional. Only if the government avoided the courts completely, for example by simply seizing the delinquent's property, might the theory of self-defensive departmentalism fail to provide the courts a chance to invalidate the unconstitutional tax. And, even here, there are some possibilities. The person whose property is seized might sue the government, or the tax collector as an individual, invoking whatever general authority Congress conferred on the courts. At that point a self-defensive departmentalist court could say, "You, Congress, asked us to resolve the kind of problem this lawsuit presents, and we can't resolve it in a way that implicates us in your unconstitutional action, so we will award damages to the taxpayer."

A different version of departmentalism might be called "independent-judgment" departmentalism. According to this view, each branch is entitled to make—and act on—its own independent judgment of what the Constitution means. At least as represented by Professor Strauss, Jefferson held this view. Congress in enacting a statute might be taken to express its judgment that the statute is constitutional; the president in refusing to deliver a commission might be taken to express his judgment that refusing to deliver the commission is constitutional. And, importantly, the fact that a court disagrees with those judgments is of no special significance. It is a datum that Congress or the president might want to take into account. So, for example, it might be that Congress did not focus on the constitutional question when it enacted the statute but that, the defect being called to its attention, it might want to revise the statute or even repeal it. Contemporary theorists have characterized one version of independent-judgment departmentalism as encouraging a view of judicial review, and more broadly of the Constitution, as encouraging dialogues among the branches about the Constitution's meaning. (The metaphor of dialogue has been particularly important in discussions of the Canadian Charter of Rights, which in turn has influenced discussions of the U.S. Constitution.)

The problem with independent-judgment departmentalism is obvious: It seems to be a formula for permanent, or at least recurrent, constitutional crisis. There are many reasons why crises might not occur all that often in a system of independent-judgment departmentalism. The courts' position is likely to have some political support. Getting Congress or the president to do something might be difficult, and not always a matter of high political priority. Compromise rather than confrontation will usually be the easier path.

Still, independent-judgment departmentalism does pose the *risk* of crisis. In the 1830s President Andrew Jackson may have said something like, "John Marshall has made his decision; now let him enforce it," when Jackson disagreed with the Supreme Court's decision in a case involving the rights of native Americans. Independent-judgment departmentalism certainly licenses, and might encourage, presidents and members of Congress to insist on their own constitutional interpretations, in situations were disagreements between the branches might disrupt the orderly functioning of government. One might hope for some way to avoid these crises.

One solution is perhaps not inherent to independent-judgment departmentalism, but might be a component of the worldview that might have made independent-judgment departmentalism attractive to the founding generation. The solution is, in short, statesmanship on all sides, and is exemplified by *Stuart v. Laird*. Precisely because forceful assertions of independent-judgment departmentalism might provoke constitutional crises, prudent statesmen would do what they could to accommodate each other. Sometimes the courts would prudently refrain from acting, as perhaps occurred in *Stuart v. Laird*; sometimes Congress would revise its statutes, perhaps grudgingly, to eliminate the constitutional problems the courts found.

Yet, as James Madison wrote in *The Federalist 10*, "Enlightened statesmen will not always be at the helm." The only other solution to the problem posed by independent-judgment departmentalism is to give someone the last word. Over the two centuries since *Marbury*, the constitutional system in the United States has come to do so by giving the courts the last word, treating judicial review as entailing judicial supremacy. Often the implications of judicial review as judicial supremacy have not been apparent to the public or even to major political actors. Barry Friedman's chapter analyzes why judicial review as judicial supremacy has not always been intensely controversial, arguing that the American public accepts the practice—perhaps because it contributes a kind of stability that would be lacking under any other system of judicial review.

Occasionally, though, judicial review as judicial supremacy becomes controversial. We may be experiencing one such moment today, as the Supreme Court invalidates statutes with broad congressional and popular support, explicitly using a theory of judicial supremacy and sometimes casting aspersions on the ability of Congress to legislate responsibly. Stephen Griffin argues for historicized normative theories of judicial review, which would support different roles for the courts at different times, and criticizes the current Supreme Court for adopting the theory of judicial review as judicial supremacy in an era where, according to Professor Griffin, commitment among legislators to protecting basic rights is quite strong. Vicki Jackson and L. Michael Seidman conclude by raising questions about the possibility of a historicized normative theory and about the extent to which even today we have a democracy of rights that could afford some theory of judicial review other than judicial supremacy.

Americans and constitutionalists around the world have been arguing about *Marbury* for generations. This collection is predicated on the hope that setting those arguments in the context of an argument of the case will contribute new elements to a long conversation.

The Oral Argument in *Marbury v. Madison*

CHAPTER ONE

Transcript of the Oral Argument in
Marbury v. Madison

(Georgetown University Law Center, February 14, 2003)

Marshal: All rise. Oyez, oyez, this honorable Court is now in session.

Judge Edwards: The matter of Marbury versus Madison. We will hear from petitioner, plaintiff please.

Professor Tushnet: May it please the Court. Judge Marbury's case depends on establishing a number of propositions. With your permission I will start with one of them and then expand into others that seem worth exploring to you.[1] I would like to start with the proposition that this Court has jurisdiction to issue a writ of mandamus if it is warranted pursuant to Section 13 of the Judiciary Act. That Act provides—to excerpt it in ways that may need exploration—that the Supreme Court shall have power to issue writs of mandamus in cases warranted by the principles and uses of law to any court appointed or persons holding office . . .[2]

---

[1] Professor Tushnet takes on the more difficult of the questions involved in the case, whether the Court has jurisdiction under the statute Marbury has invoked, expecting to have an easier time discussing the question of whether the Court has the power to declare a statute unconstitutional—an issue that would not arise unless the Court agrees that the statute gives it jurisdiction.

[2] The statute reads in full (subject to a qualification in the next note): "And be it further enacted, That the Supreme Court shall have exclusive jurisdiction of all controversies of a civil nature, where a state is a party, except between a state and its citizens, and

Judge Sotomayor: You are reading part of that sentence.

Professor Tushnet: Yes, I realize that.

Judge Sotomayor: But it's a very important part you're detaching it from.

Professor Tushnet: Yes. The structure of the statute and the policies that underlie it and then the structure of the judiciary provisions taken as a whole make it sensible to read the provision as authorizing this Court to issue a writ of mandamus in an original case.

Judge Sotomayor: Maybe sensible as a policy matter but not one of construction of the sentence.

Professor Tushnet: Let me explore the structure of the provision as a whole and then the particular sentence in which that occurs.

Judge Katzmann: Which edition are you using, the Folwell edition or the Peters edition?[3]

Professor Tushnet: I'm afraid I don't know where I've gotten this copy from.

Judge Katzmann: The Folwell edition which I understand the Court may have

---

except also between a state and citizens of other states, or aliens, in which latter case it shall have original but not exclusive jurisdiction. And shall have exclusively all such jurisdiction of suits or proceedings against ambassadors, or other public ministers, or their domestics, or domestic servants, as a court of law can have or exercise consistently with the law of nations; and original, but not exclusive jurisdiction of all suits brought by ambassadors, or other public ministers, or in which a consul, or vice consul, shall be a party. And the trial of issues of fact in the Supreme Court, in all actions at law against citizens of the United States, shall be by jury. The Supreme Court shall also have appellate jurisdiction from the circuit courts and courts of the several states, in the cases herein specially provided for; and shall have power to issue writs of prohibition to the district courts, when proceeding as courts of admiralty and maritime jurisdiction, and writs of mandamus, in cases warranted by the principles and usages of law, to any courts appointed, or persons holding office, under the authority of the United States."

[3]The Folwell version, published in 1796, has the last sentence of Section 13 punctuated differently from the Peters version, published in 1845 and quoted in the prior note. In the Folwell version, the final sentence reads: "The supreme court shall also have appellate jurisdiction from the circuit courts and courts of the several states, in the cases herein after specially provided for: And shall have power to issue writs of prohibition to the district courts, when proceeding as courts of admiralty and maritime jurisdiction, and writs of mandamus, in cases warranted by the principle and usages of law, to any courts appointed, or persons holding office, under the authority of the United States."

had access to, there the punctuation mark is a colon rather than a semi-colon and begins with a capital A. Does that make any difference to your argument?

Professor Tushnet: Our view is that whether it is a colon or a semi-colon, the structure of the section identifies four separate grounds of jurisdiction for the Court.[4] The first sentence enumerates original exclusive jurisdiction in a certain category of cases. That sentence then has a semi-colon with another section that says original but not exclusive jurisdiction. The next sentence says the Supreme Court shall have appellate jurisdiction. That's clearly a third item, and then there is this final provision referring to issues writs of prohibition and writs of mandamus. Whether that be separated by a semi-colon or a colon, it seems best read as adding a fourth ground of jurisdiction for this Court. So . . .

Judge Sotomayor: If it's not read that way and it stays attached to its preceding clause, then we would only have the right of appellate review.

Professor Tushnet: If this fourth clause or set of clauses is read as modifying the first set of clauses in that sentence, then it would justify only writs of mandamus in cases where the Court already has appellate jurisdiction with one possible qualification. The clause says "to any courts appointed or persons holding office under the authority of the United States," and although it's possible to read the persons holding office clause as tied to the existence of a case in a lower court, again the structure—again, "any courts appointed or persons holding office"— if that's read as any persons holding office, it would seem to refer more broadly to a group, not merely clerks of the court and the like.[5] We do not contend that the reading that this clause confers original jurisdiction on the Supreme Court is the only possible reading of the clause. It makes sense structurally in terms of this statute, in terms of this provision. It also makes sense as a matter of policy that Congress could reasonably make a judgment that issuing writs of mandamus to high federal officials should be something left to the judgment of this Court by conferring jurisdiction on you to do so. That would be true whether or not there

---

[4] Here Professor Tushnet begins to struggle with the fact that the natural reading of the statute is contrary to the position he is maintaining.

[5] Here Professor Tushnet offers an alternative approach to the case, suggesting that it involves a request for a writ of mandamus to a "person holding office" under the authority of the United States—that is, the Secretary of State. Again, though, a more natural reading is that the provision refers to officers of the lower courts, such as court clerks, who might have to be directed to do something by the Supreme Court.

was jurisdiction in any other court to do so. You might decide that, with respect to the Secretary of State as in this case, it's appropriate for you to be the body issuing a writ of mandamus but, with respect to some customs officials in New York, another court would be the appropriate court

Judge Edwards: Is it correct that implicit in your argument you have no other base, you are conceding there is no other possible basis for jurisdiction, you either win under Section 13 on the jurisdictional question or you are out of court?

Professor Tushnet: We do rest on Section 13, yes.

Judge Katzmann: So in part you are making a geographic argument, saying that with respect to customs officials the concerns are different than the Secretary of State.

Professor Tushnet: There is a component of a geographic concern, but—I'll get to this in just a moment—that concern could be alleviated by identifying jurisdiction in a local District of Columbia court to issue a writ of mandamus that would not be available to any other court, any other lower federal court. We believe . . .

Judge Sotomayor: Would it be a more natural reading for us to assume that our original jurisdiction is limited to those cases that the Constitution gave us original jurisdiction and to types of officers encompassed in that, ambassadors, ministers, etc., and that anybody else should be subject to appellate jurisdiction only? If a policy question was at issue the Congress established the policy, it told us who we should hear from originally.

Professor Tushnet: Addressing that argument requires, we believe, attention to the exceptions clause of Article III, Section 2.[6] If I understood your point, it was that Article III, Section 2 allocates jurisdiction;[7] let me call this exclusively, but this may be an inapt term . . .

---

[6] At this point Professor Tushnet suggests that Section 13 should be interpreted in light of the constitutional provision authorizing Congress to make exceptions to the Supreme Court's appellate jurisdiction—here, suggesting that the provision giving the Court jurisdiction to issue the writ of mandamus in its original jurisdiction should be understood to be an exception to the Court's appellate jurisdiction.

[7] Article III, Section 2, provides: "In all Cases affecting Ambassadors, other public Ministers and Consuls, and those in which a State shall be Party, the supreme Court shall have original Jurisdiction. In all the other Cases before mentioned, the supreme Court shall have appellate Jurisdiction, both as to Law and Fact, with such Exceptions, and under such Regulations as the Congress shall make."

Judge Sentelle: May be an apt term, counsel.

Professor Tushnet: That the enumeration of the original jurisdiction in this first sentence of Article III, Section 2 precludes the exercise of original jurisdiction in any other cases but . . .

Judge Sotomayor: . . . should

Professor Tushnet: Excuse me.

Judge Sotomayor: Should, can, whatever verb tense you use. Better judgment would be to leave it to that.

Professor Tushnet: If that were the only provision in Article III, Section 2, that might be correct, but the exceptions clause in the second sentence, we believe— "in all the other cases before mentioned" the Supreme Court has appellate jurisdiction with such exceptions and under such regulations as the Congress shall make. . . .

Judge Sentelle: So you would read the exceptions clause as expanding the jurisdiction awarded in the first sentence? Or at least making it possible to expand?

Professor Tushnet: As authorizing Congress to add cases, to transfer cases from the appellate jurisdiction to the original jurisdiction, yes.

Judge Edwards: Is that a bad idea just as a matter of policy to which you have referred, that is, to allow the Congress to swamp, potentially swamp, the most important court in the country with original jurisdiction, and effectively nullify the possibility of their assuming appellate jurisdiction?

Professor Tushnet: As with all exercises of congressional power of any sort, one can imagine exercises that would be extremely improvident and that might interfere with other constitutional values, so I don't want to deny the possibility, the conceptual possibility, of Congress under this reading swamping the Supreme Court. But it seems to us that the better reading of the exceptions clause, the question is what to make of the exceptions clause . . .

Judge Edwards: Why do you have to go there, why don't you simply say you're not foreclosed or that the clause does not foreclose the expansion of jurisdiction as distinguished from the retardation of jurisdiction?

Professor Tushnet: I believe that is our position; if I misstated it I apologize.

Judge Edwards: Well, you seem to refer to the exceptions clause which seems to be a part of the appellate jurisdiction—maybe I'm misunderstanding you.

Professor Tushnet: Our position is that Article III, Section 2 identifies a universe of cases and divides that universe into two parts. But the exceptions clause allows Congress to redraw the line, or shift a case out of the appellate jurisdiction and into the original jurisdiction.

Judge Edwards: The language to which you are referring, the exceptions clause, is in a sentence about the Court having appellate jurisdiction which would seem to be more naturally read to say Congress could cut away from our jurisdiction on the appellate side rather than having anything to do with whether Congress could add to our jurisdiction in sentence one.

Professor Tushnet: The question, I believe, is, what happens to those cases excepted out of the appellate jurisdiction? It's clear that that sentence does say you can take something out of the appellate jurisdiction. The question is, where can Congress put that? Now there are a couple of possibilities. One is that Congress can say no jurisdiction in the Supreme Court at all over those cases. That would raise troubling questions about "one Supreme Court," the notion of a single court that will define the federal law for the entire nation, so it seems to us that the best reading of that is to say, well yes, you can take cases out of the appellate jurisdiction, but you have to put them—once you do that, you have to put them in the original jurisdiction.

Judge Edwards: I guess what we're asking is why do you—I'm not sure why you frame it that way, why can't you add to, arguably add to, original jurisdiction without considering the question as to whether you were removing from appellate jurisdiction? What you've effectively done is if it's already in appellate jurisdiction, the Supreme Court has both original and final.

Professor Tushnet: Excuse me. I did misunderstand your question. That would be entirely consistent with our understanding of the structure of Article III. The only point that matters, we believe, in terms of understanding the structure is that Congress has authority to identify a case otherwise within the appellate jurisdiction as one appropriate for the original jurisdiction of the Supreme Court.

Judge Edwards: Why didn't you file this case in the Circuit Court of the District of Columbia, which was in existence and has mandamus authority and an esteemed scholar of our time, Susan Bloch, has enumerated the authority of that court and made it clear that they could hear this case?[8]

Professor Tushnet: This was what I was referring to as the structure of the Ju-

---

[8] For a discussion of this statute, see Susan Low Bloch, "*Marbury* Redux," in this book.

diciary Acts as a whole earlier. I think, at least in the absence of dispositive decision by this or some other court interpreting the jurisdiction of the existing circuit court, it's we believe unclear that the circuit court has jurisdiction to issue mandamus in a case like this. The structure of the lower court jurisdiction arises out of three statutes. One is the Judiciary Act of February 13, I believe, 1801, which created an extensive set of circuit courts in the country. The second is the Judiciary Act of February 27, 1801, which created the circuit court for the District of Columbia and the position to which Judge Marbury was appointed, and then, third, the Act of 1802 repealing the first of those judiciary acts, the February 13 act. Now the intervening act, the February 27 act, defines the jurisdiction of the circuit courts of the District of Columbia with reference to the jurisdiction of the circuit courts created two weeks earlier. In the absence of, sorry—the repeal in 1802 of the first of those acts seems to us to eliminate from the jurisdiction of those now non-existent courts the power to issue writs of mandamus to high federal officials.[9]

Judge Sotomayor: Then why do you need the commission at all? Why can't you just get a declaration that once Congress passed or granted the position, that that was it?[10]

Professor Tushnet: What Judge Marbury needs is some authoritative document whether it be a judgment of this Court or the piece of paper that was signed but not delivered and the reason . . .

Judge Sotomayor: Then all you need is a declaratory judgment. You don't need a writ of mandamus.

Professor Tushnet: Yes, that is right. If this Court is prepared to issue a declaratory judgment . . .

Judge Sentelle: Do we have jurisdiction to do that?

Professor Tushnet: The statute refers to writs of mandamus in cases . . .

Judge Sentelle: . . . doesn't refer to declaratory judgment.

Professor Tushnet: The reason for the . . . Just to complete my answer to Judge

---

[9] Contrary to Professor Bloch's analysis, here Professor Tushnet asserts that the circuit court for the District of Columbia did not have jurisdiction to issue a writ of mandamus—or at least that whether it had such jurisdiction was a difficult and unanswered question in 1803.

[10] The issue opened up here is, Why does Marbury care about getting the physical document that is his commission?

Sotomayer's question: Suppose Judge Marbury begins to act in a judicial capacity and awards a piece of property to one claimant in what purports to be litigation in front of him, the losing party might sue Judge Marbury and say you have engaged in, whatever the term would be, trespass to my property by purporting to authorize this other . . .

Judge Sotomayor: But that doesn't answer my question, if I don't know why your writ of mandamus is necessary to accomplish our goal. If a court, whether be it this one or circuit court, declares that Judge Marbury is a judge, what more do you . . .

Professor Tushnet: I agree entirely. Again what Judge Marbury needs is a piece of paper that he can file as a defense to this action for writ of trespass showing that he had authority . . .

Judge Sotomayor: I don't know if you're really going to the fundamental nature of my question, which is Why is a commission necessary at all to the appointment of a judge to a district court, to a D.C. court at all? Isn't it only Congress who is recognized by the Constitution as the power to whom authority is given to regulate matters in D.C. courts? Why do you need the President at all?

Professor Tushnet: To establish, an action by the President is needed to establish that this person who is purporting to exercise the authority of the United States actually has the authority of the United States.

Judge Sotomayor: Where is that in the Constitution? I see in the Constitution that Congress is given the power to regulate the matters in the D.C. district. I don't see anywhere in the Constitution that requires either a commission or any other executive act.

Judge Edwards: Let me make sure I understand this. Isn't your, the statute upon which you are relying, doesn't it require that, the commission . . .

Professor Tushnet: Requires the commission, yes.

Judge Edwards: Pursuant to what she is . . .

Judge Katzmann: Now in this case how do we know a commission even exists? Where is the evidence of it?

Professor Tushnet: This is an original action in the Court, there is no record of that. We have said that the document exists and was signed but not delivered. That is open for exploration as a factual matter.

Judge Katzmann: So you would want us to engage in fact-finding.

Professor Tushnet: In original cases you are authorized to use whatever methods seem appropriate to you to determine contested facts.[11]

Judge Katzmann: And who would you, as you understand the facts—since we don't have time to actually hear from individuals—how would you establish that the commission exists?

Professor Tushnet: You could appoint a master to serve as a fact-finder and report to you.

Judge Edwards: Just ask Chief Justice, he'll . . . He was there.[12]

Judge Katzmann: Should we ask the Chief Justice's brother?[13]

Professor Tushnet: I think it's probably important to emphasize how early in the construction of this national government we are because that is relevant to the entire problem here.[14] In 200 years we may, the people of this nation may, have a better sense of what institutions are needed to make a functioning effective national government. We're now in an exploratory period.

Judge Katzmann: Why isn't the commission, why doesn't it require delivery, why does it vest with the signing and sealing? Why not with the delivery of the commission? Where is the basis for that in law, in statute or another law?

Professor Tushnet: We believe that the best answer to that is in understanding the purposes of the judicial office to which Judge Marbury was appointed and following on that the necessity for first of all there to be some point at which his five-year term of office clearly begins. To make . . .

Judge Katzmann: Let's say that I am the President and it's signed and sealed and then I think to myself, gee you know I nominated this guy but I think I

[11] The Supreme Court has frequently used masters to investigate contested fact sin cases within the Court's original jurisdiction. It is authorized to conduct jury trials as well, although there is no record of such a trial in the Supreme Court after 1797.

[12] As noted in the Introduction to this book, John Marshall was the Secretary of State at the time John Adams signed Marbury's commission.

[13] Marshall's brother James was the federal official charged with delivering the commissions to the newly appointed judges. He delivered some before Jefferson took office, but filed an affidavit asserting that he had been unable to deliver them all.

[14] Professor Tushnet uses the family connections the judges refer to as a way of pointing out that the nation's political elite during its early years was relatively small, to emphasize the need to tolerate experimentation as the nation constructed its political institutions.

made a mistake, so I'm simply not going to deliver it. Remember we're at the beginning part of our constitutional development. So why not in essence, why not in a sense deliver a pink slip by not delivering the commission?

Professor Tushnet: I think the best response I have to that question is that it's hard to distinguish that action by the President from an action by the President either demanding that the judge return the commission, that is making the position one to be held at will, at the will of the President, which would be inconsistent with notions of the judicial role of this officer and might be inconsistent with notions of due process embedded in the Fifth Amendment.[15] So at some point the President's decision must become irrevocable. The question is at what point is that so?

Judge Katzmann: Well, if it's that clear again you come back to the question you've already been asked, why then is the matter here or anywhere?[16] And your only answer is, well the judge may be sued, well isn't the appropriate moment to litigate the matter before a court that has original jurisdiction where evidence can be submitted? It's no more or less than the evidence that you want us to consider, so apparently you think you have it and then we avoid the problem of how to try to enforce it at this point.

Professor Tushnet: That is . . .

Judge Edwards: In other words, if Judge Marbury really has the job, which is what you are asserting on the merits—there is no doubt that he has this job—why doesn't he go to the office and start working and in the event that he gets sued, that which you are arguing now can be argued then? It's better for him with the evidence properly put in.

Professor Tushnet: But that course of conduct in order to frame the legal issue necessarily exposes him to legal risk of an erroneous decision against him. And just as, well the law ought to be designed so that people in Judge Marbury's position do not have to expose themselves to . . .

---

[15] Professor Tushnet suggests here that Judge Katzmann's position would allow the president to treat officials like Marbury as employees at will, who could be fired whenever the president chose, and that such a conclusion would be inconsistent with the judicial character of the offices they hold.

[16] The discussion returns to the question Why has Marbury bothered to sue for the commission?

Judge Edwards: Are you better off, is what I'm asking, with that circumstance or a circumstance where you get mandamus from us and the President says, Not over my dead body?[17]

Professor Tushnet: I think it's inappropriate to assume that the President of the United States would direct a Secretary of State to refuse to comply with an order issuing from this Court. In the event . . .

Judge Sentelle: We've not ordered him to do an awful lot so far, counsel.

Professor Tushnet: That is correct—and it is early days, I agree—and so it's not. . . there is no guarantee of actual compliance, but in the construction of a well-designed government, and that is what we are talking about now, it seems to us inappropriate to assume that the President will refuse to comply with an order from this Court.[18]

Judge Sotomayor: We are three equal branches, so what in our Constitution stops him from making a judgment that we have acted unconstitutionally?

Professor Tushnet: Only the concern that he might have that the voters of the country would regard the system that he is now beginning to create as one that is not well designed and therefore the voters will regard him and his political party as improvident guardians of our future.

Judge Sotomayor: Isn't that what a democracy is about, to engage the people in making choices? If they don't like his choice, they will vote him out of office.

Professor Tushnet: We have no principled objection to the President refusing to comply—inappropriately refusing to comply—with an order from this Court. We believe that would contribute to the development of an ill-designed government which the people might respond to.

Judge Sotomayor: What would we do if the President refuses to comply? How do we enforce our own order?

Professor Tushnet: In the event of that behavior by the President you have the moral authority of this Court to invoke in public debate, not you of course, but

---

[17] Judge Edwards alludes to the possibility of presidential defiance of an order from the Supreme Court, an issue taken up in more detail during Professor Strauss's argument.

[18] Here Professor Tushnet again emphasizes the rudimentary state of the nation's institutions, in this context pointing out that the relationship among the courts, the president, and the people is in some sense still under construction in 1803.

people who agree with you about the propriety of the President's action and again the nature of the government that would exist were the President to be able to disregard orders from the Court.

Judge Katzmann: Let me ask you another question that is troubling me. Are the laws enacted by Congress for regulating the District of Columbia laws of the United States for Article III purposes?[19]

Professor Tushnet: We believe that again the Constitution properly interpreted makes at least laws of—I want to use the term *general* here but that's going to get into trouble as we try to specify what such laws are, but—general laws, laws roughly similar to those enforced throughout the country, laws enacted by Congress of that sort applicable in the District are laws of the United States.[20]

Judge Katzmann: Take it further, if the magistrate interprets Congress's acts for the District and if a magistrate does not have lifetime tenure and is therefore not an Article III judge, then hasn't Congress just given Article III power to non-Article III judges in ways that should trouble us?

Professor Tushnet: Here I would . . .

Judge Katzmann: Maybe even being unconstitutional. Could be the next thing we declare . . .

Professor Tushnet: Here again I would stress the need for flexibility and caution in the process of constructing a new national government. We don't know what the exigencies of judicial administration in the next fifty to one hundred years will be. And it therefore seems improvident to construe Article III to require that every person exercising something characterizable as the judicial power of the United States have life tenure. Obviously some significant portion of those people who do exercise that power must have life tenure—that is the clear import of Article III—but it seems appropriate to construe the Constitu-

---

[19] The difficulty Judge Katzmann is raising is this: Marbury holds a judicial position, but lacks the guarantee of life tenure that judges appointed pursuant to Article III have. But, as a federal appointee, Marbury appears to be exercising the judicial power of the United States, which, Judge Katzmann suggests, only life-tenured judges can exercise.

[20] Professor Tushnet's response suggests that the Court could distinguish between actions of Congress in its capacity as the local legislature for the District of Columbia and its actions in its capacity as a national legislature, and that the Constitution requires only that judges enforcing laws enacted in the latter capacity have life tenure.

tion to authorize Congress to either experiment or be flexible in the construction of subordinate judge-like actors who would not have guaranteed . . .

Judge Sentelle: The first section of Article III refers to inferior judges, inferior courts, and says the judges both of the Supreme and inferior courts shall hold their offices during good behavior. Doesn't that preclude the argument you just made?

Professor Tushnet: We believe not. Again, the question is whether this justice of the peace is properly characterized as an inferior court within the meaning of Article III rather than as a judicial actor authorized by Congress's power to make regulations for the District of Columbia, if nothing else to implement federal statutes, statutes enacted subsequently pursuant to Article I.

Judge Edwards: I'm going to give you a couple of minutes on rebuttal, but your time is up. If you could wrap up with a sentence or two.

Professor Tushnet: The only conclusion that I want to offer you is an acknowledgment that this case is in all of its aspects not open and shut for our side or for the other side. That the words of the statutes and the Constitution are amenable to interpretations that would lead to the issuance of the writ of mandamus by this Court on behalf of Judge Marbury and that the constructions of the statutes and the Constitution that lead to that conclusion will contribute to the development of a more effective functioning national government than the alternative constructions would. Thank you.

Judge Edwards: Thank you, counsel. Mr. . . . .

Professor Strauss: Mr. Chief Justice and, may it please the Court, the Secretary of State wishes to deny that this Court has jurisdiction, to deny that mandamus is available against the Secretary, to deny that mandamus be an appropriate remedy in this case even were it available and although the Court should not reach this issue, to deny that any legal wrong was done here that requires a remedy.

Judge Sentelle: Start at the beginning of that. Does not the statute seem to grant us this jurisdiction?

Professor Strauss: Justice Sentelle, if I may just do one more thing before I answer your question. The Secretary has also instructed me to . . .

Judge Katzmann: You have to answer the Justice's question.[21]

---

[21] Professor Strauss's express refusal to answer the question posed before he made his next point is the first indication of the tensions between the Court and President Jefferson.

Professor Strauss: Well, this is a preliminary matter. I apologize, Justice Katzmann. The Secretary has instructed me to suggest with all deference that in view of the Chief Justice's involvement with the facts that gave rise to this case and the fact that the Chief Justice sealed the commission that was not delivered, the fact that the Chief Justice was Secretary of State at the time the commission was not delivered, the fact that an affidavit by the Chief Justice's brother was filed by Mr. Marbury in support of his case, that the Chief Justice may wish to consider recusal.

Judge Katzmann: Before we get to that, your client failed to appear the first time we set this case for oral argument. Why shouldn't we simply award a default judgment against you?

Judge Edwards: And hold him in contempt.

Professor Strauss: Well, I have been dispatched to represent my client, Justice Katzmann, I have been dispatched by the future. The denizens of the future are fond of attributing to my client Mr. Madison various views that he didn't hold and it's of a piece with that . . .

Judge Katzmann: Don't we have a problem, I mean he's got these notes hidden somewhere about what went on at the Constitutional Convention we don't have access to it.

Professor Strauss: The Secretary's position is that those notes are not relevant to the interpretation of the Constitution.

Judge Sentelle: Get back to the statute for a moment. Does not the statute seem to grant us precisely the jurisdiction which Judge Marbury asserts?

Professor Strauss: No, Justice Sentelle, I don't see that all in the statute.

Judge Sentelle: Read the fourth clause.

Professor Strauss: The jurisdiction Mr. Marbury claims as original jurisdiction in this Court—and the statute seems to me quite clear in all of its versions, Justice Katzmann—that original jurisdiction is limited to cases involving ambassadors, public ministers and states. The clause purporting to provide the issuance of writs of mandamus is if anything appended to the clause providing for appellate jurisdiction or else is not appended to any clause. I don't see any plausible construction of the statute, quite frankly, in which that clause provides original jurisdiction in this Court. I would add to that, that if it did provide for original jurisdiction there would be constitutional issues and the Court would be warranted in interpreting the statute to avoid those as it has done in the past.

Judge Sentelle: Assuming that we decided that the construction advanced by Mr. Marbury is the correct construction, do you have a fall-back position with reference to the Constitution?

Professor Strauss: Our position, Justice Sentelle, if you mean the Court concludes that Section 13 purports to grant jurisdiction in original actions, we do not believe, Justice Sentelle, that there is a general power in the courts to declare acts of Congress unconstitutional.[22] We do believe there are instances in which a branch of government may, especially if it is being asked to exercise prerogatives it believes it does not have under the Constitution, decline to exercise those prerogatives. I believe that would be the advisable course in this case should . . .

Judge Sotomayor: What is the remedy for someone wronged by an unconstitutional act? Where do they seek redress?

Professor Strauss: There are a variety of remedies, Justice Sotomayer. The remedies are available at common law for people wronged by allegedly unconstitutional government action. They can bring actions in trespass, actions in assumpsit. In this case were Mr. Marbury wronged, which he was not, he would be free to sue for his salary, an appropriate common law action in a court that had jurisdiction over common law action, which this Court of course does not. That, we believe, is the remedy available. Mandamus is not an available remedy.

Judge Sotomayor: You would suggest that it is more appropriate as a matter of constitutional principle that lower state courts would make decisions about the acts of the Secretary of State or our President, that these would not be more appropriate in federal questions?

Professor Strauss: In appropriate cases. If for example there were diversity of citizenship, a case could be brought in the lower federal courts.

Judge Sotomayor: So what meaning do we give to Article III, Section 2 that says the judicial power shall extend to all cases in law and equity arising under this Constitution, the laws of the United States, and treaties made?

Professor Strauss: Justice Sotomayor, I believe that clause says that Congress may authorize the federal courts to hear cases arising under the constitutional laws of the United States.

---

[22] The reference to the absence of a "general" power to declare statutes unconstitutional is Professor Strauss's second suggestion of the possibility of presidential defiance of an order from the Supreme Court.

Judge Edwards: Then you can see that if we construe Section 13 as Judge Sentelle first suggested, the case is properly here and we can consider the constitutional issues fully.

Professor Strauss: The Court is of course free to consider the constitutional issues fully. The question is whether the Constitution permits the Court to substitute its judgment about the constitutionality of a statute for that of the legislature.

Judge Edwards: I don't see how we can consider a case as the Constitution empowers us to do without considering all of the legal factors including constitutional that would come into play. You are stripping us of that which the Constitution gives us.

Professor Strauss: I don't disagree with you, Mr. Chief Justice, that the Court should consider all constitutional issues. One of the constitutional principles in play, however, is the principle that the branches are coordinate and no branch can claim supremacy over another.[23]

Judge Edwards: Is that the separation of powers or some such notion? Where is that, and which provision should I look at that says separation of powers?

Professor Strauss: The Constitution of course establishes three branches of government and affords all of them . . .

Judge Edwards: Right, and my branch has the authority to hear cases that may involve, as Justice Sotomayor just said, constitutional questions. All cases in law and equity arising under the Constitution and laws of the United States. I don't know how I decide a case if I can't consider all that which is implicated.

Professor Strauss: Mr. Chief Justice, the question is, what purpose is served by that clause of Article III if not to empower the courts to declare acts of Congress unconstitutional? One answer to that question is: the question whether this Court may declare acts of state legislatures unconstitutional is an entirely different matter. And if the Court has that power, that would explain to the extent if I understand the Chief Justice correctly one point he is suggesting is that clause of Article III appears redundant unless this Court has the power to declare acts of Congress unconstitutional. I do not agree with that. The clause is not redundant because the state issues remain.

---

[23] Professor Strauss here is making the subtle point—not one readily accepted by judges—that the proper interpretation of the Constitution as a whole requires that judges accept the interpretations of specific provisions that are inherent in Congress's decision to enact a statute that a litigant challenges as unconstitutional.

Judge Sentelle: Are you proceeding from the assumption that no branch has the final say in the constitutionality of an act?

Professor Strauss: My general proposition, Justice Sentelle, is each branch has a final say on matters within its purview. That's my proposition.[24]

Judge Edwards: A case is brought to us and the question includes a question of constitutionality, we are entitled under Article III pursuant to the power given to us to decide whether or not in our view, it is repugnant to the Constitution and whether as a consequence we will enforce it.

Professor Strauss: That is correct, Mr. Chief Justice, but in doing that the Court must acknowledge that the President has constitutional prerogatives.

Judge Edwards: The President can exercise constitutional prerogatives in a number of circumstances without regard to whether or not we refuse to give a remedy or grant a remedy. In our view of the Constitution, pardoning, for example, vetoing bills, Congress can decide not to pass a bill, they can disagree with our views. That in no way suggests that we are foreclosed in cases that are properly before us from saying in our view it's repugnant and we will not give the remedy or we will give the remedy pursuant to our view, and that's final.

Professor Strauss: In doing that, Mr. Chief Justice, the Court must take into account the fact that the legislative branch has expressed its conscientious judgment on the constitutionality of the act and that judgment simply cannot be overridden because this Court disagrees. Now there is a category of cases specifically implicating the prerogatives of this Court in which I would say the Court may refuse to exercise powers.[25]

Judge Edwards: Where is it in the Constitution, to what are you looking that says, if Congress passes an act, one, that we assume that they assume it was constitutional and, two, we are required to accept that in deciding cases under Article III?

Professor Strauss: I see that in the fact Congress is empowered to pass laws under Article I of the Constitution and I also see that, Mr. Chief Justice, in the fact that the Constitution nowhere says as one would expect it to say, that the courts and the courts alone have the final word on the constitutionality of acts of Congress.

[24] Again, Professor Strauss hints at the possibility of presidential defiance.

[25] Here Professor Strauss offers a version of departmentalism in which the courts have the power to declare unconstitutional, and refrain from acting under, statutes that call upon them to do something the Constitution says courts cannot do.

Judge Edwards: You are creating a bogus issue. You are assuming something that we are not suggesting by our questioning. It isn't the courts alone. I've already indicated to you that there are a number of instances when the President and Congress will state a view that we . . . assert, for example. None of my colleagues nor I are suggesting that we can offer advisory opinions. If we see something that we disagree with, we can't say, bring it here and we'll override the act of the President or Congress. But we certainly do have the authority under the Constitution to take any cases within our power and properly brought to us as cases under the Constitution and to issue a judgment on its constitutionality.

Professor Strauss: We have no disagreement with that.

Judge Katzmann: What if you had a case involving an interpretation of a statute, Congress passes a statute, its words are unclear, the courts interpret the words of the statute, is that appropriate?

Professor Strauss: Yes, that is Justice . . .

Judge Katzmann: Why is that appropriate? If in one case, the case of statutory interpretation, you are willing to say that the words of Congress can be determined in essence by the courts, why is that appropriate and the review of constitutionality inappropriate?

Professor Strauss: The Constitution, Justice Katzmann, is not just another statute. The Constitution is something altered not by the legislature but by the people in convention assembled. And the power to interpret . . .

Judge Katzmann: I had thought that statutes are the product of the people's will through their elected legislators.

Professor Strauss: Well, statutes are the product of the legislature but there is no reason to apply to a constitution the rules that apply to statutes given their different provenance and given the coordinate authority of the three branches. The Court would be assuming for itself the power that the other branches don't have.

Judge Sotomayor: No, the branches certainly have the power to declare an unwillingness to pass a law. Both the Congress can say something is unconstitutional and not pass it, the President can veto an act because he feels, because he feels it's unconstitutional. That's not the issue, the issue is, do we have the power to say it's not, and why don't we share that power?

Professor Strauss: Justice Sotomayor, I don't want to deny that within a limited purview the Court does have that power. I also don't want to deny that sometimes defining that purview . . .

Judge Sentelle: So you do concede or you do agree that there is some realm within which the Court can review acts of the coordinate branches for constitutionality?

Professor Strauss: Yes, I meant to acknowledge that from the start, Justice Sentelle, just as there is a realm within which the President may say notwithstanding anything the other branches have instructed me to do, my constitutional prerogatives require me not to do it. The President has that authority as do the courts.[26]

Judge Sentelle: And that's the only area in which the Court can act on constitutional basis?

Professor Strauss: I don't see any other way in which the power to assess constitutionality can be reconciled with . . .

Judge Sotomayor: You're saying two different things. You are starting with the proposition that we are empowered to say an act is unconstitutional. And at the same time saying, but you have no power to enforce that judgment. That's really what you're taking issue.

Professor Strauss: It is not exactly that, I think, Justice Sotomayor. My position is that the Court does have fully legitimate power within a limited realm to say we may not exercise this authority even though it has been granted to us. What I am denying is that the Court can say in any case whatever this act of Congress is unconstitutional.

Judge Katzmann: And that realm is, so I understand, what?

Professor Strauss: I acknowledge it's difficult to define, Justice Katzmann, just as it is difficult to answer the comparable question for the executive.

Judge Katzmann: What are we as a court to do if you can't define for us what that area is? What is the principle by which we're supposed to act?

Professor Strauss: My definition, Justice Katzmann, would be that if power is assigned to you that you believe you cannot exercise under the Constitution, you may decline to exercise it in order to protect the prerogatives of the court.

Judge Sentelle: But going back to Article III, Section 2, Clause 1, the judicial powers shall extend to all cases in law and equity arising under this Constitution. Later in the same Constitution it says that the Constitution is the supreme law. How can we decide cases under the law of the Constitution if we cannot construe the meaning of the Constitution, counsel? If we construe its meaning

---

[26]This is an almost explicit threat of presidential defiance.

and Congress has done something inconsistent therewith, must we not be able to say that's unlawful, that's unconstitutional?

Professor Strauss: Justice Sentelle, I think when any official exercising authority under the Constitution who has a responsibility to uphold the Constitution, when any official exercises that authority, one thing he or she must take into account is, what have other branches of government, other agencies, other officials said? Every . . .

Judge Sentelle: We can take that in account, but nonetheless we're left with the charge of extending, exercising the judicial power on cases in law and equity arising under the Constitution and the laws of the United States and treaties and so forth. And we're told later in the same Constitution that that Constitution is the supreme law. How can we decide the applicable law without being able to decide whether the highest law has been transversed by some lower element of law?

Professor Strauss: It's the Secretary's position, Justice Sentelle, that except within the purview I have described, the Constitution requires that the Court defer to the judgments of other branches.

Judge Sentelle: Where does it do that?

Professor Strauss: This it seems to me the only way to construe . . .

Judge Sentelle: Where does it do that?

Professor Strauss: It does not do that, but by the same token it does not provide that the Court may set aside legislation on grounds of unconstitutionality. What we are trying to do here is to construe the document in a way that acknowledges the coordinate power of the three branches.

Judge Edwards: Those are not equally forceful propositions. You stated them as if they were. They are not. Yours is terribly weak. And the one that Judge Sentelle is enunciating is based on the literal terms of the Constitution. Yours is based on a policy notion and finds no literal support whatsoever in the Constitution save for proposition of separation of powers which we can't find. We may in history construct one later on, but it's not there.

Professor Strauss: Mr. Chief Justice, I fail to find literal support for the proposition in the Constitution that this Court may declare acts of Congress unconstitutional. It would have been a simple matter for the drafters of the Constitution to include in Article III a clause giving this Court the power.

Judge Edwards: Can a case as the Constitution refers to include a challenge to an act of Congress?

Professor Strauss: A case within the meaning of Article III? A case can of course include such a challenge. The question is the proper disposition of the challenge.

Judge Edwards: It is within our authority to decide cases right?

Professor Strauss: Absolutely.

Judge Edwards: And a case can include, can properly include, a challenge to a statute

Professor Strauss: Absolutely.

Judge Edwards: Either on it own terms or constitutional . . .

Professor Strauss: Absolutely.

Judge Edwards: And we are entitled to give a disposition in law and equity.

Professor Strauss: Right. No disagreement with that.

Judge Edwards: And give a remedy because that is what you do in law and equity.

Professor Strauss: The remedy is, you are entitled to give an appropriate remedy, that's right. One of the things that the Court must consider when it is deciding the constitutionality is whether another branch's judgment of constitutionality is entitled to deference.

Judge Edwards: That's the part where I'm losing you because I can't find that anywhere here. By definition we understand that they have reached a judgment. We're not sure whether they've even considered the constitutionality but we know they've reached a judgment. It's now under challenge and you agree that can properly be a case before us, and it says we have the authority to consider that such cases in law and equity historically law and equity allow the Court to reach a conclusion and give a remedy to the winner.

Professor Strauss: I don't know, Mr. Chief Justice, whether your question is about remedy and about whether mandamus is appropriate.

Judge Edwards: Well, you are suggesting that there be no remedy if Congress has passed a statute and we find it to be unconstitutional because in fact if they passed a statute, they assumed it was constitutional.

Professor Strauss: And the Court should find it constitutional because one of the things the Court should consider . . .

Judge Edwards: And we have no business to do, it's not a case, if it can be a case before us, it's a case of a sort that I can't comprehend. It isn't a case that I as a judge can truly consider, because you are saying one party to the case always wins. That's not within the notion even the one they had in England be-

fore we carried forward whatever we carried forward, that isn't the way it operates.

Professor Strauss: My proposition is not that one party always wins, Mr.
Chief Justice, it is that there are legal principles that even this Court must observe.

Judge Sentelle: Interestingly on the won/lost question if we can declare
statutes unconstitutional and we decide that this one is unconstitutional, you
win, right? If we say we don't have jurisdiction to grant this mandamus because
the statute is unconstitutional, you win.

Professor Strauss: If the Court concludes that is correct, Justice.

Judge Sentelle: So if we disagree with you, you win.

Professor Strauss: Well, I think in this, in my proposition which I have tried
to advance consistently from the start, that there is no general power in this
Court to declare acts of Congress unconstitutional. For example, should this
Court six days from now declare unconstitutional . . .

Judge Sotomayor: Constitutional or unconstitutional?

Professor Strauss: Declare unconstitutional . . .

Judge Sotomayor: Why do we have the power to declare them constitutional?

Professor Strauss: The Court has the power to, the Court follows the law as it
is, and if the Court's conclusion is that the law is constitutional there is no difficulty.

Judge Sotomayor: But I don't understand how we can have the power to do
the affirmative and not the negative. What creates the case unless we have the
power to decide a controversy? Inherent in the concept of a claim is the notion
that one side is claiming X and the other side is claiming Y. If we can't adjudi-
cate that, how do we have a case before us?

Judge Edwards: I just can't understand your notion of case.

Professor Strauss: Well, there is a case when as the Court recognized, in I
think it was Hayburn's case, when there is a live controversy between the parties, but let's try this as a . . .

Judge Sentelle: Hayburn's case was decided by justices on the circuit, that was
not decided by the Court.

Professor Strauss: That's true. I stand corrected, Justice Sentelle. I should have
said as some Justices of this Court have recognized, thank you. Lower courts are
obligated in our system, this has been settled, to follow the decisions of this

Court. In cases that come before the lower courts they may reach a judgment on the meaning of statutes, the meaning of the Constitution, the meaning of the common law, that is different from the judgment of this Court. They are nonetheless required to give effect to the judgment of this Court. That doesn't mean that there is no case before those courts, that doesn't mean one side always wins, that just means that sometimes it's an obligation on a branch of government to accept the judgment of other branches of government when the branches are co-equal. And that is the proposition I'm advancing. It seems to me nothing in the Constitution contravenes that and it is . . .

Judge Edwards: I don't understand the notion of co-equal: you're saying that as if we are co-equal in all respects. We are not. We don't legislate. And we don't have an army. We can't decide whether to prosecute or not, and the other two branches don't decide cases. So we're not co-equal in the sense that I am referring to. They have responsibilities that are theirs alone. We have a responsibility that is ours alone, and that is to decide cases within the judicial power. They do not have that authority.

Professor Strauss: That is correct, Mr. Chief Justice, of course, which is why we take such strong exception to the proposition advanced by my learned friend that this Court may direct an officer in the executive branch how to do his job. The executive branch is in charge of the executive, and the courts should not be directing by writ of mandamus the Secretary of State about how to do his job. When I say co-equal, I do not mean they have identical responsibilities. Among other things, Mr. Chief Justice, the head of the executive branch was elected by the people recently. And this branch . . .

Judge Sentelle: No, he was elected by the Electoral College.

Professor Strauss: With substantial popular support. We'll take our chances on the people, Justice Sentelle. If the Court has no further questions.

Judge Edwards: Thank you. Two minutes on rebuttal.

Professor Tushnet: Thank you. I only want to make two points in connection with the discussion of power of the Court to hold statutes unconstitutional that you've most recently engaged in. The first point—there is a weaker point and a stronger point. The weaker point is that, to use the language of the Chief Justice, it is not necessary to say that the Court is required to accept the determination by Congress and the President that a statute is constitutional, it's not necessary to say that, in order to say that the judgments that they have made about constitutionality are relevant to your independent determination of constitutionality. So, for example, on the assumption that Section 13 confers jurisdiction to issue an original writ of mandamus, it is not irrelevant to you that this is a provision in the first Judiciary Act drafted by people who were active participants in the Constitutional Convention. That is the weaker position. The stronger position is that while . . .

Judge Sotomayor: Why is that the weaker position? Why shouldn't we give deference absent some clear contradiction meaning unless a statute is clearly unconstitutional, why shouldn't we assume the good faith of our executive and legislative branches?

Professor Tushnet: That is what I was about to characterize as a stronger position. If you are willing to call that one also a weak position, I am not going to disagree with you. That position I think has to be reconciled with your concern that you've expressed that you are authorized to articulate and determine what the law is. But constitutional law, while law, is a special kind of law. It is more closely tied to the understanding of the people of this nation about what this nation is and what it is to become. And because of that special nature of constitutional law, when you construe the Constitution you are not doing the kind of thing that you do when you construe a statute. You are dealing with the construction of this nation, and the people acting through their representatives in Congress and through the President have—I don't want to make claims about equality but—a very important role in constructing that nation through its Constitution.

Judge Edwards: What should we be thinking about when we deliberate? There are two things to worry about, do we ignore, assuming that you simply cannot prevail on Section 13—it just does not say what you want it to say as a jurisdictional matter—do we ignore that because in our view we will better serve the future of the country by simply granting some policy issues and deciding now for the better good in our view and if we do that, what does that say to judges, justices who will succeed us and judges below us about the proper order in disposing of cases, do you ignore jurisdictional issues that are there because you want to get to the merits and you take on constitutional issues when there are nonconstitutional issues which are dispositive?

Professor Tushnet: Our view is that if we are wrong, as we believe we are not, in our interpretation of Section 13, then this Court has no authority to order the

President to deliver the commission or rectify the wrong that has been done to Mr. Marbury. Your jurisdiction depends upon statutory decisions made by Congress and signed by the President.

Judge Sotomayor: So in essence you're telling us, don't reach the merits unless you find you have jurisdiction.

Professor Tushnet: Absolutely. Thank you.

Judge Sentelle: Thank you both. Our pleasure.

Judge Edwards: We are not going to deliberate and we are not going to decide anything. Nor call the next case.

CHAPTER TWO

On Having Mr. Madison as a Client

DAVID A. STRAUSS

Marbury v. Madison is celebrated for holding that courts may declare Acts of Congress unconstitutional. That makes it natural to suppose that an advocate preparing for oral argument in *Marbury* would have focused on the various arguments for and against judicial review. But Secretary of State James Madison's lawyer would, I think, have approached the case in a different way, and a present-day lawyer assigned to "represent" Madison in a two-hundredth anniversary reargument of *Marbury v. Madison* enters quite a different world. The client—Thomas Jefferson's Administration—had a relationship with the Supreme Court that is much more adversarial than the relationship between the Executive Branch and the Supreme Court is today, or has been at any time in recent history. The Court's view of itself is different, and the Executive's view of the Court is different. Defiance of a Supreme Court decision—something that the Executive Branch would be very unlikely even to contemplate today— was, apparently, a realistic option in 1803.

Beyond that, President Jefferson's Republicans, who had just taken over in 1801 after an acrimonious election, were fully prepared to try to intimidate the Federalist-dominated judiciary in ways that went even beyond selectively threatening to defy its decisions. In 1805, just two years after *Marbury*, the Republicans impeached Justice Samuel Chase at least in part to send a message to Chief Justice Marshall and the other Federalists on the Court and in the judiciary. Part of the task of Madison's lawyer would have been to convey to the Court an unyielding attitude and an implicit threat that Madison's allies would attack the Court if it ruled against him—an approach that is nearly the opposite of that which an Executive Branch lawyer would instinctively take today.

On the merits, the issues before the Court in *Marbury* would also seem very different to Madison's lawyer in 1803 than they seem to us today. Madison and Jefferson probably would have been most concerned with the question whether a court may issue a writ of mandamus to an Executive Branch official. Today, of course, the general power of the courts to mandamus federal officials has long been recognized, and it would be pointless or counterproductive for an Executive Branch lawyer to make sweeping arguments to the contrary. On the other hand, the issue for which *Marbury* has become famous—the constitutionality of judicial review—was probably less important to the Republicans in 1803 than it appears to us in retrospect. And the Republicans' position on that issue would have been complicated; their interests were best served by being very skeptical about judicial review but not quite unequivocally opposed. For a present-day lawyer, the overall picture is disorienting. Both the attitude with which you would approach the Court and the positions you would assert are foreign to what you would do today.

I

The first oddity in representing Secretary Madison is that the present-day reargument on his behalf is not exactly a reargument: no lawyer representing Madison appeared before the Court in 1803. This was not, of course, an oversight, or an indication that Madison thought the case was trivial. It was, by all appearances, a way of casting doubt on the Court's authority, and probably an implicit threat that Madison would not comply with an adverse ruling by the Court.

Today, it is close to unthinkable that the Executive Branch would demonstrate that kind of disrespect for the Court. After the Court decided *United States v. Nixon*, President Nixon released incriminating evidence that precipitated his resignation; he apparently did not seriously consider defying the Court. After *Bush v. Gore*, Vice President Gore immediately conceded the Presidential election, even though that case was decided by a narrow margin and was, in the view of many, a decision of very questionable legal soundness. Today, everyone expects that a government lawyer appearing before the Court would, if asked, assure the Court that whatever the Executive Branch's position on the merits of the case, the Executive will—of course—comply with the Court's decisions. Any suggestion that the Executive might consider defiance would be truly extraordinary.

Apparently it was not so extraordinary in 1803, and that different relationship between the Court and the Executive Branch would affect an advocate's approach in important ways. Unlike a present-day government lawyer, Madison's counsel did not have to be a respectful supplicant, propitiating the Justices by reassuring them that the Secretary of course would defer to their ultimate authority. Madison's lawyer would have had another weapon; he or she could let the Justices know that if they ruled against the Secretary, the Secretary might ignore their order, and the Court's institutional authority might be seriously damaged.

Madison's lawyer could also let the Justices know that Jefferson's party was fully prepared to attack them politically and to try to remove them from office through impeachment. In order to be most effective, an advocate would have to convey these kinds of threat subtly, of course, but the threat could be conveyed. In a case like *Marbury*, an advocate vigorously representing the Administration probably would make a point of conveying it. Today such a threat would be wildly out of place; in fact, today a government lawyer would ordinarily go to the greatest lengths to reassure the Court that he or she intended no such threat.

There is a second oddity that confronts Madison's present-day lawyer right at the outset of the case. By modern standards, at least, Chief Justice John Marshall's failure to recuse himself was unconscionable. Marshall was the Secretary of State who sealed Marbury's commission; he was Secretary of State when the commission was not delivered; and Marshall's brother filed an affidavit in support of Marbury's petition for a writ of mandamus. It is inconceivable that a Justice today would participate in a case in which he or she had such a personal involvement with the very controversy that was before the Court.

Today, if an advocate believed that a Supreme Court Justice should not participate in a case, the challenge would be twofold: to argue that the Justice should recuse him- or herself, but to be sure not to alienate the other members of the Court by pressing the argument too aggressively. If that failed, the next best thing, from the advocate's point of view, would be to do as much as possible to discredit that Justice in the eyes of his or her colleagues, again as respectfully as possible so that the effort would not backfire. But in *Marbury*, probably neither of these approaches would have had any serious chance of succeeding. Marshall obviously knew of the extent of his involvement in the case, and if he did not recuse himself on his own motion it is unlikely that anything Madison's lawyer might say would persuade him. And the rest of the Court was composed of Federalists who were hostile to Jefferson; trying to undermine Marshall's credibility in their eyes would, again, almost certainly be futile.

In these circumstances, the best way for Madison's counsel to use Marshall's failure to recuse himself would be to signal that the Administration was prepared to attack the Court publicly if need be. Tactically, I think it would have been best for Madison's lawyer to have sought Marshall's recusal in open court. But the reason for doing so would have been not to try to persuade the Court, as an advocate normally would, but instead to embarrass Marshall, and again to convey the Jeffersonians' implacability and their willingness to confront the Court in the future.

II

On the merits, Madison would, I think, have been intensely concerned with the question whether Executive Branch officials are subject to writs of mandamus issued by federal courts. Today, we take it for granted that Executive Branch officials can sometimes be ordered by courts to perform a legal duty. But in 1803, when the Constitution was barely a decade old, this was not so clear. It would have been plausible to argue that, under the Constitution's separation of powers, the President alone is responsible for ensuring that his subordinates within the Executive Branch faithfully execute the laws. If those officials unlawfully infringed on the common law entitlements of an individual—by taking that individual's property, for example, or perhaps by withholding money lawfully due—then the individual could pursue a common law remedy. But if the only complaint was that the official failed to perform a legal duty, in circumstances where that failure did not deprive anyone of an interest protected by the common law, then the President alone had the power to insist that the official comply and to dismiss the official if he or she did not. So, at least, it might have been argued by the Executive Branch in 1803.

This argument certainly would have appealed to a Republican administration faced with a hostile, Federalist-dominated judiciary. Of course, even without the power to issue writs of mandamus, the federal courts could have done many things to interfere with the Administration's agenda. But the power to compel officials to comply with the Federalist judges' conception of what the law required would have been, potentially, a substantial hindrance. *Marbury* provided an opportunity for the Jeffersonians to obtain a favorable ruling on this important issue. It seems likely that, had they chosen to contest the case, they would have taken advantage of the opportunity and tried to settle the issue in their favor. Or at least, if they were thinking clearly about their interests, they should have done so. And there was no apparent reason for the Administration *not* to press this issue. If they succeeded they would lose nothing and possibly win quite a lot.

By contrast, the more famous question in *Marbury*—the constitutionality of judicial review—presented a somewhat more complex issue for the Jefferson Administration. On the one hand, it was a question of great importance to the Republicans, and they would have been determined to prevent the Supreme Court from asserting this power—but not necessarily in *Marbury* itself.

The big case, for the Republicans, was not *Marbury* but *Stuart v. Laird*. In February 1801, after Jefferson's victory and just before leaving office, the Federalist-controlled Congress enacted a statute that relieved the Supreme Court Justices of the duty to ride circuit and created a new set of circuit courts. President John Adams filled the sixteen vacancies on those courts with Federalist appointees; these were among the so-called Midnight Judges. In 1802, the Republican Congress repealed the 1801 Act. *Stuart v. Laird* was a challenge to the constitutionality of the 1802 repealer. The challenge asserted, among other things, that because the 1802 Act deprived the sixteen new appointees of their positions, it violated the clause of Article III, Section 1 that provided that judges hold their office "during good Behavior."

The constitutionality of the 1802 Act was, obviously, much more important to the Republicans than whether Marbury got his commission. There were plausible arguments that the 1802 Act was unconstitutional. Six days after *Marbury* was decided, the Supreme Court, in *Stuart*, upheld the 1802 Act without reaching the question whether it violated the tenure provision of Article III. But for Madison's lawyer, appearing before the Court in *Marbury* with *Stuart v. Laird* still pending, one of the most important tasks would have been to avoid saying anything that the Court could possibly use as a basis for invalidating the

1802 Act. Beyond that, Madison's counsel would surely have wanted to convey the message that the Court would be ill advised to strike down such an important piece of legislation and would encounter the most vigorous opposition from the Republicans if it did. In other words, the argument about judicial review in *Marbury* would have been conducted mostly with an eye toward *Stuart v. Laird*, not Marbury's commission, and part of the task of Madison's counsel would have been to send a warning shot across the Court's bow.

At the same time, the Republicans' position would have been somewhat complicated. It was probably not in the Republicans' interest to assert that the courts entirely lacked the power to invalidate Acts of Congress. The Court's assertion of that power in *Marbury*, of course, resulted in a victory for Madison. While Jefferson was famously displeased about Marshall's maneuver in *Marbury*—Marshall had asserted the power to invalidate Acts of Congress while ruling in favor of the Executive Branch, thus obviating any risk that the Court's decision would be defied—the Administration probably preferred a victory on that ground to a loss.

More importantly, however, the Republicans surely wanted to preserve, for the Executive Branch, the power to refuse to enforce certain laws enacted by the previous, Federalist-controlled Congress on the ground that the President considered them unconstitutional. It would have been difficult to assert that prerogative for the Executive without acknowledging some symmetrical power in the judiciary.

For this reason, I think the Jefferson Administration, had it been forced in *Marbury* to take a position on the constitutionality of judicial review of Acts of Congress, probably would have worked out a narrow and carefully qualified view. It might have said, for example, something to the effect that there is no general power in the courts to declare statutes unconstitutional, but that a court may, in a limited range of cases, refuse to exercise powers that Congress purports to grant but that the Constitution precludes. That formulation would have enabled the Court to refuse to accept jurisdiction in *Marbury*. Something like that formulation would also have made it easier for the Republican Administration to assert that it had the power to refuse to enforce unconstitutional statutes. But, crucially, if the position were framed narrowly enough, it would not have given the Court anything it might use against the Jeffersonians in *Stuart v. Laird*.

III

In other respects, the argument on Madison's behalf would have been relatively straightforward. Madison's counsel would have asserted that Section 13 of the Judiciary Act of 1789 did not purport to grant the Court a general jurisdiction to issue writs of mandamus, but only authorized the grant of mandamus in cases otherwise within the Court's original or appellate jurisdiction. If the Court had accepted that construction of Section 13, of course, it would have had no occasion to assert the power to declare Acts of Congress unconstitutional, and it would have dismissed Marbury's petition for want of jurisdiction. The Court had previously shown a willingness to construe statutes so as to avoid a constitutional doubt, and that canon of construction would have supported the argument that Section 13 did not purport to confer jurisdiction.

On the merits, Madison would have argued that Marbury had no right to his office because the right did not attach until the commission was delivered. And Madison would have argued vigorously that mandamus would not lie to enforce Marbury's claim against an executive branch official.

But as I have said, the principal challenge for Madison's counsel would have been to convey a certain attitude to the Court. The Republicans had, relatively recently, won a clear victory over the Federalists—dispatching the Federalist Party permanently, as it turned out. Jefferson was famously magnanimous in his Inaugural Address, but partisan animosity still ran high. The Federalists were entrenched in the judiciary. As the Chase impeachment showed, the Republicans were prepared to attack that redoubt. There is no reason to think that Madison's counsel would have been vituperative or uncivil, but there is also no reason to think that he would have taken positions that were in any way conciliatory toward Chief Justice Marshall and his Court; quite the contrary. Madison surely did not understand, before the fact, how significant a decision *Marbury* would become. But I think that he and the Republicans, like Marshall, would have recognized that it was a potentially important case in one respect: it might help determine whether the Federalist-dominated judiciary would be able to interfere with the Jeffersonians' program. That is, it was part of a struggle over who was to be the boss. That struggle, rather than abstract issues about judicial review, would have been the central concern of Madison and his lawyer.

Perspectives on *Marbury v. Madison*

CHAPTER THREE

The Intellectual Background of *Marbury v. Madison*

SUZANNA SHERRY

Introduction

The intellectual background of *Marbury v. Madison*, like its political background and its legal precedents, is messy and contested. Over the years, Marshall's opinion has been attacked from all sides and subjected to potentially devastating critiques (and equally powerful paeans). Rather than enter the fray, I propose to ask a different question: Given the fragility of the Supreme Court in 1803 and the vulnerability of Marshall's analysis, why did the decision *work*?[1] In other words, why was the contemporaneous criticism muted and feeble; why did judicial review expand in scope and in reach; and why did *Marbury* increase rather than decrease the power of the Court so that when it decided more controversial cases over the next two decades, it spoke from a position of strength?

I suggest that *Marbury*'s success was primarily the result of its congruence with the American intellectual currents of the day. Marshall's ability both to synthesize existing intellectual consensus and to insert, almost seamlessly, his own innovations allowed him to create an opinion that provided a foundation for the development of modern judicial review. In particular, I will examine three of the most important eighteenth-century intellectual tenets that Marshall drew on and subtly altered: the idea that the judiciary was the keeper of the common law, the belief in natural law as a limit on government, and the newly emerging "science of politics." I will show how Marshall, in his opinion in *Marbury*, captured these ideas in crystalline language that simultaneously evoked virtually universal contemporaneous agreement and set the stage for momentous changes.

I. *Marbury* in Perspective

In 1803, the Supreme Court was a "fragile institution," besieged on all sides. Its first three Chief Justices had left under inauspicious circumstances. Two had resigned for supposedly more prestigious appointments: John Jay as special ambassador to England and later governor of New York, and Oliver Ellsworth as special minister to France. John Rutledge, who had previously resigned as Associate Justice in order to serve on a South Carolina trial court, was a recess appointment and ultimately failed to gain Senate confirmation. A number of other prominent attorneys declined nomination to the Court.[2]

This lack of enthusiasm for service on the Court was unsurprising, as it seemed to be the neglected—or even abused—stepchild of the Congress. When the seat of government was moved from Philadelphia to Washington in 1800, no provision was made for the Supreme Court. It was eventually accommodated in a tiny room in the Capitol. Things were to get worse, however. In the wake of the 1801 battles between outgoing Federalists and incoming Republicans, Congress cancelled the Court's 1802 term, mostly to prevent the Court from reviewing the repeal of the 1801 Circuit Courts Act; the repealer stripped newly appointed lower court judges of their posts. Three years later the House impeached Justice Samuel Chase, who was acquitted in the Senate by a narrow margin, with a majority—but not the required two-thirds—of Senators voting to convict on some charges.[3]

The early Court suffered from multiple disabilities. As the least dangerous branch, it lacked respect, but as the most undemocratic branch it was feared. Having decided only a handful of constitutional cases in its first decade, the Court had nevertheless already been reversed once by constitutional amendment. Moreover, as a result of life tenure, the Justices' political affiliations were out of synch with the rest of the country: it was the only remaining Federalist institution in the new Republican government. The appointment of John Marshall did not help matters. A personal and political enemy of Jefferson, appointed at the last moment (and as a second choice) by the lame-duck John

Adams, he had no judicial experience and spent his first few weeks as Chief Justice simultaneously serving as Secretary of State.[4]

Added to these trying circumstances were two excruciatingly difficult cases that pitted the Court against the other branches of the federal government. The 1803 term saw not only *Marbury v. Madison*, but also *Stuart v. Laird*, which challenged the constitutionality of the 1802 repeal of the Circuit Courts Act.[5] It would have been no wonder had the Court flexed its judicial muscles only to be met with defiance or, worse, utterly ignored.

Marbury itself is, as many scholars have reminded us, a deeply flawed opinion. Marshall was personally involved in the events that led to the case, having failed, as Secretary of State, to deliver the commissions that Marbury and his colleagues brought suit to obtain. Much of the opinion can be characterized as dicta, since once the Court found itself without jurisdiction it should not have ruled on the merits. Scholars have also suggested, quite plausibly, that Marshall made egregious legal errors, without which the question of judicial review would not have arisen. He may have misconstrued the precedent on the law of commissions and the nature of mandamus, thus creating the conflict that set up the opinion's ability to simultaneously rebuke Jefferson, claim the power of judicial review, and insulate the decision from outright defiance. Marshall probably misread §13 of the Judiciary Act when he interpreted it to grant original jurisdiction to the Supreme Court, thus raising the question of its constitutionality. He almost certainly misinterpreted Article III by suggesting that its list of cases within the Supreme Court's original jurisdiction could be *neither* contracted nor expanded: neither logical argument nor historical evidence supports the idea that the list was meant to be exhaustive. These multiple mistakes have led some critics to contend that the opinion borders on legal fraud.[6]

For all that, however, Marshall's coup was remarkably successful. Despite some contemporaneous criticism of the mandamus ruling, the decision itself was largely uncontroversial. The establishment of judicial review, in particular, garnered little criticism. The idea of judicial review spread, first to state courts and, eventually, to much of the rest of the world. Most important, the Supreme Court itself gained sufficient strength to allow it, less than two decades later, to issue truly controversial opinions in cases such as *McCulloch v. Maryland* and *Martin v. Hunter's Lessee*. Although those cases were heavily criticized, they did not bring down the Court, as they might have had they been issued in 1803.[7]

In light of both the politically charged circumstances and the problems with the opinion, how did Marshall succeed so well? Was he merely a clever politician, "advanc[ing] in one direction while his opponents are looking in another"?[8] I suggest in the next section that a large part of Marshall's genius was his ability to synthesize and crystallize inchoate currents of the day into enduring forms, while subtly and seamlessly weaving in his own ideas to lay the foundation for further development.

II. The Mirror of *Marbury*

We know that the Supreme Court necessarily reflects—at least in part—the felt necessities of its time. The difference between *Plessy* and *Brown*, between *Bowers v. Hardwick* and *Lawrence v. Texas*, is one of a changing national consensus in which the Court can hardly fail to join. No Supreme Court doctrine is likely to succeed for long if it strays too far from what a majority of Americans desire. Consciously or not, justices take public opinion into account; they, no less than the man on the street, are part of the public. John Marshall turned this reflective quality into an art form.[9]

Three related intellectual ideas current in the late eighteenth century informed Marshall's opinion in *Marbury* and were transformed by it. First was the idea that judges are the keepers of the common law. This notion was familiar to eighteenth-century Americans from their English heritage and remains the hallmark that distinguishes us from civil law countries. A related, but less familiar aspect of eighteenth-century American thought, inherited mostly from English opposition thinkers, was that principles of natural law—enforceable by those same common law courts—limit the powers of government. Finally, supporters of the new Constitution were enthralled by the emerging idea of a science of politics, epitomized by James Madison's views on divided government. I turn to each of these ideas in turn, examining how Marshall both drew on them and altered them.

A. *The Keepers of the Common Law*

One of the hallmarks of Anglo-American jurisprudence is the reliance on common law as well as legislation. Unlike legislation—which the judges interpret and apply but do not create—the common law is created by judicial decisions in individual cases, which then provide the guiding principles for later cases. The notion that judges developed and applied the common law—which could be changed or preempted by the legislature but was in the control of the judiciary until and unless the legislature acted—is probably the most familiar part of *Marbury*'s story. Developed over the centuries, first in England and then in the colonies, this judicial role is still taught in large parts of the first-year curriculum in American law schools. Interesting historical disputes rage about the level of independence of English (and early American) judges, and about whether the impetus for their independence and the source of their importance lay in themselves or simply because they served as useful pawns in the ongoing battles between King and Parliament. The uniquely American idea of separation of powers left the significance of the judiciary even more unclear, and one accomplishment of *Marbury* was to place judicial independence firmly within the system of checks and balances created by the Constitution.[10]

There is no dispute, however, that judges' primary role was as expositors of the common law. On this, even Coke and Blackstone agreed. Blackstone, after recounting the historical development of the various English courts, opined: "But at present, by the long and uniform usages of many ages, our kings have delegated their whole judicial power to the judges of their several courts; which are the grand depositories of the fundamental laws of the kingdom." Coke agreed: "The common law hath no controller in any part of it but the high court of parliament; and if it be not abrogated or altered by parliament, it remains still." (In *Dr. Bonham's Case*, Coke went further, suggesting that even Parliament could not alter natural law principles.) Both jurists reflected the ordinary English jurisprudence of their age regarding the role of judges.[11]

American colonists were well schooled in this common law tradition. Blackstone's *Commentaries* were published in multiple American editions. The views of Coke and other challengers of parliamentary supremacy found favor among colonists chafing under the yoke of a parliament in which they were not represented. And the colonists had even more reason than their English cousins to trust courts. Parliament and the King were distant institutions, with whom Americans had little contact except through intermediaries. Colonial courts, on the other hand, were staffed by lawyers and judges who were both more accessible and more locally connected. While statutory law was decreed by a remote and alien parliament, justice was dispensed by one's friends and neighbors. This fact only increased the American attachment to the courts as keepers of the common law.[12]

During the immediate Revolutionary period, there was some discontinuity as Americans rejected all things British. All the newly independent states declared their readiness to abrogate English common law where necessary, and some even toyed with the idea of rejecting English common law altogether, even as a default option. But the Revolutionary fervor was primarily anti-British, not anti-common-law, and ultimately all states reverted to a common law regime. Although the content of the common law might be different on either side of the Atlantic, the Blackstonian description of judges as the "grand depositories" of the common law remained a fundamental principle of Anglo-American legal thought.[13]

Marshall drew on this principle in his opinion in *Marbury*. It is reflected best in what is perhaps the most famous line in the opinion: "It is emphatically the province and duty of the judicial department to say what the law is." No American of 1803 would disagree with that statement; it resonated with centuries of tradition. But Marshall used this traditional idea in a new and potentially transformative context. Judges had always been interpreters of the *common* law, but here Marshall was referring to *constitutional* law. By equating the Constitution with ordinary (common) law, Marshall simultaneously evoked and transformed the traditional understanding. The innovation was subtle and drew on half-formed ideas that had been haltingly expressed as early as the debates in the constitutional convention of 1787. Part invention, part tradition, part encapsulation of ideas that were present but inchoate in American political thinking, this single sentence illustrated Marshall's extraordinary talent for remaking American law without provoking alarm from traditionalists.[14]

By treating constitutional law as ordinary law, Marshall accomplished several things. The least important was the achievement for which the opinion is most often celebrated: the reaffirmation of judicial review. Although *Marbury* is sometimes thought to have established judicial review, in fact its existence was generally assumed by the time of the constitutional convention and statutes had indeed been invalidated by a few state courts beginning in the mid-1780s. Many of Marshall's theoretical arguments in favor of the practice were taken almost verbatim from Hamilton's *Federalist 78*.[15]

Had Marshall relied solely on Hamilton's political theory and on the precedent from state courts, however, the power of judicial review might have remained weak and rarely used. The additional effect of equating constitutional law with common law was to make judicial review seem ordinary and usual rather than a last resort required by Federalist political theory. Even in the phrasing of the claim Marshall went beyond his contemporaries. The prevailing view of common law judges was that, as keepers of the law, they said what the law was only as an incident of deciding the cases before them. Marshall seemed to acknowledge that limitation elsewhere in his opinion, when he argued that the Court *must* resolve the conflict between statute and Constitution simply in order to decide the case. But the majestic declaration that "the law" is the province of courts suggests a much broader responsibility, subtly hinting that the judiciary is the supreme arbiter of all constitutional language.

Marshall thus sowed the seeds for the growth of judicial review from its original narrow form to the broad power the Court exercises today. In *Marbury* itself, after all, the Court simply refused to follow what it viewed as a congressional dictate to act unconstitutionally. It did not purport to pass judgment on unconstitutional acts by other governmental entities, as long as the Court was not asked to participate in the unconstitutionality. Today, of course, the Court frequently orders governmental actors to cease acting unconstitutionally. That reaching out beyond its own sphere might be seen as controversial were it not for the two-hundred-year-old understanding that the Constitution, no less than statutes or the common law, is ordinary *law*, and thus squarely within the authority of the judiciary to interpret. Marshall's seemingly banal description of a fundamental tenet of Anglo-American jurisprudence was, in context, a powerful assertion of potential judicial might.[16]

B. Unwritten Natural Law

Less familiar to modern American lawyers and legal scholars is a second important eighteenth-century belief: that unwritten natural law principles limit governmental authority just as written constitutions do. Eighteenth-century Americans inherited their traditions from a country that had neither a bill of rights nor judicial review, but they nevertheless developed—partly because of the mother country and partly in spite of it—a strong belief that there were certain inalienable rights that legitimate governments could not infringe upon. Natural law, in this context, is the body of law that trumps the positive law (whether enacted or common law) because it is binding on all nations. While different scholars used a variety of labels for the rights protected by natural law, the common thread is that certain rights predate the establishment of the government and exist regardless of whether they are enumerated in a written bill of rights.

Derived from Locke as well as from English opposition thinkers like Coke and Bolingbroke, the colonists' invocation of natural law pervaded political theory from the 1760s through the first few decades of the nineteenth century. It could be seen in countless political speeches and sermons that referred to "God-given rights," the "rights of Englishmen," and rights which no government "hath a right to take away." James Otis in 1761 echoed Coke when he argued that "an act against natural equity is void," and Thomas Jefferson expressed the same sentiments in the Declaration of Independence's appeal to "inalienable rights." Many early state constitutions contained "declarations" of "natural," "inherent," "essential," or "inalienable" rights—rights that their drafters clearly assumed existed even before enumeration in the Constitution. James Madison defended the proposed Ninth Amendment—which states that "[t]he enumeration in the Constitution of certain rights shall not be construed to deny or disparage others retained by the people"—on the ground that it was necessary to avoid an implication that unenumerated rights "were intended to be assigned into the hands of the General Government, and were consequently insecure." Language similar to that of the Ninth Amendment was added to many state constitutions after 1791.[17]

If judges were the keepers of the law, and "the law" included natural law, we would expect to find examples of courts striking down legislation on the ground that it violated natural law. And, indeed, in at least six cases in state courts between 1780 and 1803, that is exactly what we find. These courts claimed—and exercised—the power to invalidate statutes as inconsistent with *unwritten* fundamental law. Both state and federal courts continued to do so well into the nineteenth century, in some states even up to the eve of the Civil War. Courts invalidated legislation involving property rights, jury trials, *ex post facto* laws, and other fundamental principles even where such protections were not present in any clause of the written Constitution.[18]

Marshall, like other judges of his time, sometimes interwove natural law and constitutional arguments. In *Fletcher v. Peck*, for example, Marshall wrote that a state legislature was "restrained, either by general principles which are common to our free institution, or by the particular provisions of the constitution of the United States" from passing certain retroactive legislation. Marshall's invocation of natural law principles was not as vivid in *Marbury* as it was in *Fletcher*, or even in *McCulloch v. Maryland*, but it was nevertheless an important part of the opinion. His answer to the question of whether "the laws of his country afford [Marbury] a remedy" is a majestic declaration of the rights of citizens that appears to depend primarily on notions of natural law. He proclaims, with virtually no citation, that providing a remedy for civil wrongs is "the very essence of civil liberty," and "one of the first duties of government."[19]

But in relying on these arguments, Marshall also subtly expanded on the views of his contemporaries about the content of natural law. Prior to *Marbury*, most discussions of natural law focused on the *limits* on government: fundamental principles preventing the government from infringing inalienable rights and engaging in tyranny. By articulating a natural right to a legal remedy for civil wrongs, Marshall suggested that the government also has *duties* arising from natural law. Again, his reformulation captured ideas that were as yet inchoate but very much in keeping with the times. Americans were, in the early nineteenth century, in the process of changing their views about the purposes of government. The older notion viewed law as fixed and immutable, and the purpose of government was therefore to prevent changes that might stray from traditional principles. But Americans were gradually accepting a more modern view: that law was neither transcendent nor immutable, and that government was therefore required to make policy choices that might in fact change both the law and the society. Thus Marshall's imposition of natural law duties on government was new, but it was not frighteningly radical.[20]

Marshall envisaged a relatively narrow notion of governmental duties: natural rights included a previously unarticulated enforcement component. But that incremental move past his contemporaries carried the potential for a later and much more radical transformation, to the affirmative government of the modern administrative state. Marshall's vision did not go as far as the administrative state, but he nicely captured its newly emerging precursor.

Moreover, while Marshall's claim about the essence of liberty and the duties of government—and his use of natural law principles—were uncontroversial, the context in which Marshall made these assertions increased their significance. His straightforward presentation of questions and answers—some invoking precedents or statutes, some invoking the constitution, and others invoking fundamental but unwritten principles—implied that natural law, like constitutional law, was ordinary law and a normal source of judicial decisions. This in turn allowed judicial review to grow beyond the narrow confines of the written Constitution and its original historical meaning.

We have since lost the idea that unwritten natural law is judicially enforceable against the government. It is, as John Ely reminds us, as quaint an idea to us as is a belief in ghosts. But Marshall's accomplishment has still borne fruit. Partly as a result of his matter-of-fact appeal to sources of fundamental law outside the written Constitution, and partly as a result of his later cases packing fundamental law into the grander clauses of the Constitution, the Supreme Court has often enforced unenumerated rights without acknowledging that it was doing so. Both substantive due process—protecting economic liberty during the *Lochner* era and privacy in our own—and the idea of the Constitution as a living, changing document rather than a frozen historical one, have roots in Marshall's reliance on multiple sources of law as equally valid.[21]

C. The Science of Politics

On the cusp of modernity, the founding generation still clung to old notions of natural rights while simultaneously embracing the new scientific ideas of the Enlightenment. In particular, they viewed the American experiment as an implementation of Enlightenment ideals, and politics—including the creation of the Constitution—as a scientific endeavor. Benjamin Rush wrote in 1788 that "Government is a science, and can never be perfect in America, until we encourage men to devote not only three years, but their whole lives to it." James Madison epitomized this view in his meticulous preparation for the Annapolis Convention of 1786, a precursor to the 1787 constitutional convention in Philadelphia. As described by one historian, Madison, in the months before the convention, "undertook a course of reading in the history of 'ancient and modern confederacies,' drawing upon the two trunkloads of books that Jefferson had sent him from Paris. . . . He closed each section of his notes on this reading with a short but pointed list of the 'vices of the constitution' of the particular confederacy he had just studied, the peculiar structural and political defects that compromised its strength and vigor." The practical application of this scientific course of study is evident in the Constitution itself and in Madison's most famous defenses of it in *Federalist 10* and *51*.[22]

Marshall was, like Madison, a child of the Enlightenment. He was an ardent supporter of the Constitution, defending it in the Virginia ratifying convention against attacks from Patrick Henry and George Mason. His use of deductive logic in *Marbury*—while ultimately flawed in execution—illustrates the same view of politics (and constitutional interpretation) as science. But where Madison's arguments were largely theoretical, Marshall's contribution was more practical. His opinion in *Marbury* paints a perfect portrait of three intertwined but mutually constraining branches, exactly as Madison's science of politics would predict.[23]

The opinion's combination of a decision on the merits made impotent by the power-grabbing judicial review maneuver has been praised as political strategy. But it was also a masterful way to show the science of politics in action. By ruling that *some* court (if not the Supreme Court) could issue mandamus to the Secretary of State, he established that the Executive Branch was subject to judicial oversight. By striking down §13 of the 1789 Judiciary Act, he showed that the legislature, too, could be reined in by the courts. But lest this lead to fears of an unchecked judiciary, he simultaneously disclaimed power over political decisions by the Executive and, in striking down §13, appeared to circumscribe the power of the judiciary. Denying legislative omnipotence, restraining any tendency toward an imperial presidency, and self-deprecatingly describing the judiciary—all in a single opinion involving whether a justice of the peace could obtain his commission—is quite an accomplishment. It helped ensure that no branch of the federal government would easily be able to overshadow the others, as well as paved the way for later decisions resting on the idea of checks and balances.

III. Marshall's Luck

Marbury's success, however, was not due entirely to Marshall's talent. While *Marbury* required Marshall to confront Congress and the president, it did not raise what was at the time an even more politically sensitive issue: the spheres of authority of the state and federal government, which now fall under the rubric of federalism. Judicial review of federal legislation was not especially controversial, and judicial review of executive action was only somewhat more so. But had Marshall faced, in 1803, a case that pitted the fledgling Supreme Court against states' rights, he would have had a much more difficult task.

In 1793, the Court had tried to deny a claim of state sovereignty in *Chisholm v. Georgia.* The case merely held that the language in Article III providing for federal court jurisdiction over cases "between a state and citizens of another state" allowed a citizen of South Carolina to sue the State of Georgia in federal court to recover debts arising from bonds issued by the state. It took only two years for the decision to be reversed by constitutional amendment. The states continued to chafe under federal rule, and, after *Marbury,* the Marshall Court continued to rebuff them. In 1809, Pennsylvania passed a statute attempting to nullify a federal court decision in admiralty, and there was much popular grumbling when the Court struck down the state statute. When the Court next took on a state, in 1816 in *Martin v. Hunter's Lessee* and again in 1819 in *McCulloch v. Maryland,* both decisions were met with a firestorm of criticism. Indeed, federal supremacy over the states was not finally established until 1865, when Lee surrendered to Grant at Appomattox.[24]

By 1816, Marshall's Court had gained sufficient strength to weather the attacks launched at *Martin* and, a few years later, at *McCulloch.* But what if those cases, instead of *Marbury,* had come to the Court in 1803? It is interesting to speculate about whether Marshall could have successfully captured a consensus on the divisive issue of federalism. If not, then it was Marshall's good fortune—which ultimately redounded to the benefit of the Court and the nation—that his primary antagonist in 1803 was merely the President of the United States.

Conclusion

Ultimately, what matters of *Marbury*'s intellectual background is what we make of it. I have tried to suggest that Marshall succeeded in *Marbury* by simultaneously synthesizing and innovating. His great strength lay in the fact that his innovations were small and subtle and resonated with contemporaneous beliefs. He did not seek to turn conventional wisdom on its head, nor did he provocatively proclaim the novelty of his ideas. Instead, he wove them seamlessly into the opinion. We would all—scholars and judges alike—do well to follow his example of integrating tradition and change.

Marbury Redux

A Comment on Suzanna Sherry

SUSAN LOW BLOCH

As Professor Suzanna Sherry observes, the Supreme Court in 1803 was, indeed, a fragile institution. Professor Sherry also accurately notes that Chief Justice John Marshall's opinion in *Marbury v. Madison* was "brilliant political strategy." In one unanimous opinion for the Court, Marshall was able to establish that the executive branch was subject to judicial oversight, that the legislature, too, could be reined in by the courts, and that the judiciary would modestly decline to accept jurisdiction if Congress had given it more power than the Constitution authorized. As Professor Sherry notes: "Denying legislative omnipotence, restraining any tendency toward an imperial presidency, and self-deprecating the judiciary—all in a single opinion involving whether a justice of the peace could obtain his commission—is quite an accomplishment." My question is: How was it that Chief Justice Marshall found himself with such an opportune moment to accomplish so much? Was it simply luck or, more likely, creative opportunism on his part?

As I will show, the only way Marshall and the Court could accomplish all that this opinion did without ordering anyone to do anything, thus avoiding any possibility of defiance, was if Marbury and his colleagues sued initially in the Supreme Court. They did, but why? Why sue in a court that, it turned out, had no jurisdiction to hear their case, when there was another nearby court available, with jurisdiction and the ability to grant their requested writ of mandamus? This article will explore several possible explanations for this propitious choice. Let me start with some background.

In an earlier article, *The* Marbury *Mystery: Why Did William Marbury Sue in the Supreme Court*,[1] I showed that there was an alternative court in which Marbury could have sought his requested writ of mandamus. The court we now call the U.S. Court of Appeals for the D.C. Circuit was created in the same legislation that created the justice of the peace positions to which Marbury and his brethren were appointed, the Judiciary Act of February 27, 1801.[2] This court was up and running when Marbury filed his claim in December 1801. The court had jurisdiction to grant a writ of mandamus in this type of case and did so several years later in *United States ex rel. Stokes v. Kendall*.[3] Marbury and his lawyer, Charles Lee, clearly knew about this court. Not only was the D.C. Circuit created in the same legislation that created the justice of peace position, but Charles Lee had been the Attorney General in the Adams Administration at the time and was instrumental in appointing the judges for the D.C. Circuit.[4]

Given this, I suggested that it is possible, indeed likely, that Marbury, his co-petitioners, and their lawyer Charles Lee, all ardent Federalists, deliberately by-passed the D.C. Circuit and went instead to the U.S. Supreme Court to give the Supreme Court the opportunity to establish exactly what it established in *Marbury*. Had they filed initially in the D.C. Circuit, there were a number of alternative scenarios, but none would have offered the opportunities that filing in the Supreme Court provided. Specifically, the following scenarios were possible:

1. The D.C. Circuit might have denied the writ. Then, if Marbury and his colleagues appealed the denial to the Supreme Court, the Court presumably would have still believed they were entitled to the writ. Under the Supreme Court's understanding of Section 13 of the Judiciary Act of 1789 and Article III, as expressed in *Marbury*, the Supreme Court would have had jurisdiction to hear the appeal, would have reversed the lower court's decision, and would have issued the writ. By so ruling, the Supreme Court would have established the power of the judiciary to review the actions of the executive, but it would not have established the power of judicial review of legislative action. And, even more significantly, it would have invited a confrontation with President Jefferson, a battle that most people believe the Supreme Court would have lost and been seriously weakened by.

It is, of course, possible that the Supreme Court, preferring to avoid a confrontation with President Jefferson, would have seen the law differently than it did in *Marbury* and would have denied the writ on appeal. But that is not only a cynical view of the Court, it would also mean that virtually nothing interesting would have been established by this case.

2. Alternatively, the D.C. Circuit might have granted the writ. That could have led to several possibilities:

a. Secretary of State Madison might have appealed to the Supreme Court. Presumably, the Court would have found that Marbury was entitled to the writ, as it did in the *Marbury* case, and would have affirmed. As in the above scenario, this would have established the power of the judiciary to review the legality of executive branch actions, but would have said nothing about the judiciary's power to review the constitutionality of acts of Congress, and would have risked defiance by Madison and Jefferson.

b. Madison might have ignored the D.C. Circuit and not bothered to appeal. That is the more likely scenario, given Madison's refusal to appear in the Supreme Court in the actual *Marbury* case. Seeing the executive branch so dismissive of the court's order would have severely damaged the federal judiciary. Thus, this scenario not only would have failed to establish any power of judicial review but also would have shown that the whole federal judiciary could be ignored.

c. Madison could have complied with the D.C. Circuit's order. This, of course, was highly unlikely, given what Jefferson and Madison were saying. But even if Madison had complied, the case would have established judicial power over the executive with respect to ministerial duties, but would have said nothing about judicial power to review the constitutionality of Acts of Congress.

The *only* way to accomplish what the *Marbury* case in fact achieved—to present what Professor Sherry's appropriately labels "a masterful way to show the science of politics in action"—was for Marbury to sue initially in the Supreme Court. So that brings me back to my earlier question: Was the decision to sue in the Supreme Court just luck or a calculated decision? I believe that luck had very little to do with this choice of forum or this outcome.[5] Choosing the Supreme Court was, in my opinion, a masterly deliberate choice.

Not all readers were convinced. Several commentators offered me alternative suggestions as to why Marbury and his colleagues might have chosen to bypass the D.C. Circuit in favor of the Supreme Court.

Professor Terry Sandalow of the University of Michigan suggested that Marbury and his counsel might have feared that the circuit judges would be too timid to grant the relief. After all, it was an unusual suit, seeking to order the Secretary of State to defy his own President's orders.[6] That conjecture is certainly possible, but it does not explain why, after Marbury and his colleagues received these presumably welcome words from the Supreme Court—declaring that they had been legally wronged, that a judicial remedy was appropriate, and that in fact mandamus was warranted—they did not run down the street to the D.C. Circuit with that kind of authority. What better brief could they want than a unanimous Supreme Court opinion written by Chief Justice Marshall, older brother of one of the D.C. Circuit judges, saying they were entitled to a writ of mandamus? It certainly was not too late; more than half of their five-year term still remained. And they and their attorney clearly knew of the court's existence. Their failure to follow through suggests they cared little about actually securing the requested writ of mandamus.

Professor Alvin Goldman of the University of Kentucky suggested that Marbury and his lawyer might have feared that James Marshall, one of the three judges on the D.C. Circuit and John Marshall's younger brother, would have decided to recuse himself since he was personally involved in the nondelivery of the commissions[7] and that, without James's vote, they might have lost.[8] But fear of recusal seems unlikely. John Marshall was at least as involved in the nondelivery of the commissions as James Marshall,[9] and obviously no fear of John's recusal kept Marbury and his colleagues from seeking relief from John Marshall in the Supreme Court. And their lack of concern was correct—such a fear was unfounded. Under the ethical standards of that time, only financial conflicts required recusal.[10] Indeed, in conformity with this understanding, when John Marshall had a financial interest in a case a few years later, he did recuse himself.[11]

But even if Marbury and his lawyer did fear that the D.C. Circuit might not issue the writ, that concern does not explain why, after Marbury and his colleagues received the Supreme Court's opinion, they did not go directly to the Circuit Court to get the relief they had said they wanted. Again, having John Marshall's opinion in hand should have amply bolstered their resolve.

Recently, Seth Waxman, former Solicitor General, suggested that Marbury and his lawyer may have thought the Supreme Court had original jurisdiction to issue the writ and that Section 13 of the Judiciary Act was constitutional because they may have believed that Secretary of State Madison was a "public minister" under Article III of the Constitution.[12] Waxman also opined, somewhat along the lines of Professor Sandalow's and Professor Goldman's suggestions, that Marbury and his lawyer might have assumed the D.C. Circuit couldn't, or wouldn't, issue such a writ.

The problem with this argument is that there is no indication that Marbury and his lawyer believed that the Secretary of State was a "public Minister" under Article III. Nothing in Charles Lee's argument supports that. Of course, that could have been because the Secretary of State made no appearance in the Court and presented no arguments; thus, Lee had little to argue against.[13] But that more expansive reading of Article III does not seem to have been an accepted theory at the time[14] and was explicitly rejected by the Supreme Court many years later when the Court made it clear that the reference in Article III to "public ministers" referred only to ministers of foreign countries.[15]

Even crediting these commentators' conjectures with some plausibility, no one has explained why, after Marbury and his colleagues lost their case in the Supreme Court, they failed to take advantage of the Supreme Court's essentially favorable opinion.[16] It was a short walk down the street to the D.C. Circuit, a court they knew existed and with which they were familiar. It would have been simplicity itself to present Marshall's opinion and ask for the writ to which the Supreme Court had just found them entitled. I believe the reason they did not do so is that they did not really care about these commissions. The more compelling conclusion is that they wanted to offer the Supreme Court this incredible opportunity to establish judicial review without risking defiance—and they did it very well, indeed perfectly.

So, after all this debate, I still believe that Marbury and his colleagues went directly to the U.S. Supreme Court because they knew it was the only way they could achieve everything they wanted to achieve. Specifically, it was the only way to give the Court the opportunity to establish the power to review the constitutionality of the laws of Congress, the actions of the Executive Branch, and still order no one to do anything, thereby avoiding any risk of defiance. Whether Marbury and his co-petitioners originated the idea or were inspired by others, I do not know. Nor do I know whether these commissions were deliberately withheld by the Marshall brothers. But I do know—and believe they knew—that had they gone first to the D.C. Circuit, there were an array of alternatives, but, as I indicated above, none was nearly as attractive as that offered—and delivered—by suing originally in the Supreme Court. Marbury and company's choice of forum was neither accident nor oversight. It was an intentional, clever, and—for all of us—valuable decision for which we are all in their debt.

CHAPTER FOUR

The Myths of *Marbury*

BARRY FRIEDMAN

There are three types of stories told about *Marbury v. Madison* and the establishment and maintenance of judicial review.[1] They are all, in their own fashion, wanting. The reason is that none of these stories takes sufficient account of popular will as the primary force in establishing and maintaining the judiciary's power to say what the Constitution means.

It is often said that in *Marbury v. Madison*,[2] the greatest judicial decision ever rendered,[3] the legendary Chief Justice John Marshall created the power of judicial review. But this is demonstrably incorrect. The power of judicial review is noteworthy because it commands the compliance of officials with the rule of law. *Marbury* may have declared an enactment unconstitutional,[4] but the judgment in *Marbury* required nothing of anybody save the judges themselves. Had John Marshall required something of those in power, he likely would have been rebuffed.[5] In reality, it was long after *Marbury* that the power of judicial review would command acquiescence from government officials on a regular basis.

There are those who take a considerably less grandiose view of *Marbury*, but even those who tell a more modest *Marbury* story apparently share a belief that judges have the power to establish and maintain the practice of judicial review. According to the modest story, all that happened in *Marbury* is that the Supreme Court (speaking through Marshall of course) recognized the obvious: that in deciding a case, judges—just like other government officials—must consult and follow the Constitution. Still, these *Marbury* minimalists acknowledge that today judicial constitutional pronouncements are supreme. This, we are told, occurred through a process of judicial "usurpation."

Not everyone accepts that the judges are so powerful. There is a third group who believes that as a matter of naked politics, the judiciary is indeed "the least dangerous branch," and that "possessed of neither the purse nor the sword" judicial authority requires explaining.[6] Under this account judicial review depends on the grace of the political branches, and especially the legislature. Judges have the power they do, it turns out, not because they took it, but because those in power gave it to them, or at least let them have it.

Frequently lost in these accountings of judicial power are the rest of us: The People. There is an entirely different story of *Marbury* that can be told, and probably should be. It is a story that rests the power of judicial review squarely on the back of popular acquiescence. This recounting does not necessarily claim popular support for the establishment of judicial review, which turns out to be a remarkably complex question. But the maintenance of judicial review is unequivocally a function of popular acceptance. And in this exercise of popular will, our elected representatives are not a perfect proxy for our views. When it comes to protecting judicial review, the People may stand on their own, apart even from their elected agents.

The discussion that follows largely is devoted to explaining why the stories we tell about the establishment and maintenance of judicial review are problematic. It is an exercise in clearing the way for alternative understandings about the politics of judicial review. Part I tackles "judicial power" stories, i.e., those that rest the power for creating judicial review on the backs of judges, explaining that this was not the case. Part II critiques the many different theories regarding why it is that those who have political (or other) power would choose to accept judicial review, showing how these stories are wanting. Part III offers a brief sketch of an alternative—the notion that judicial supremacy arose as a function of popular acquiescence, and that popular support maintains the institution today—and notes the implications for this alternative theory.[7]

I. The Myths of Judicial Prerogative

The predominant view in the legal academy has been that the establishment and maintenance of the power of judicial review is the work of the judges themselves. This point of view is found in the work of two very disparate groups of scholars, *Marbury* minimalists and *Marbury* maximalists. Mark Tushnet contrasts these two readings:

> Marshall's statement can be read in at least two ways. . . . He might have been saying, "Look, if you pass a statute asking us to do something—in *Marbury*, hear a particular class of cases—you can't keep us from saying what the law is. And the Constitution itself says that it is law—indeed supreme law." . . . The second reading . . . does treat the courts and not just the Constitution as supreme: "It is emphatically the province and duty of *the judicial department*—and no one else—to say what the law is. Once we say what the law is, that's the end of it."[8]

A. The Creation Story

The most familiar story is that of the *Marbury* maximalists, what might be called the Creation Myth. In this story, the power of judicial review sprang fully born from the pen of John Marshall. No ordinary man was Marshall, and no ordinary opinion was *Marbury*.[9] Witness the words of Alexander Bickel, an iconic figure in the legal academy, describing *Marbury* in his classic work, *The Least Dangerous Branch*:

> [T]he institution of the judiciary needed to be summoned up out of the constitutional vapors, shaped, and maintained; and the Great Chief Justice, John Marshall— not singlehanded, but first and foremost—was there to do it and did. If any social process can be said to have been "done" at a given time and by a given act, it is Marshall's achievement. The time was 1803; the act the decision in the case of *Marbury v. Madison*.[10]

B. The Creation Story Debunked

This is a good story, but it is not quite right. In *Marbury* the Chief Justice seems to have asserted the power of judicial review. But he did not create it. In one sense, judicial review preexisted Marshall,[11] in another it did not become established for almost another one hundred years.

To say this is to require a little in the way of definition. If all judicial review means is that judges can interpret and rely upon the Constitution in the course of deciding a case, then even if the Creation Myth were true it would also not be that interesting. What makes judicial review interesting is if constitutional pronouncements in ordinary litigation are—at the least—heeded by the parties

before the court. What gives it even greater force is if, once judges have pronounced what the law of the Constitution is, government officials are duty-
bound to adhere to that interpretation. Typically we call this judicial supremacy.[12]

Oversimplifying, there have been three periods in the rise of judicial supremacy in the United States. During all of these periods claims were made
about judicial supremacy that would sound familiar to modern ears, but
through most of history these sorts of claims were contested. It was only in the
last period that claims of judicial supremacy obtained widespread acceptance
(although there remain dissenters, of course). It is not an exact science saying
when one period began and when one ended. Judicial review has evolved, with
progress and backsliding intermingled. Today's prevailing understanding of judicial supremacy took root at the end of the nineteenth century and was not
fully upon us until almost the middle of the twentieth century.

The first period of judicial review's history in the United States was one of
nonsupremacy.[13] During this period judges could say whatever they wanted,
but there was no widespread belief that anyone necessarily must listen. *Marbury*
itself exemplifies this period. John Marshall had a great deal to say about the
Constitution, but if he had the need to make someone follow his word then he
was probably out of luck unless those in power agreed with him. Marshall's
constitutional decisions either approved the work of the governing branches—
McCulloch v. Maryland[14] comes to mind here, but so does *Stuart v. Laird*[15]—or
like *Marbury* required nothing of them.

This state of affairs persisted at least until mid-century, with defiance of constitutional rulings being a real problem.[16] Commonly it was state governments
who were the object of constitutional decisions during this period. And not un-
commonly when they disagreed with the Supreme Court, they simply did as
they saw fit. Judgments went unenforced, judges were forced from office, and in
at least one instance a person was executed despite a Supreme Court order to
the contrary.[17]

Over time government officials came to recognize judicial constitutional
pronouncements as binding, but this came at a price: the independence of the
judges themselves. This was the second period in the rise of judicial supremacy.
As society came to accept the binding force of judicial pronouncements, it also
toyed with means of holding the judges accountable. Emphasizing the difficulty

in periodicization, there were surely instances such as this stretching back to Marshall's day. Judgments enforcing the Alien and Sedition Acts were obeyed, but when Jefferson's party took power, judges were threatened with impeachment and their security threatened until they foreswore blatant political activity.[18] By the Civil War the story was mixed. Chief Justice Taney's decision in *Ex Parte Merryman*[19] was defied by President Abraham Lincoln,[20] echoing tactics of an era that was coming to a close. During Reconstruction judicial decisions that might be binding in an uncomfortable way were avoided by manipulating the size of the Court or stripping its jurisdiction.[21]

This sport of challenging judicial independence continued until at least 1937. During the populist and progressive eras there were numerous proposals to bring the judges to book.[22] The federal judiciary remained largely, though not entirely, unscathed. In the states, however, judicial selection systems underwent constant "reform," and rarely in the direction of more independent judges.[23] Had the Supreme Court ruled in 1935 against the constitutionality of taking the United States off the gold standard,[24] Roosevelt was prepared to defy the Court.[25]

The Court-packing fight in 1937[26] can be seen as the great battle that signaled serious concern with threatening judicial independence or manipulating the judiciary to implement governmental preferences. Thus began the third period, during which judicial supremacy took root. Roosevelt paid a price for his attempt to manipulate the Court, but then again he might have lost the battle and won the war. Soon thereafter he had his subservient Court. Perhaps the last serious fight in the federal system over judicial supremacy was in 1957, when a Congress unhappy with the Communist decisions,[27] but reflecting a lot of dissatisfaction with the desegregation decisions as well,[28] came close to stripping the Court's jurisdiction.[29] There certainly have been shots taken at the Supreme Court since then,[30] but this was the last major skirmish over the independence of the judges and judicial supremacy.

In light of all this, it becomes impossible to maintain the Creation Myth. John Marshall undoubtedly did something important. His opinion in *Marbury v. Madison* remained the touchstone throughout the ages for those who saw the importance of judicial supremacy to the rule of law. But Marshall's act was an organic one, not bearing full fruit for some 150 years.

C. The Usurpation Myth

This would seem to put the *Marbury* minimalists in the driver's seat. According to them, Marshall did not establish judicial supremacy.[31] He did not even set out to do so. Instead what he did was what everyone realized a judge should do. In a case before the Court, where the Constitution was implicated, Marshall realized that judges are just like other government officials operating under a Constitution. They must read that Constitution, and if it bears upon their work, they must follow it.[32]

Of course, rare is a minimalist who denies the fact of judicial supremacy (as opposed to its propriety, about which there is obvious dispute). Minimalists just think it happened at some point down the road. At some point judges simply seized power.[33] We can call this the Usurpation Myth.

D. The Usurpation Myth Questioned as Well

Like the Creation Myth, the Usurpation Myth has its serious problems. Some are found in facts about *Marbury* that seem to cut in the maximalists' favor. For one, nothing one reads of Marshall makes him out to be as modest as the minimalists would have it.[34] Minimalists tend not to support their assertion of Marshall's modest intent with historical sources. For another, the language of *Marbury* seems to bear out a maximal interpretation. *Marbury* is most famous for this sentence: "It is emphatically the province and duty of the judicial department to say what the law is."[35] Note the absence of modesty in that sentence. It is quoted time and again for the assertion of judicial supremacy,[36] probably because that is what it seems to say.

Marshall's opinion in *Marbury* appears to undercut the minimalist story. As others have pointed out, constitutionalism does not inherently mean that judges may trump the legislature's reading of the Constitution. In other countries that claim the rule of law, judges defer to legislative judgment that what has been done is perfectly constitutional.[37] Marshall seemed to be reaching for something beyond modesty. Moreover, because *Marbury* arguably did not present the constitutional question regarding judicial review, Marshall grasped to reach it.[38] This seriously undercuts the notion that mere minimalism was all that was happening.

But perhaps the most problematic thing about the Usurpation Myth is that to hear it told, the usurpation happens over and over, such that judges seem to keep usurping power after they already have it. History finds the usurpation story trotted out regularly by those opposed to what the Court is doing at the moment. Though the claim of judicial usurpation is not a new one, it must feel new to every generation that levels it.[39] As the brief recounting of supremacy's history explained, however, once supremacy took hold at the turn of the twentieth century, there was no looking back. That is not to stay things must remain that way; only that "usurpation" may be more a cry of the discontent than a depiction of what has occurred.

II. The Theories of Legislative Grant

There is a much more fundamental problem with these stories of judicial aggrandizement: one of power. Those who tell us that judges seized this awesome power of judicial review—and here, most minimalists and maximalists differ only on the timing—barely pause to explain how it was that the judges launched such a coup. One might reasonably stop and wonder. By what act of magic could judges possessing no armies manage to seize such authority against the will of those who otherwise would have wielded it?

An entirely different group of scholars, recognizing that judicial authority must rest ultimately on the consent of those who wield power, have developed a number of theories as to why judicial review actually is advantageous to those in power.[40] These theories are various, and not all of them are consistent with one another. But they share the common notion that to understand why judicial decisions are treated as supreme, one must locate the benefit such supremacy confers on those who have the power to strip judges of their authority.

These various theories shed a great deal of light on the role judicial review might play in society, although at bottom they are all problematic, for a variety of reasons. First, the theories commonly do not distinguish between the establishment of judicial review and its maintenance today. It is not only possible, but probable, that the two are not entirely related. Second, the theories—surprisingly—often fail to account for challenges to judicial power. If judicial review in fact confers benefits upon those in power, it becomes more difficult to explain periodic attacks on judges. Finally, those theories typically fail as an explanation of how judicial review actually is exercised. In other words, a theory about the benefits of judicial review to those in power must account for the decisions themselves, but most such theories do not.

A. *Gradual Accretion*

Mark Graber argues that a number of antebellum Supreme Court cases invalidating "naked land transfers" played a role in the establishment of judicial review.[41] Obviously a theory as to how judicial review took root requires some understanding of when it was exercised initially. It is commonplace to observe that between *Marbury* and *Dred Scott*[42] the Supreme Court did not invalidate any federal statutes.[43] But through careful research, Graber has unearthed a variety of cases in which, long prior to *Dred Scott*, the Supreme Court used creative statutory interpretation to invalidate statutory enactments that appeared to take land from A and give it to B.[44] Graber argues persuasively that these were cases in which the Court clearly indicated that constitutional principles prohibited what would be the more obvious reading of statutes.[45]

Graber's implication from these cases is that "[b]y routinizing the process of judicial review in politically uninteresting matters, the Marshall and Taney Courts fostered beliefs that the judiciary was the appropriate forum for resolving all controversial constitutional issues."[46] Indeed, Graber claims, this routinization of judicial review in property cases is precisely what made it easier for the Court to assume the authority to decide *Dred Scott* itself. Prior to *Dred Scott*, both sides of the slavery dispute had called upon the Supreme Court to resolve it. "If past scholarship is correct," Graber tells us, "pro-slavery advocates were the most irrationally successful optimists in American history."[47] After all, having not held a statute unconstitutional for half a century, they nonetheless assumed the Supreme Court would invalidate the Missouri Compromise. But in light of these naked land transfer cases, Graber argues, Southern optimism made much more sense: The optimism was more than warranted, given that "[a]ll prominent persons endorsed the central constitutional principles the justices relied on to resolve disputes over title."[48]

Graber's work is an important contribution to constitutional history and constitutional theory, but it does not on its face solve the puzzle facing us. Graber unquestionably has contributed to our thinking about the establish-

ment of judicial review, but his history does not tell us why those in power necessarily have maintained the institution of judicial review. Routinization undoubtedly was an important part of getting the institution in place, but a rou-
tine can be unsettled quite quickly if it is threatening to the regime in power.
Between the antebellum period and today there have been numerous serious
attempts to do just that with regard to judicial review. We need more than routinization to explain why we have judicial review, and judicial supremacy, today.

B. Helping Out the "Ins"

There is in Graber's work the germ of another theory regarding judicial review, one that also finds tacit support in an interesting article by Michael
Collins.[49] Collins has studied diversity cases from the post-Reconstruction era,
and from that study concludes that often the courts relied upon general constitutional law principles to decide the cases in favor of national concerns looking
to curtail state authority over them.[50]

The theory suggested by the work of Collins and Graber is that judicial review emerged when it did because it advantaged those in power. Graber, for example, argues that the statutory provisions eliminated by creative interpretation in the antebellum period were mistakes.[51] Whether he is correct in this or
not—an alternative interpretation being that they were the result of one faction
triumphing in the legislature—certainly those decisions taught observers—
propertied ones at that—that judicial review could be a welcome friend against
legislative tyranny. Similarly, what is implicit in Collins's work is that powerful
national interests learned that the courts, speaking in the name of the Constitution, could be a good friend in reining in the state legislatures.

Today there are scholars who recommend just this sort of strategy for helping establish judicial review in emerging democracies. The advice goes something like this: build support for judicial review by showing those in power that
it can be to their advantage, while avoiding stepping on the toes of those that
can hurt you. An example of this is Epstein, Knight, and Shvetsova's analysis of
the establishment of judicial review, with special attention to the case of the
Russian Constitutional Court.[52] Their conclusion was that the Russian Constitutional Court got into trouble by wandering out of its tolerance zone—i.e.,
where the parties in power would accept what the Court was doing—and into

the minefield of presidential power, ultimately putting itself at odds with a strong Boris Yeltsin.[53] Small wonder that when push came to shove, Yeltsin shoved and the Court toppled.

This theory that judicial review is established and maintained because it benefits those in power has a great deal of intuitive appeal. It forms the basis for another recent challenge to common wisdom, in the area of the Supreme Court's race decisions. It is often fashionable to think of the Supreme Court as the protector of minority rights against majority will. Superficially the decisions in desegregation cases such as *Brown v. Board of Education*[54] seem to fit this model, and thus pose a real challenge to the "benefit the 'ins' " argument. But of late scholars such as Derrick Bell, Mary Dudziak, Michael Klarman, and Gerry Spann have questioned the minority-rights model as it applies to race cases specifically and to judicial review generally. Their argument is that the majority in fact tolerates these decisions because they are consistent with majority preferences or wishes. In this way, for example, scholars explain the civil rights decisions: Despite Southern opposition to desegregation, the fact is that by the 1950s segregation was a real problem for American foreign policy, which had a hard time condemning Communist oppression abroad while maintaining an apartheid system at home.[55]

It undoubtedly is true that judicial review needs the support of those in power both to get started and to be maintained. But the difficulty with a "theory" like this is that it is overdetermined and far too general. There is often a story that can be told about why the "ins" actually favored a particular judicial outcome, but if this always is true it becomes unclear why they need judicial review at all.[56] If the "ins" always get to do what they want, what is needed is some theory of why we have a Constitution and judicial review at all. We need a story about why the "ins" are better off getting what they want with judicial review than without it.

C. The Transitional Power Story

There are several more specific versions of the "ins" story.[57] One theory garnering a great deal of attention lately is that the "ins" realize they may not be in forever, and so they favor judicial review as a protection for when they are out. This theory surfaced first, perhaps, in the work of Mark Ramseyer regarding judicial independence to Japan.[58] Ramseyer observed that despite superficial safe-guards of independence of Japanese judges, in practice there was a very elabo-rate system of ensuring judicial decisions were consistent with the wishes of the governing party. Why the difference, Ramseyer wondered, between Japan and the United States?[59] Why do those in power in the United States not bring the judges to heel, as they apparently are in Japan?

As Ramseyer sees it, judicial review is a thorn for the "ins," but one they tol-erate looking toward the day when that thorn may be pricking someone else in power. Japan's ruling power has been in power a long time and expects things to remain that way. Power transfers regularly in the United States. Ramseyer hy-pothesizes that "ins" who realize they may be out have much more to gain from an independent judiciary than "ins" who don't plan on going anywhere anytime soon. Thus, an independent judiciary is tolerated in the United States, but not in Japan.[60]

This theory of transitional power is now being used to explain the develop-ment of constitutional courts and judicial independence in a variety of differ-ent contexts. For example, Lee Epstein and her co-authors have used it to ex-plain the differing term lengths and features of security of constitutional courts.[61] Richard Drew is using it to explain the emergence of judicial selection and retention systems in the state governments of the United States.[62]

Although there may be some truth to this theory under some circum-stances,[63] it does not explain the establishment of judicial review in the United States. One would think that upon obtaining the reins of government in 1800, the Jeffersonians realized that their tenure might not be indefinite. After all, they had just replaced the Federalists in a heated partisan contest.[64] Yet, as soon as it became clear the courts could be a problem, the Jeffersonian Republicans attacked them. Maybe this does not rule out the transitional power hypothesis. Perhaps it just took several plays of the game to learn that today's "ins" could be tomorrow's "outs." But it is equally plausible that hubris overtakes "ins" who come to believe that they will be in for a long time. The theory runs into seri-ous difficulty when one observes sporadic attacks on judicial review through-out history, long after any reasonable party in power should have seen that power transfers regularly.

Moreover, this transitional theory is inconsistent at some deep level with the "ins" theory generally. If judicial review just serves the "ins" needs while in power, then it is not going to protect "ins" when they are "out." On the other hand, if it protects "outs" who used to be "ins," one would have to assume at some point the current "ins" would get tired of the "out-protecting" Court. Indeed, today's "ins" might figure they are likely to stay in power longer if courts are not always interfering with their agenda while protecting the "outs." So, which is it? Are judicial decisions in-supporting or out-supporting? In truth, the results are mixed, and thus we have a more complex story on our hands.

D. Interest Group Theories

There are a variety of theories that have been devised to explain precisely why the "ins" would prefer judicial review while they are in. All of these operate under the rubric of interest group theory, which states that government is responsive to groups that can demand (and pay for) favorable legislation. These theories all shed some light on our problem, but as we will see they are inconsistent with one another and ultimately with the realities of judicial review.

1. Sealing the legislative deal

The most famous of these theories is one offered by William Landes and Richard Posner, who suggest that judicial review serves to seal legislative bargains, permitting legislators to obtain maximal rents for the legislation they enact.[65] The problem, it turns out, is that you can go to the legislature to buy a good deal, but what is to keep the next legislature from overturning the deal you bought? Independent judges, it seems, can enforce these deals, thereby maximizing the price of legislation. The proof of this offered by Landes and Posner is that so few statutes are overturned by constitutional review. What judges actually do is enforce bargains that were struck, rather than invalidating them. Judicial review thus ensures the permanency of legislation.[66]

Independent judges are important to this story, according to Landes and Posner, because otherwise the judges would be beholden to the party presently in power, and of little use protecting deals acquired from the prior government. If Group A got a deal from the legislature at time A, and Group B wants to repeal that law at time B, Group A's deal is protected in part by the difficulty of getting another deal through the new legislature. But still, the original deal might not be enforced by the judges. "[I]f the judges are the perfect agents of the current Congress, they will refuse to enforce the [old deal], and the effect will be the same as a legislative repeal."[67] "[A]n independent judiciary would, in contrast, interpret and apply legislation in accordance with the original legislative understanding."[68] Why would judges want to do this? Because, Landes and Posner explain, this is how they maintain their value to those in power, thereby avoiding attacks.

With all due respect to the genius of Landes and Posner, this story is simply not persuasive. If the advantage of judicial review is that it does not undo legislative deals, then why have it at all? Their answer—that it ensures the permanence of legislative deals—suggests they have looked at the wrong evidence. The question is not how many statutes the judges did not overturn, but how many deals were enforced by the judges. Of course, there need not be explicit enforcement, but Landes and Posner need—and do not have—evidence that legislative deals are more permanent somehow in a regime where there are constitutional principles that could be enforced by courts than in a regime where judicial review is not a possibility. This evidence does not exist in their work. Indeed, in a long footnote they candidly explain they do not have it.[69]

Besides, in practice judges are sometimes attacked by those in power. The New Deal is not the only example, but it might be the best one for these purposes, because in a sense the judges were doing what Landes and Posner posited they should be. The New Deal judges were standing firmly in support of what might be thought of as preexisting deals (or understandings), and in opposition to a regime that would have overturned many of them. Yet, apparently overturning old deals was more important to those in power than the permanency of the deals they might adopt. This comports with an observation above: When in power, the "ins" may have the best chance of remaining there by doing well by those who support them at present.

2. *Unsealing the deal*

The Landes and Posner view was challenged in theory and empirically by Nicholas Zeppos, who argued that in fact far more deals are undone than Landes and Posner realized.[70] Zeppos reached this conclusion on the strength of an important insight and some hard work. The insight was that courts often engage in just the sort of clever statutory interpretation Graber identified, modifying legislative deals substantially without simply striking the legislation down.

Courts can undo what it is a legislature has done by creatively interpreting the statute rather than simply striking it down as unconstitutional. (This is just the sort of thing Landes and Posner realized was a problem with their own empirical evidence.) Zeppos then went to the United States Reports and found that judicial modification of legislative deals was far more common than the Landes and Posner data suggested, and that this was even more true for "important" statutes.

With new evidence, Zeppos gave us a new theory of why the "ins" might prefer judicial review: his argument was that deal "undoing" was actually in the interest of groups because sometimes they strike bad deals they later regret. Or, they get caught in deals they just do not like. Thus, Zeppos suggested, judicial review serves the wishes of the interest groups that support the "ins." Groups can go to the legislatures and get the deals they want. But if they subsequently realize that their deal was a bad one, or if they are disadvantaged by someone else's deal, then they have recourse.[71]

The difficulty with the Zeppos theory is that when one looks at the list of "groups" identified by Zeppos as advantaged by judicial review, they turn out to reflect many interests that are not necessarily the "ins." For Zeppos, groups include labor unions, dissenting members of groups themselves, and even individuals. Among the cases of courts identified by Zeppos as modifying or invalidating "important" legislation we find *Webster v. Doe* (holding a gay former employee has a right to challenge dismissal from the CIA as unconstitutional);[72] *Shapiro v. Thompson* (invalidating residency requirements in the Social Security Act);[73] and *Marchetti v. United States* (invalidating reporting requirement of illegal activity under the Internal Revenue Code).[74]

In fairness to Zeppos, his self-assigned task was not to prove that judicial review helped the "ins" but that "groups" (broadly defined) might support aggressive judicial review. In this, what Zeppos ultimately offers is support for a more classic theory of judicial review, one that sees judges as protecting minority rights. Indeed, if anything, Zeppos raises questions why so much of judicial review occurs under a rational basis test, which, in practice gives great deference to the "ins" that passed the original legislation. If, as Zeppos argues, all these "groups" prefer judicial review, the question is why judicial review is not more aggressive, even in the area of economic rights.

3. Why judicial review is inevitable

The final entrant in this dialogue is William Eskridge's point that whether judicial review is good or bad for groups (he thinks the latter), they are going to keep pursuing it, and so it is an inevitability.[75] Eskridge reaches this conclusion by coming at the question from a very different branch of rational choice theory: positive political theory. Positive political theory looks not only to the preferences of those who demand legislation, but also to those who supply it.[76] Eskridge's point is that if the judiciary is independent, judges are going to have their own preferences. In enacting legislation—putting deals into law, as it were—the parties are going to have to take account of those judicial preferences, in order to see that their laws are not invalidated when courts exercise judicial review. Not only will this increase the transaction costs of players in the legislative game—one reason groups might not like judicial review—but judicial preferences are not likely to be the same ones interest groups would prefer. Thus, Eskridge is skeptical that rational interest groups would prefer judicial review at all, given the choice.[77]

What Eskridge adds to this story is the important insight that even if in the aggregate judicial review is disadvantageous to groups, they cannot enter into a binding agreement to forego it in specific cases. Eskridge sees the problem as a Prisoner's Dilemma. The best state of affairs for groups, he believes, is no judicial review. But in any given situation some group that is hurt in the legislative process is going to go running to the judiciary for help. Given that sometimes such a group will prevail, it becomes impossible to police a norm of no judicial review.[78] Whether or not Eskridge is right that over time groups might prefer no judicial review, he certainly reinforces the idea that when the "ins" are out, or even just the "outs" are out, they are going to want to turn to the courts if that is a place they can turn.

Of course, what Eskridge does not tell us outright, but suggests, is that the institutions themselves might not prefer judicial review either. Echoing Landes and Posner, perhaps unintentionally, Eskridge hypothesizes that the judges, being independent, are not likely to share the same values as those in power.[79] But if this is true, then what Eskridge is saying is that so long as judicial review is tolerated it will be utilized, but we still need some reason to understand why it is tolerated.

E. In Sum

We have been examining theories as to why those in power might prefer to have judicial review in place. Obviously there are a limited number of possibilities. Either the "ins" benefit in the here and now from judicial review, or they tolerate it because they believe they will benefit in the future. But we have not seen any clear evidence that either is regularly the case; and the theories tend to conflict with one another. It may be true that sometimes judicial review benefits the "ins," and sometimes it does not, but then we need a more complex story as to why it generally is tolerated. In a pithy article, John Ferejohn draws attention to just this fact.[80] Ferejohn recognizes that the political branches inevitably pose a threat to the independence of the judiciary as an institution, and thus is skeptical that "interest-based theories" are able to account for the American system. "Why, if judicial independence is a good thing for some interest-based perspective, leave the door open for political meddling in the future by allowing the political branches to influence the judiciary as a whole?"[81]

Of course, when we look to history we learn that judicial review is not always tolerated, that judges sometimes are attacked. They were attacked after Reconstruction era decisions, after Progressive era decisions, and after New Deal decisions, with the last serious attack being 1957. Challenges to judicial authority continue, of course—including some recent ones[82]—but the level and seriousness of threats has diminished over time. The theories we have been considering do not really explain the attacks themselves, or why they have been diminishing. In other words, they do not explain why those in power have responded as they have to judicial review.

Just as the theories fail to explain the attacks on judges, they also fail to explain many instances of judicial review in which there were no serious attacks, or to explain the output of judicial review generally. Judges struck down legislative apportionment schemes that benefited those in power. The "ins" grumbled and threatened, but nothing was done about the judges. During the 1960s the judges decided important cases according rights to criminal defendants. It took a long time for those in power to see a problem in this, and ultimately when they did so the problem was addressed through the gradual process of judicial appointment. Judges struck down the death penalty, but have permitted it again. Judges protected abortion rights, but have backed away. Judges have struck down many statutes protecting rights that were passed by recent (but different) Congresses, in the name of federalism. Judges said people may not be punished for burning the flag to make a statement. Everyone complained, but the judges persisted.

III. The People's Courts

Here is where we stand. It seems unlikely that the judges could establish the power of judicial review on their own, and maintain it, if it was truly not in the interests of those in power. By the same token, we do not have an account that seems entirely persuasive of why those who are in power tolerate judicial review. It could be that the explanation is simply more complex than can be captured in any one theory. This likely is the case.

And yet, missing from all these other accounts—the judicial power story, and the political power story—is something that may have important explanatory value. That something is the rest of us, the People. Everyday ordinary citizens with the everyday, ordinary level of political engagement, sitting on their sofas, watching television, stirred occasionally to some small gesture of political involvement, be it voting, answering a poll, sending in a check, or writing a letter.

As a matter of naked power, looking to the people rather than the political branches may not seem to make sense. After all, the political branches have direct power to control the judiciary. In the article quoted above, Ferejohn inevitably places the button of power in the political branches themselves.[83]

And yet, in that same article Ferejohn alludes several times, in passing, to the importance of the people. "It seems clear," he says, " that the basic reason constitutional protections for judges have remained strong and stable over the years is that the political branches, or, perhaps, *the people themselves*, have not really wanted to alter them—at least not badly enough (or for long enough) to incur the substantial costs and political risks associated with such an effort."[84] He later declares that "the practical security the judiciary as a whole enjoys is entirely dependent on the whims of the popular branches *and of the people themselves*."[85] While continuing to focus on the political, power-wielding, branches, Ferejohn recognizes that at some deep level ultimately the resolution of such a conflict rests in the people:

However these crises are resolved, the resolution tends to restore a circumstance of equilibrium between judicial action and popular preferences. Whether the new political majority loses popular support by overreaching itself, or the courts shift their behavior in such a way that it becomes acceptable to the other branches, it will no longer be possible to find majorities to produce further changes in political behavior.[86]

It is precisely this point that requires development, because it is the missing piece of explanatory theories of judicial review. Understanding the role of the people can help explain a great deal about why a system of judicial review and judicial supremacy is maintained in this country. It may offer some insight into the outcomes of judicial decisions. And it might help us to comprehend the bounds of judicial authority, for it necessarily is true that judicial authority rests ultimately in political power.

A response to this story might be that the idea of popular maintenance of an independent judiciary is no different than one about the "ins": our governors are our agents and act for the rest of us. Indeed, many (if not all) of the theorists whose work is described in Part II would doubt that there is a will of the people independent from that of their elected representatives.

Historically, however, that has not necessarily been the case. It is no secret that there is some slack between the will of the people as principals and their elected agents.[87] During times of tension over judicial authority, that slack has revealed itself. A clear example is the 1937 fight over Franklin Roosevelt's Court-packing plan, discussed at greater length below. Of course, the preferences of politicians may come to reflect popular will during such times of struggle. But the point here is that it is only during the course of such struggles that voter-representative slack reveals itself and adjustment occurs. The discussion of "popular will" refers to the potential gap in preferences between voters and politicians that reveals itself during such struggles.

The idea of popular support for the maintenance of judicial review receives remarkably little attention in the legal academy. The task here is twofold, then. To expand upon the point itself and to suggest what attention to it might reveal.

A. *The Point*

It became clear during the New Deal battle over judicial independence that the public was taking on the role as the judiciary's ultimate defender. Franklin

Roosevelt's attack upon the Supreme Court plainly was frustrated at least in part by public opinion. Even taking into account some principled opposition to the plan among Democrats, Roosevelt had the votes in Congress to move his plan. But public opinion was against him, and ultimately the plan failed.[88]

It is true the Court itself might have had a hand in influencing public opinion, but that only serves to support the main contention, that there is a relationship between public opinion and the maintenance of judicial review. Greg Caldeira's study of public opinion during the Court-packing fight suggests that public opinion shifted in response to Supreme Court decisions that seemed to "switch in time" and to the retirement of Justice Van Devanter.[89] What this means is that the public might have let the political branches get away with it, if the Court had not turned at the last minute.[90] Nonetheless, it seems apparent that public opinion was riding shotgun on the Congress as it deliberated Roosevelt's plan.

Less clear is whether public opinion always did or could play this role. There is evidence during prior attacks on the courts regarding the exercise of judicial review that popular opinion was being touted and perhaps actually taken into account. References are made to the people and popular opinion during the Jeffersonian attacks on the courts and during Reconstruction.[91] On the other hand, the people's will was advanced frequently in attacks on the courts during the populist-progressive era, and those attacks came to naught.[92]

It is easy to understand why the New Deal might have been a turning point. Just as there has been a growth of judicial supremacy over the years, so too has there been a rise of democracy. The extension of the franchise, the increasing influence of interest groups, the role of the media and public opinion polls are familiar territory.[93] Without aiming for precision, the New Deal seems as likely as any time for the confluence of these to begin to play an important role in discussions of curtailing judicial review. Roosevelt's Court-packing plan was a high salience event among a very broad public.[94]

In any event, it simply seems a given that no wholesale attack on judicial supremacy could succeed at present absent public support. It is very difficult to imagine the political branches stripping judges of the power of judicial review or otherwise disciplining them, in the face of contrary popular opinion. Thus, popular views play an important role in the maintenance of our system of judicial review.

Whether the popular role is indirect only, or can be more direct, it is difficult to say, as is the question of whether popular support for curbing the judiciary will ensure success of such a measure. In other words, it seems obvious that attacks by the political branches upon the judiciary must be vetted in the Court of Public Opinion. But whether the political branches are likely to be moved to action by the public, and whether those branches will defy a judge-thirsty public, is more difficult to know. The events of the Progressive era suggest politicians might fail to accede to the wishes of a public looking to discipline the judiciary, but it is hard to know what the majority of the public wished at the time, and times may well have changed.

Not only does the public have a hand in maintaining the system of judicial review, it may well have an important voice in the scope of the exercise of that power. This, concededly, is a more difficult contention to defend. But given that a weakness of the other theories is the failure to explain judicial outputs, it at least is worth considering whether judicial decisions at present follow popular wishes.

Popular opinion may well account for the direction of the Supreme Court following the defeat of Roosevelt's Court-packing plan. Scholars speak frequently of the "New Deal settlement."[95] By this they mean the withdrawal of the judiciary to a more deferential stance of judicial review in economic matters and more aggressive review in individual rights.[96]

It is worthwhile noting that none of the other theories of judicial review can do much of a job of explaining this. Certainly not judge-powered theories. We have had liberal judges, conservative judges, Democratic judges, and Republican judges, and, within certain bounds of tolerance to be sure, the practice of judicial review has been roughly similar—or at least was from the 1940s to the early 1990s. But legislative and interest group theories fare no better. It is difficult to take the actual cases and explain why powerful groups, and the legislature in particular, would have made the choices judges made, and not others.

On the other hand, there is a great deal of evidence that the post–New Deal Court pursued the agenda that popular opinion desired of it. Popular opinion supported Roosevelt's position that new solutions were needed to entrenched economic problems, that the Constitution had to be kept up with the times, and that the judiciary—the Nine Old Men in particular—should retire from the field of aggressive review of economic legislation.[97] Yet, popular opinion balked at Roosevelt's attempt to make the judiciary compliant.[98] And the reason is that the very same popular opinion saw a threat to overweening government power when it came to individual liberties.

Add these two parts of the equation together and you have the New Deal settlement: withdrawal from the field of economic legislation, but judicial intervention to protect individual rights from governmental power. At least until recently, much of the exercise of judicial review in the post–New Deal era reflects what the public was thinking and saying during Roosevelt's attack on the judiciary.

The similar point may be made with regard to the present Court. Many scholars complain that the Supreme Court is trumping popular will in its recent binge of striking congressional statutes, primarily on federalism grounds. Yet, a few scholars have observed the congruity between the Republican devolution agenda and the Court's decisions.[99] At the end of the Supreme Court's 2002 term, the Court surprised many people with its seemingly liberal decisions upholding remedies against the states under the Family and Medical Leave Act, sustaining affirmative action in higher education, and its turnaround decision striking down state laws that criminalized homosexual sodomy. In the 2003 term the Court once again backed away from its strong federalism position[100] and ruled against the federal government in the closely watched terrorism war cases.[101] Pundits note, once again, that shifting public opinion may have played a role.[102] And a swing Justice on the Court, Sandra Day O'Connor, suggested as much in extrajudicial writings.[103]

B. *The Significance of the Point*

This greatly simplifies a complex story, but it is worth doing so to get where this takes us, one part of which is thinking about why the legal academy has been so slow to recognize that judicial power rests on popular acquiescence. Whether the story of popular influence is precisely correct or not, there is enough to it to bear close examination. There is every reason to believe popular opinion supports the direction of judicial review as well as its existence.

There is a great deal of research in the social sciences that examines, and supports, just this supposition. The research takes a variety of approaches, but its central conclusions tend to be relatively constant. Supreme Court decisions in the main are consistent with public opinion, and public support exists to protect constitutional decision making, even if the public disagrees with particular decisions.[104] The causation story is complicated, to be sure, but the evidence is sufficient that one cannot easily be blind to it.

Yet, for many years the legal academy seems to have staked out quite a contrary perspective. When one reads legal scholarship, it tends to take one of two positions.[105] One position is that judicial review is contrary to popular will, but that is a good thing that simply needs justification in a democracy.[106] The other position is to complain that judges are acting contrary to popular will and urge reining them in.

It is really quite difficult to understand the persistence of this perspective in the legal academy. But perhaps it is because judicial review holds out a hope and a threat. The threat is that judges, being too independent, will frustrate the will of a democratic majority. Of course, there is an implicit sense here that the informed majority will do what is right, and thus the judges will be a bane upon society.

The hope is that judicial review will have a moderating influence on a majority will that is not always right. There are different versions of this hope. One version is that the judges will be more enlightened generally than the majority, protecting minority rights, seeing us through to a better society however one defines that.[107] Of course, differences of opinion on what constitutes a better society tend to make the hope an illusory one if it requires universal acclamation. Another version is that the judges will save us from ourselves when we are really misguided or stupid, and that the very exercise of judicial review will temper particularly oppressive instincts or moves by the political branches, fed by momentary popular passion.[108]

The significance of all the discussion about public opinion is that understanding the relationship between public opinion and judicial review may offer some guidance on whether the hope or threat perspective is the right one to take. There are many variables. The answer will depend on how much support for courts there is even if people disagree with the decisions and the extent to which the public will shelter an unpopular court from political reprisal. It will also depend, importantly, on issues of intensity of preference, the degree to which the public pays attention to judicial decision making, and the extent to which public opinion is subject to manipulation on the subject.[109]

Admittedly, answering these questions is difficult. But the important point at present is that we will not pursue answers so long as we adhere to the myths of *Marbury*. So long as we believe judges can take the power for themselves, or that judicial review exists only because those in power prefer it, we will miss the vital role of the public. Once we recognize that role, we can begin to tackle the question of whether the relationship between judicial review and popular opinion is a healthy one.

Judicial Review and the Stages of *Marbury*

A Comment on Barry Friedman

DOUGLAS S. REED

In the sociology of legal education, the emergence of *Marbury v. Madison* as a classic and important text is worthy of several chapters. From the identification of the case as "foundational," to its perceived justification for a judicially led effort to restrict meanings of the Constitution to judges, to the copious theoretical efforts to respond to the "problem" of *Marbury*, the developments in the many meanings of *Marbury* are creations of the twentieth century and the early years of the twenty-first. As others have stated, the primacy of *Marbury* in constitutional syllabi tells us vastly more about the judicial politics of our day (and recent past) than it does about the conflicts, constitutional designs, and legal theories of the Founders. Its strength as both precedent and as a guide to the legal and constitutional problems of American politics has little to do with the contexts and rationale and reasonings of the case as it proceeded between 1801 and 1803. Instead, like any good classic, *Marbury* is reinvented for and by each new generation. These plural meanings and our capacity to invest those meanings with political values ensure that its normative appeal and political significance will be far greater than its actual judgment and narrow ruling.

In these narrowest of senses, the judgment of *Marbury v. Madison* meant that William Marbury could not hold office as a Justice of the Peace in the District of Columbia and the Supreme Court could not issue writs of mandamus in original proceedings. In its broadest meaning, the authority of *Marbury* is that the Supreme Court can save American society from the worst impulses of its impassioned demagogues and unenlightened masses, or, alternatively, that the Court now governs Americans as judicial tyrants, suppressing the capacity for self-governance. The invention of both the "problem(s)" and "solution(s)" of *Marbury* has sustained generations of legal academics, who have used *Marbury* to respond to the judicial and constitutional developments of these times. Clearly, there is a need for a "foundational" text to play this role, but the casting of *Marbury* into that leading role stems from the place the judiciary came to play in American politics during the twentieth century, not from any inherent majesty of *Marbury* itself. *Marbury* is the stage for our judicial politics and constitutional theories, not their foundation. *Marbury*'s virtue as a stage lies in its capacity to support any number of actors, declaiming an enormous variety of lines.

Onto this stage now comes Barry Friedman, arguing that the maintenance of judicial review (which, according to both *Marbury* maximalists and minimalists, flows from *Marbury*) lies neither in the work of judges themselves, seeking to acquire and defend power nor in legislative acquiescence to the increasing use of judicial review, but in a vastly simpler mechanism of legitimation: acclamation by the People. As a nation, we are wedded to the institution of judicial review, if not judicial supremacy, because We, the People, in a democratic sense, have legitimated judicial review. Moreover, contends Friedman, public support for the institutions of both the Supreme Court and judicial review, in effect, obviate the concerns constitutional law scholars have advanced about the dangers of judicial review and, indirectly, *Marbury*'s role in the development of judicial review. Thus, on the occasion of the two-hundredth anniversary of *Marbury* we should, in Friedman's view, respect the wishes of the American people and value the institution of judicial review for its democratic legitimacy.

Friedman's analysis is important because it asks us to reflect deeply on the role and structure of judicial review in American politics. Constitutional lawyers and legal academics have only recently begun to explore, in an empirical sense, how judicial review radiates or extends beyond the operation of the courts and intersects with other political institutions, as well as with political attitudes and behaviors. That kind of analysis is important because it reorients the discussion of judicial review away from normative theory and shifts the investigation of judicial review into a realm where we can begin to understand its real world consequences on the organization of American politics. If judicial review has achieved a democratic legitimacy, analysts should be able to demonstrate that legitimacy (and its attitudinal foundations) empirically through an examination of expressions of democratic support. In addition, by placing an empirical (rather than normative) frame around judicial review, Friedman's account prods scholars to explore whether and how judicial review endows particular political interests and actors with political advantages and whether the public deems those advantages legitimate.

One clear objective of Friedman's project is to reorient the scholarly examination of judicial review. Friedman's challenge, as I see it, is to understand the relationship between judicial review and at least two dimensions of American politics. First, if the longevity of judicial review is the result of popular approval, we need to more fully understand the process of judicial legitimation and how it differs from the processes of legitimation undergirding other national political institutions. Second, we need to distinguish the kinds of support the public expresses for the Supreme Court, primarily exploring the difference between support for the institution as a whole and support for the particular policies embodied in the decisions of the Supreme Court.

Processes of Institutional Legitimation

Because proponents of a strong theory of judicial review assert that judges need to be able to restrain the abuses of legislative majorities, it makes the most sense to compare the processes by which judicial actions and legislative actions attain legitimacy in the eyes of the polity. If the durability of judicial review in the American context stems from its broad popular support, as Friedman claims, we should at least be able to discern a process or mechanism by which the practice of judicial review gains legitimacy. Moreover, it is important to distinguish the ways that judicial legitimation takes place and how it is different from legislative legitimation.

First, let's consider the bases for legitimacy of legislative action. Obviously, elections form the cornerstone of legitimacy for all legislative acts. Not only are individual legislators accountable to the electorate, but the policy direction of Congress as a whole receives a very public stamp of approval (or disapproval) through elections. Electoral legitimation not only has a normative resonance within constitutional democracies, but it puts a distinctive stamp on institutional organization and activities. That is, Congress organizes both its institutional processes and its work product in such a way as to make winning elections easier for its members.[1] The individual-level electoral demands on members of Congress create an institutional context in which credit-claiming, symbolic politics, and pork-barrel provision of discrete benefits to home districts and constituents are all part of the game of legitimation.

This dynamic stems from the relative frequency of House elections and assumes that these elections have the potential, at least, to be competitive—especially if members of Congress do not respond to their constituents' demands and other ambitious politicians back home are all-too-eager to fill their seats. The electoral calendar—and the growing need to raise large sums of campaign funds within relatively short periods of time—combined with a ready pool of capable politicos biding their time in state legislatures, city councils, and county commissions create intense pressures, especially on first-term representatives, to hew very closely to the script of electoral legitimation, in which representatives deliver the goods, claim credit for those goods, and move on to the next fund-raiser.

An essential feature of congressional legitimation is its geographic orientation. Because members of Congress represent people residing in places, the needs and priorities of those places imbue members of Congress with a sharply localist attitude. The American public values and rewards an exceedingly local perspective in its members of Congress, and any member of the House (and to a lesser extent the Senate) who is unable or unwilling to maintain a parochial attention to the interests of key players in their home districts will soon find themselves out of a job. Voters in single-member districts care less about members of Congress's stance on important national policy directions than on their actions on behalf of local constituents and local needs.

Finally, the process of legislative legitimation is exceedingly nonreverential. There is little respect for Congress, at large, among the electorate, and challengers frequently campaign on an incumbent's leadership position in Congress as evidence that he or she no longer has the interests of the home district at heart. Legislative office-holding, in itself, confers little glamour or celebrity status, and while the Senate may lay claim to its heritage as a body that values debate and deliberation, poll after poll suggests that the American electorate views Congress as a whole as a largely ineffective and nonresponsive institution. Certainly, social prestige attaches to the office of Senator, but members of the House, in general, enjoy little in the way of society page notices. While certain members of Congress may achieve celebrity status, that position, more likely than not, precedes rather than follows their election to Congress. Electoral challenges, campaign promises, ever-present political exigencies, and the relentless need to cut bargains and to raise funds all contribute to an image of congressional representative as supplicant rather than revered public servant.

In toto, these characteristics of Congress, members of Congress, and electoral legitimation result in a legitimacy of legislative processes that rests on a messy reality: the act of holding elections—even when the retention rate is high—changes the conduct of members of Congress, as well as the organization and work product of Congress. Elections are a potentially powerful point of coercion the public holds over individuals who, presumably, want to retain their jobs.

In contrast, the processes of judicial legitimation are untethered from the unseemly necessity of elections, at least at the federal level. Appointed for life, confirmed just once (unless willing to be appointed to a higher judgeship), federal judges enjoy a real world immunity from serious sanction by the public. They may be vilified in print or on air, or even shot at, but absent violence the public has no direct recourse to affect their work or their job security. Instead, any public sanction or approval of judicial decision-making is expressed obliquely, through the random samples of the public expressing support or opposition to the specifics of judicial decisions via public opinion polls. It is rather clear that federal judges take little direct notice of these in the vast majority of Supreme Court, appellate court, or district court decisions. Indeed, public ratification of judicial decision making seems to be one of the lowest priorities of the federal judiciary as a whole, although there is official concern about conflicts of interest and any public perception of possible impropriety. But these concerns center on the potential for the maladministration of justice, in which the vast power of the judiciary is deployed in an unfair or partial fashion.

Instead, the formal legitimacy of judicial acts has more to do with how judges act than the public approval of their substantive rulings. Martin Shapiro has argued that the central political problem of courts is to ensure that judicial proceedings do not become a game of "two-against-one."[2] Much of the formality of legal proceedings and courts' attention to process, Shapiro argues, are efforts to demonstrate to the parties before the bar that the court has no interest in the outcome. If Shapiro is correct, the legitimacy of judicial action flows primarily out of judges' adherence to lawfully authorized processes and their ability to effectively "split the difference" between claimants. If a judge is installed in her office through proper processes (i.e., appointment and confirmation) and she adheres to clearly specified processes of adjudication, then there is little room to deny the formal legitimacy of the judicial act—no matter what its substantive content. Even if a judicial decision is reversed on appeal, the lower court ruling is not "illegitimate"; it is simply voided through another lawfully created process.

Thus, the formal legitimacy of *Bush v. Gore* stems not from the logic of the majority opinion or the substantive outcome of the case, or even from any popular approval of the ruling, but solely because both the lower courts and the Supreme Court adhered to a particular set of procedures and that particular individuals, properly nominated and confirmed, articulated some sufficiently generalizable reasons and handed down a ruling. Accordingly, any denial of the legitimacy of *Bush v. Gore* has to be placed within the framework of rules and roles. From this perspective, the primary grounds for claiming *Bush v. Gore* to be illegitimate stems from Supreme Court Associate JusticeAntonin Scalia's apparent act of prejudgment, as evidenced by the injunctive relief granted to George W. Bush to stop the statewide recount ordered by the Florida Supreme Court. When Scalia wrote, "It suffices to say that the issuance of the stay suggests that a majority of the Court, while not deciding the issues presented, believe that the petitioner has a substantial probability of success,"[3] he opened the Court up to the criticism that the unfolding judicial process was less important to the resolution of this case than the partisan commitments of the Justices.

Scalia's act of apparent prejudgment suggested to critics that the Court's proceedings were simply for show, that because Republican appointees had the votes, they were engaged in a game of "two-against-one" and nothing could prevent their awarding the election of 2000 to Bush. If we conclude that the strongest basis for rejecting what many see as the most aggressive display of judicial power in U.S. history lies predominantly in a process and role-based argument, then it seems reasonable to conclude that the processes of judicial legitimation have more to do with rather vague sentiments about the act of judging, the cultivation of a vague quality known as "judicial temperament," and the maintenance of the spirit of open-mindedness, than with substantive agreement over the outcome of any particular case. In short, the process by which judicial acts are legitimated in the eyes of the public are deeply bound up with public perceptions of what the judicial role should be.

Keith Whittington's examination of the impeachment power offers an insightful perspective on the development of the idea of the judicial temperament. In *Constitutional Construction*, Whittington explores the process by which the details of our constitutional blueprint are filled in, through political conflict and contestation.[4] An early episode of this constructive process was the debate over what constituted an impeachable offense for federal judges. The conduct of Associate Justice Samuel Chase in his vigorous judicial enforcement of the Sedition Act during the John Adams administration provoked enormous controversy, and after the Federalists were swept from office in the election of 1800, articles of impeachment against Chase passed in the House and a trial was held in the Senate. Following shortly on the heels of the impeachment of Judge John Pickering, for clear mental incompetence, Chase's impeachment trial, argues Whittington, stood for a larger issue about the independence of federal judges and to whom they would be accountable in the new Republic. The trial not only required the Senate to determine the standards it would employ for the removal of judges from office, but it also forced federal judges themselves to evaluate what constituted "good behavior" in the performance of their constitutional authority and duties. Chase's conduct served as a kind of negative template—a how-to manual of how not to act—and helped defined the notion of a federal judiciary that is nominally nonpartisan.

The legitimacy of judicial acts—and, therefore, the legitimacy of judicial review itself—cannot be distinguished from the legitimacy of the roles that judges play in political life. That kind of role-playing and role-definition has little to do with congressional or even presidential legitimacy. Members of Congress can play virtually any kind of role—gadfly, legislative craftsman, wrench-thrower, the Great Compromiser, parliamentarian, or maverick independent. And while it is true that the judicial policy-making function both expects and allows judges to play some of the roles that legislators play, federal judges are nonetheless far more constrained in their ability to explicitly assume the mantle of law-making. The fact that elected politicians can gain political favor from voters by denouncing judges who "legislate from the bench" illustrates that judicial legitimacy depends in part on the ability of judges to couch their policy making within the idioms and practices of legal interpretation, to play the role of a judge while engaging in policy making.

Yet unlike members of Congress, once federal judges profess that self-restraint, they are largely unconstrained by popular views. Because the institution properly creates no space for popular inputs or decision making, public sentiment about any particular case is largely irrelevant to either the resolution of that case or the broader operation of the institution of the federal judiciary—especially at lower levels of the court system, which resolves, by far, the great majority of civil and criminal actions. Popular legitimacy of judicial acts, then, unlike legislative legitimacy, emerges from a judicial internalization of public sentiments about the judiciary's proper role in the affairs of state. As a result, the legitimacy of judicial review is focused less on substance than on process, less on popular will than on explicit rules and roles.

Anchoring the legitimacy of judicial actions on rules and roles means that public perceptions of judicial decision making will be far more influenced by the "cult of the robe" than the perceptions of legislative decision making will be influenced by "cult of the Congress" (if such a thing can even be said to exist). Moreover, just as we can track institutional organization in Congress back to its electoral modes of legitimation, so, too, we can identify within the Supreme Court's operation, organization, and agenda-setting various tactics and policies calculated to increase its likelihood of legitimation through its expression of its own role as a court and its members' self-conception as judges. The ban on cameras in the Court, its collegial handshakes at the beginning of each term, the Justices' simultaneous and stirring entry into the courtroom from behind the velvet curtains on the bench, the ritualized swearing in during Court sessions of new members of the Supreme Court bar, even the recent costuming flourishes of William Rehnquist, Sandra Day O'Connor, and Ruth Bader Ginsburg all heighten and stress the Court's public emphasis on its "courtly" attributes, perhaps in demonstration of its devotion to its self-imposed judicial role. The public face of the Court seeks, at almost every turn, to emphasis not the raw policy-making power of the Court, but its very real operation as a court of law. In a constitutional democracy, the trick of legitimating unelected judicial power to reverse the decisions of legislative majorities requires the Supreme Court to represent its considerable power not as an individualistic or personal attribute of the Justices, but as a collective responsibility of a body devoted to a higher law, the Constitution.

It is perhaps easiest to see the script when a judge deviates from his or her lines. The judicial sin of Alabama Chief Justice Roy Moore, the act that led to his removal from office by his colleagues, was to adhere to an individualistic sense of judicial power, rather than submit to the collective wisdom of his judicial brethren. Judges are allowed—even encouraged—to make principled stands of defiance through their dissents. But those principled stands must come only in words, and not in deeds. By refusing to cabin his view that the Ten Commandments form the foundations of Western law to a written opinion and by using his administrative authority as Chief Justice to display those Ten Commandments (and refusing to remove them when ordered by a federal judge to do so), Chief Justice Moore lost sight of the process of judicial legitimation. Perhaps convinced that the court of public opinion would rescue him (not an illogical view in Alabama), and mistaking popular support for judicial legitimation, Moore abdicated the required role that the reality of judicial power required of him. To insist that one's view of the law is correct—in the face of reversal—is an admirable position for plaintiffs and defendants, but not for judges. That insistence, combined with his commitment to translate his convictions into deeds, meant he was, literally, no longer fit to be a judge.

The plight of Chief Justice Moore helps us better understand the difficulty of sweeping the theoretical thorns and briars of judicial review under the rug of public approval. Moore deployed the tactics of electoral legitimation to validate a judicial interpretation of what the law required. He sought cover in public opinion, but public opinion cannot provide sufficient cover for judicial officials. The act of judging and the legitimacy of judging require more than a knowledge that the public approves of the job one is doing (the practice of judicial elections at the state level notwithstanding). Public approval may be nice, it may make one's job easier, but it does not justify the job itself, nor does it provide meaningful insight into the choices one must make while on the job. The persistence of judicial review in the American experience may have less to do with the popularity of the institution, per se, and more to do with the fact that the American public recognizes that judicial decision making requires that a judicial temperament, a judicious frame of mind, will, at times, run counter to popular sentiment. And, perhaps even more importantly, the American people want, in their judges, the capacity for judicial temperament to prevail, for judges to reject the prevailing understanding, and to find value in an individual claim.

When we look at the reasons people express for supporting judicial decisions—even decisions that run counter to their own claims—we find that individuals are far more likely to comply with a decision if they feel that the process was fair and that the judge heard and understood the claimants' or defendants' point of view. As Tom Tyler has found in his investigations into public attitudes toward judicial officials, procedural justice looms larger than substantive justice.[5] Indeed, it appears that the most important legitimating activities of judges are simply listening and understanding the claim, even if the ruling goes the other way. While there often is intense policy disagreement over the substance of particular court rulings, the legitimacy of a court's ruling is rarely directly attacked. Individuals may disagree or wish judges had ruled the other way, or even seek to evade the strictures of the ruling, but once the process has run its course, most will not dispute the authority of the court to rule in the fashion it did. While courts (like bureaucracies) will often face problems of implementation and compliance, in the vast majority of cases legitimacy, per se, will not be an issue. The campaign of "massive resistance" in the South in the post-*Brown* era is striking for its singularity. The legitimation of courts, and their power to exercise judicial review, has little to do with substantive agreement with the outcomes of particular decisions and more to do with broad agreement about the roles judges ought to play in American life. But agreement on that role is, in large part, conditioned on an understanding and agreement that judges are not partial and are not partisan. Judges exercising judicial review, in this light, have undergone a kind of American legal apotheosis, in which they can do no wrong, as long as they seek to aid no party.

The next relevant question, then, is whether judicial review, as an institution, is neutral to policy outcomes. Does a judicial constraint on electoral majorities prevent particular policy outcomes that would be achievable in the absence of judicial review, or under a weaker form of judicial review? One way of examining this is to explore Friedman's claims about the relationship between democratic self-governance and the democratic acceptance of judicial review. If a democracy can choose to regulate itself through judicial review, then we have removed at least one theoretical objection to the exercise of judicial review. The problem lies, however, in capturing the nature of that consent.

Courts, Polling, and the Organization of Democracy

Friedman's argument that the people have legitimated the ongoing practice of judicial review rests, ultimately, on arriving at some understanding of public support for the Supreme Court (and consequently the practice of judicial review). That claim, while clear, creates an obvious empirical problem: What counts as public support? In today's political world, polling is perhaps the most widely accepted means to gauge public support of political institutions and public policies. Friedman does not suggest we simply submit judicial review to a public referendum, but if the institution of judicial review enjoys the kind of public support he claims it does, then public opinion, as measured by polls, ought to register at least some significant support for the practice of judicial review that exists independent of the public's support for the substantive policy positions of the Court, at any given moment in time.

Public opinion polls, as they relate to politics, emerged as social science developed a relatively robust technique of inferring from population samples the views of the entire polity. While undoubtedly useful for predicting outcomes of elections and gauging broad levels of support for relatively straightforward policy options, polling is, nonetheless, not a necessary element of democratic life. Indeed, historically, American democracy has endured for a much longer period without polling than with it. One consequence of Friedman's anchoring the evaluation of public support for the institution of judicial review in the language of public opinion is to assume an organization of political life that makes polling and public opinion sensible. That organization, however, does not lend itself well to the kind of robust and well-informed political reflection that can provide any meaningful evaluation of judicial review.

This point is perhaps clearer if we can historicize the practice of tapping public opinion. Friedman writes that "There is evidence during prior attacks on the courts regarding the exercise of judicial review that popular opinion was being touted and perhaps actually taken into account." He then mentions briefly Jeffersonian and Reconstruction attacks on the court, as well as the New

Deal episodes. While political scientists of today can, in some ways, reconstruct historical public attitudes toward the court, it is less clear that politicians of those earlier episodes used the information (to the extent it was even available) the same way politicians (or the media) would today. What counted, in political terms, during those episodes of political conflict over Supreme Court politics is not necessarily public opinion as we understand the term today. The public's "mood" or "mind" in those settings (with the possible exception of the New Deal) was, at best, party elites' and bosses' perceptions of how events were playing out in their immediate and local area. Party leaders engaged in conversations with both lower level officials, as well as prominent local citizens, gauged the level of support and conveyed those messages upward in conversations with office holders. That is a very different kind of information-gathering process than a ten-minute poll with somewhere around one thousand randomly selected individuals who have far less information and inclination to respond to these questions. The subtlety of the answer to the question whether the public "likes" judicial review depends largely on the sensitivity of the instrument being used. Our politics today is deeply concerned with both the tallying and media depiction of survey data, but in order for those bits of information to have political salience, politics has to be organized in a particular way. We have organized our politics in such a way as to give maximum credence to polling and media depictions of polling numbers only in the last thirty years or so. Over the course of American history, public views and public sentiments were aggregated and distributed in very different fashions and through very different political forms. Friedman's imprecision on this point is important because not all forms of gathering and distributing opinions are comparable and they can yield very different forms of support for institutions.

Finally, it is important to explore how Friedman accounts for the relationship between agreement and consent. Friedman regards public opinion support—perhaps as registered by polls, perhaps gleaned through some other unspecified mechanism—as synonymous with consent. In doing so, he may very well be conflating majority acceptance of the products of judicial review with a democratic politics that sees judicial review as playing a useful role. If we limit our tallying of public sentiment to those kinds of agreement that are visible through the lens of public opinion, the two may look identical. In settings in which there is extensive agreement with the constitutional policy making engaged in by the Supreme Court, public support of judicial review would be high, as it might be under a system in which the American people duly considered the pros and cons of conducting their democratic politics under the supervision of a Court empowered by judicial review. Both settings, conceivably, could yield significant polling support for the Supreme Court, but it is unclear whether supporters like the output of judicial review (i.e., the substance of the rulings) or the institution of judicial review. From the perspective of public opinion polls, these positions may look the same, but the two are, in reality, very different: The first may exist because there is little capacity for meaningful democratic politics that could actually challenge the ongoing practice of judicial review. The latter would be a considered reflection and acceptance of the role of judicial review.

This is an old criticism. James Bradley Thayer made it at the turn of the twentieth century when he wrote that excessive judicial interference with legislative decision making weakened the democratic capacities of the people. When legislative mistakes are corrected outside legislatures, wrote Thayer: "The people lose the political experience, and the moral education and stimulus that comes from fighting the question out in the ordinary way, and correcting their own errors. The tendency of a common and easy resort to this great function ... is to dwarf the political capacity of the people."[6] But if we explore public acceptance of judicial review only through the lens of polling support for the institution of the Supreme Court, then we have lost any analytical ability to distinguish between acquiescence and consent. How do we know that Americans like the policy positions adopted by the Supreme Court or like the fact that the Supreme Court offers a relatively definitive resolution for policy decisions for which there is not necessarily an easy answer? Public opinion polling can give us the answer to the first question, but I think the second question is more important, particularly for our capacity to engage in democratic self-governance.

There is some empirical evidence to bolster Thayer's point. Philip Klinkner has examined over a long historical period the simple correlation between voting turnout of the American electorate and the rates at which the Supreme Court struck down legislation. He found a strong correlation between the higher rates of the exercise of judicial review and lower rates of voting in national elections during most of the nineteenth and twentieth centuries.[7] Indeed, as Figure 1 indicates the two rates seem to almost mirror one another over this time period.

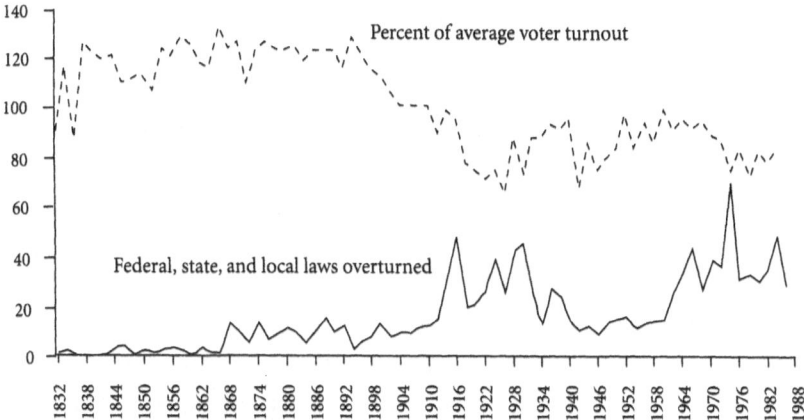

FIG. 1. Percent of Average Voter Turnout vs. Number of Federal, State, and Local Laws Overturned by Supreme Court. Source: Philip A. Klinker, *Dwarfing the Political Capacity of the People? The Relationship between Judicial Activism and Voter Turnout, 1840–1988*," 25 Polity 633 (1993).

Although these are simple correlations and other factors may be driving both the exercise of judicial review up and voter turnout down, Klinker's demonstration of such a relationship suggests a tension between the two forms of organizing national political life.

The relationship between judicial review and democratic self-governance is typically studied at the institutional level. The typical normative objection to judicial review lies in its ability to defeat majorities, but if judicial review is related, at a more fundamental level, to individual-level inclination to participate in elections, then we have on our hands a more troubling objection to a robust vision of judicial review. From this perspective, judicial review does not simply prevent the realization of some majoritarian policy perspectives, it may reduce the likelihood of some policy perspectives being even articulated. To the extent that democratic capacity is reflected in voting, it is possible that judicial review is potentially corrosive of that democratic capacity. If this is the case, then it then strikes me as odd for Friedman to point to "democratic" politics as the basis for continued support for judicial review. I fear that he is conflating two very different things.

Finally, by shifting the discussion of the maintenance of judicial review onto the terrain of public opinion, Friedman is diving, headlong, into an area of study fraught with a number of methodological problems, the most prominent of which is teasing out the reasons individuals have for supporting the Court. These issues, which have bedeviled political scientists are directly relevant to the important question of whether Thayer and Klinkner are right: Is public support for the Supreme Court and the institution of judicial review considered and reflective or is it substantially ignorant of Supreme Court decisions and conduct? As Friedman notes, the framing effects of polling are enormously significant in the study of support for the Court. Political scientists typically make a distinction between "diffuse" and "specific" support for the Supreme Court, with diffuse support indicating a reservoir of support for the Court, independent of any particular policy position or direction of the Court. For large segments of the American populace, individuals support the Supreme Court as an institution, even if they might disagree with the particular policy positions the Court has pronounced. Some political scientists have interpreted that difference between diffuse and specific support as an indication that the American public has a broad faith and trust in the institution of the Supreme Court.

The troubling aspect of the relationship between diffuse and specific support—particularly for Friedman's argument—is that as individuals learn more about the actions and decisions of the Supreme Court, the gulf between an individual's disagreement rate with specific Court positions and an individual's degree of diffuse support for the Court begins to collapse. That is, diffuse support begins to look a lot like specific support for individuals with higher levels of education and greater awareness of Supreme Court activities. The more one knows, the more one's diffuse support is predicted by one's specific support for the positions adopted by the Court. And since specific support is largely ideological support for the outcome of particular cases, the difference between diffuse and specific support is largely, then, a function of knowledge and ideological support for what the Court is doing. If Friedman wants to argue that diffuse support is evidence of support for judicial review, he is then indirectly arguing that Americans support judicial review largely out of ignorance. That, to be sure, is a rather tricky ground upon which to justify the institution of judicial review.

Conclusion

Friedman's aspiration is a good and sensible one. He seeks, in part, not to defend judicial review or to advance a normative theory of its desirability, but to explain its long life through an accounting of its congruence with American democratic politics. The difficulty of the argument lies not with judicial review's inherent incongruence, but with what counts as evidence of democratic support, particularly when the operation of judicial review exerts a powerful influence on what we think of as democratic self-governance. *Marbury*'s stage is perhaps best thought of as the platform for a kind of national political theater, in which we continually watch actors struggle for advantage or slink away in defeat. Sometimes the characters we love win and sometimes they lose, but the only constants are the cheers and boos of the crowd and the existence of the stage itself, which renders the play intelligible to both the players and the audience. In some ways, the legitimacy of the stage is irrelevant—what may be more important in the long run is whether the play is sufficiently engaging to all the audience or whether the scripts become so timeworn and tiresome that most of the audience drifts away. *Marbury* may make the staging of our politics possible, but it certainly does not determine the kinds of plays we stage.

CHAPTER FIVE

The Age of *Marbury*: Judicial Review
in a Democracy of Rights

STEPHEN M. GRIFFIN

The age of *Marbury* is our own age, the age of unchallenged judicial supremacy.[1] The fact that the exercise of judicial review by the Supreme Court did not become a political issue in the aftermath of *Bush v. Gore*[2] illustrates this perfectly. No public official opposes or even argues tentatively for any limitation on the power of judicial review. The proclamations of judicial supremacy by the Rehnquist Court and its recent invocations of *Marbury v. Madison*[3] show that the Court no longer feels the need to justify itself by means of a theory of judicial review.

From a scholarly perspective, this is puzzling. Theories of judicial review that emphasized the democratic limits on the Supreme Court's power were once at the center of American constitutional law and theory.[4] It has been quite some time, however, since they served as the organizing ideas to which scholars responded, willingly or not. This scholarly and theoretical development has arguably had an influence on the Court. As Mark Tushnet recently noted, "the Justices in the new constitutional order in fact do not seem to have the same anxiety about justifying judicial review that characterized the early years of the New Deal constitutional order, and which continued to dominate scholarly concern through the Warren Court years."[5]

Over the last forty years, American constitutional theory has moved from a period in which theories of judicial review dominated the field to a period, still ongoing, in which theories of constitutional interpretation hold sway. In 1962, Alexander Bickel, perhaps the most influential constitutional theorist of his generation, began his important book *The Least Dangerous Branch*,[6] not with his soon to be famous "countermajoritarian difficulty,"[7] but with a critique of Chief Justice John Marshall's reasoning in *Marbury*.[8] But the energy scholars of Bickel's generation poured into critiquing *Marbury* has mostly died out.[9] It is likely that the two-hundredth anniversary of *Marbury* will be dominated by praise, not critique.[10]

What does the Constitution mean? And who decides? These two questions have been at the heart of constitutional theory for decades, although there has been a consistent conflict over which question has primacy. In this essay, I focus on the latter question and offer a theory of judicial review that is responsive to our democratic values and political circumstances without being subject to the many lines of criticism brought against Bickel's countermajoritarian difficulty. I think it is worth walking down this well-worn path again because in recent decisions the Supreme Court has signaled that we are entering a new era in which rights created through democratic deliberation will be subject to judicial challenge.[11] This means that issues debated exhaustively under the aegis of the countermajoritarian difficulty can be analyzed in a new light. The question posed by the Court's recent decisions is not one of defending minority rights against majoritarian incursions, but rather the institutional question of which branch of government is in the best position to protect constitutional rights.

It is my impression that constitutional scholars have become somewhat complacent about the justification of judicial review in a democracy. It appears to be taken for granted that the flaws of the countermajoritarian difficulty eliminate the possibility of a valid democratic critique of judicial review. I have long had the intuition that it was possible to develop a critique of judicial review that was democratic without relying on the countermajoritarian difficulty or the view that democracy is essentially a matter of majority rule. My intuition was based in part on the fact that scholars had been ignoring the accomplishments of the Executive and Legislative Branches in protecting constitutional values through civil rights legislation. The purpose of this essay, then, is to advance a theory of judicial review that is democratic without being majoritarian, does not rest on the countermajoritarian difficulty, and provides a realistic perspective on the comparative abilities of the different branches of government to protect rights.[12]

It is, of course, appropriate to begin a theory of judicial review by considering *Marbury*, quite apart from any considerations of bicentennial commemoration. I suggest, however, that there is a more important reason for beginning with *Marbury*. Recent constitutional scholarship shows that Marshall's reasoning in *Marbury* remains persuasive for many.[13] Yet the kind of judicial review endorsed in *Marbury* is really quite remote from the institution of judicial review as it exists today.[14] In the first section I show how these differences undermine the relevance that Marshall's reasoning has for us. I focus especially on the popularity of the doubtful case rule and the different understandings of the law/politics distinction prevailing in Marshall's era. Justifications of the contemporary institution of judicial review must proceed on a different basis.

In the second section I offer a theory of judicial review that is responsive to our democratic values and political circumstances. While I agree that the countermajoritarian difficulty was not a sound basis on which to build, I attempt to learn from the errors of scholars like Bickel in order to create a theory that has greater descriptive and normative credibility. First, I contrast Bickel's theory with Robert Dahl's famous study of the Supreme Court's influence[15] to show that both works were dependent on the political context of their time. I draw the conclusion that any theory of judicial review must be rooted in a realistic understanding of contemporary politics. Second, I provide a political context for my theory of judicial review by highlighting the importance of a closely divided government and the politicization of constitutional issues and the federal judicial appointment process. The phenomenon of politicization is key for me, as it has permanently undermined the judiciary's comparative advantage in matters of principle. Third, I provide an account of the value of democracy that does not rest on majoritarianism. Rather, I appeal to the concept of a "democracy of rights,"[16] based on the equal dignity of all ordinary citizens. This sort of democracy is led naturally to consistently protect constitutional rights through legislation. Fourth, I apply this account to contemporary judicial review to argue that the judiciary should defer to legislation that protects constitutional rights. Moreover, I argue that the creation of a democracy of rights and the politicization of constitutional issues have led to a point where vigorous judicial review can no longer be justified.

In the third section I explore the implications of my theory by critiquing two powerful defenses of judicial review recently offered by constitutional scholars. The defense of judicial review by the distinguished scholars Daniel Farber and Suzanna Sherry is part of their more general critique of contemporary constitutional theory.[17] Christopher Eisgruber's subtle justification of the judiciary's comparative advantage in matters of principle is woven into his account of constitutional government.[18] Both defenses provide a useful contrast to a critique of judicial review based on the concept of a democracy of rights.

I. Judicial Review in the Marshall Era

Judicial review as established by Chief Justice John Marshall and the Supreme Court in *Marbury v. Madison*[19] was very different from judicial review as it exists today.[20] Unfortunately, the widespread use of the term "judicial review" to describe both eighteenth- and twenty-first-century practice promotes the idea that when we debate the role the Supreme Court should have in American government and politics, we are continuing a debate begun two centuries ago. Legal scholars, political scientists, and historians all use "judicial review" to refer to the practice advocated by Alexander Hamilton in *The Federalist 78*[21] and Chief Justice Marshall in *Marbury*.

From another point of view, however, it is a mistake to use "judicial review" to refer to the practice advocated by Hamilton and Marshall. This is true in the trivial sense that neither Hamilton nor Marshall used this term. But it is also true in the important sense that the practice they advocated does not match the twenty-first-century institution with which we are familiar. The eminent historian Gordon Wood has stated this point of view forcefully. He argues that to ask whether the founding generation intended to establish judicial review is anachronistic because "no one meant to establish what eventually became judicial review; it could scarcely have been imagined. Like most developments in history, judicial review was unplanned and unintended."[22]

I will follow these suggestive remarks by demonstrating that the founding generation did not advocate or establish some of the most important contem-

porary elements of the power of judicial review. Moreover, the founding generation was committed to an understanding of the scope of judicial review that is
no longer accepted. I will argue that these historical circumstances undermine
beyond repair the relevance that Marshall's reasoning in *Marbury* has for us.

A. Understanding Judicial Review as an Institution

The practice we call "judicial review" that is the focus of contemporary debate over the role of the Supreme Court is more a creation of the twentieth century than an accepted idea of the era in which Chief Justice Marshall lived. In
general, the contemporary debate is about whether the Court's exercise of judicial review is justified or is legitimate in light of our constitutional tradition and
democratic principles.[23] The influence the Court wields over American law,
politics, and society, however, does not derive simply from the discrete power
that Hamilton referred to as "the right of the courts to pronounce legislative
acts void."[24]

The contemporary power of judicial review consists not only of the practice
Hamilton defended (which I will call the "voiding power"), but also of other
important elements. Some of these elements were present in the Constitution
from the beginning, but others were acquired only over time. Two elements
present in the Constitution were judicial independence and life tenure, both of
which are just as important to the institution of judicial review as the voiding
power. If, for example, justices served for a nonrenewable six-year term or were
elected, the power of judicial review would be affected significantly. In such a
world, judicial review would operate more in the shadow of the political
branches. Judicial review is thus a complex institution composed of a number
of elements, not just a discrete power.

Another key element of the contemporary power of judicial review that only
developed over time is the doctrine of judicial supremacy, the idea that the
Supreme Court is the final authority in matters of constitutional interpretation.
When the legitimacy of judicial review is debated today, the doctrine of judicial
supremacy is part of the institution under debate. Yet the voiding power defended by Hamilton and Marshall is analytically distinct from judicial supremacy.

The use of the term "judicial review" to denote both what I have called the
voiding power and the complex contemporary institution of judicial review

thus introduces an important ambiguity that has affected the debate over the role of the Supreme Court. When we debate the legitimacy of judicial review, are we concerned with the voiding power or with judicial review considered as an institution? The contemporary power of judicial review consists of a number of elements, and while some of them were present in the early republic, others were not. If we are to understand how the contemporary power of judicial review differs from judicial review in the early republic, we must take care to identify these elements as clearly as possible. In the discussion that follows I will distinguish among: (1) those elements that existed in the early republic and continue to exist today; (2) those that existed in the early republic but no longer exist; and (3) those that were created by later developments. The particular point I want to emphasize in this discussion is that to use the term "judicial review" to describe both present practice and practice in the early republic ignores the crucial issue of what *conditions* were attached to the exercise of judicial review in the early republic.

1. *Judicial review in the early republic*

I suggested above the three elements of judicial review that existed in the early republic and continue to exist today: (1) judicial independence; (2) the voiding power; and (3) life tenure. As argued first by Wood and, more recently, by Jack Rakove, the most overlooked element on this list is judicial independence.[25] Before the founding generation could properly consider what sort of power the judiciary should have, they first had to conceive it as a truly separate, coequal branch of government.[26] Unfortunately, as Wood notes, "we still have no history of the emergence of what Americans called an 'independent judiciary' at the end of the eighteenth century and the beginning of the nineteenth century—perhaps because we take a strong independent judiciary so much for granted."[27]

Many scholars have seen Hamilton's famous argument justifying judicial review in *The Federalist 78* as a forerunner of the argument Chief Justice Marshall provided in *Marbury*. But Hamilton's argument also well illustrates how all three of these elements were important to the founding generation. Hamilton's general topic is judicial independence. After briefly defending life tenure, Hamilton begins his discussion of "the right of the courts to pronounce legislative acts void"[28] by stating, "[t]he complete independence of the courts of justice is peculiarly essential in a limited constitution."[29] The Constitution is limited in that it "contains certain specified exceptions to the legislative authority; such for instance as that it shall pass no bills of attainder, no *ex post facto* laws, and the like."[30] Hamilton declares that it is the duty of the courts "to declare all acts contrary to the manifest tenor of the constitution void."[31]

Hamilton then responds to the charge that this kind of judicial independence makes the judiciary superior to the legislature. Hamilton's denial rests on the character of the Constitution as a fundamental or supreme law and the doctrine of popular sovereignty. The power of the people in establishing the Constitution is superior to both the legislative and judicial powers. If a legislative act is contrary to the Constitution, it therefore must be invalid. The courts are in a good position to enforce the will of the people as "an intermediate body between the people and the legislature, in order, among other things, to keep the latter within the limits assigned to their authority."[32] This is confirmed by the idea that the "interpretation of the laws is the proper and peculiar province of the courts."[33]

Although Hamilton argues in favor of judicial independence and life tenure, it is understandable that scholars have seen his argument in favor of the voiding power as the most significant part of *The Federalist 78*. For all practical purposes, the judicial duty to declare unconstitutional acts void seems equivalent to what we call judicial review. But making this easy equivalence would be a serious error. The critical point that is missed is that Hamilton's idea of the voiding power might have certain limiting conditions attached to its exercise that would make it quite remote from the contemporary institution of judicial review.[34] To see the force of this point, we must consider the possibility that there were elements of judicial review in the early republic that no longer exist.

2. *The forgotten elements of judicial review*

Recent scholarship has been concerned with exploring the idea that there were important elements of the institution of judicial review in the early republic that no longer exist. There are two candidates: (1) the doubtful case rule and (2) a much different understanding of the relation between law and politics. Sylvia Snowiss's study of the origins of judicial review played an instrumental role in bringing the relevance of the doubtful case rule back to the attention of scholars.[35] This was the "rule of administration" cited by James Bradley Thayer in his famous article arguing for what is now called judicial restraint.[36] Thayer by no means presented all the evidence that this rule was part of the debate over the judicial power in the early republic. As Snowiss argues, the debate over judicial power in the late eighteenth century "reflected the understanding that this power was confined to the concededly unconstitutional act. This understanding was expressed on the U.S. Supreme Court by repeated use of the doubtful case rule. Under this rule legislation could be overturned only if there was no doubt about its unconstitutionality."[37]

Hamilton's discussion of judicial review in *The Federalist* and Chief Justice Marshall's argument in *Marbury* both reflect the assumption that the voiding power be exercised only in a clear case. Hamilton argues that the judiciary has a duty to strike down any law contrary to the "*manifest* tenor of the constitution"[38] and his examples all involve absolutely clear cases of constitutional violation. In *Marbury*, Marshall contends that because "[i]t is emphatically the province and duty of the judicial department to say what the law is," a statute conflicting with the Constitution must be held invalid. Marshall states that any other result would allow the legislature to do "what is expressly forbidden."[39]

Marshall then gives three examples that have to do with the legislature expressly violating a clear provision of the Constitution. For instance, he comments that the Constitution "declares that 'no bill of attainder or *ex post facto* law shall be passed.' If, however, such a bill should be passed and a person should be prosecuted under it; must the court condemn to death those victims whom the constitution endeavors to preserve?"[40] Of course, there is only one answer to Marshall's rhetorical question. When a provision of the Constitution is expressly violated, the judiciary must take cognizance of the case and uphold the Constitution's status as supreme law.

As historian Charles Hobson notes,[41] Marshall endorsed the doubtful case rule in important cases such as *Fletcher v. Peck*,[42] *McCulloch v. Maryland*,[43] *Dartmouth College v. Woodward*,[44] and *Brown v. Maryland*.[45] On balance, the evidence is clear that the rule played an important role in debates over judicial review in the early republic.[46]

It is also clear that the doubtful case rule is not part of the contemporary institution of judicial review. The rule becomes highly problematic once it is accepted that the judiciary has the duty to interpret and enforce the Constitution in ordinary cases. As a practical matter, the rule counsels the judiciary to ignore probable cases of constitutional violation. In contemporary terms, the rule threatens judicial independence by asking for extraordinary deference to the

legislature. The rule does not ask so much for judicial restraint as judicial abdi-
cation.[47]

Another good candidate for an element of judicial review in the early republic that no longer exists is the different understanding the founding generation had of the relation between law and politics. This understanding had several overlapping dimensions. One was that the judiciary had no power to
resolve all of the constitutional questions that might arise. The judiciary could
hear only legal cases, not political disputes. As Marshall stated in a largely overlooked speech to the House of Representatives in March 1800: "the constitution
had never been understood, to confer on that department [the judiciary], any
political power whatever."[48] Marshall's discussion of "political questions" in
Marbury reflected this point of view.[49] To some extent, Marshall was making the
point, familiar to constitutional lawyers, that the judiciary could consider only
concrete cases and controversies. Also implicit in his remarks, however, was the
idea that there was some sort of additional limit on the kinds of cases the judiciary could hear. Presumably, for example, the Supreme Court should refrain
from hearing a political dispute masquerading as a properly brought case.

A second dimension of the relation of law to politics was that judges were
not understood to be making law. From the perspective of the eighteenth century, the law was not the product of individual will, but of general reason.[50]
This point is quite important, but it can be difficult to understand. We are used
to the idea that in some cases, the justices of the Supreme Court change the law.
But for the founding generation, the very idea of changing the law through judicial decisions was almost unthinkable. As William Nelson comments, "[t]hey
understood law as fixed and immutable, not as something that government
could change in response to shifting conceptions of social good."[51] In the specific case of constitutional law, members of the founding generation like
Hamilton believed that judges did not make new law by enforcing the Constitution, they merely implemented the will of the people.[52]

The third dimension of the relation of law to politics had to do with the
method the judiciary employed to decide cases. This point has been illuminated
by Nelson's study of *Marbury*. Nelson argues that "in *Marbury v. Madison*, Chief
Justice John Marshall drew a line, which nearly all citizens of his time believed
ought to be drawn, between the legal and the political."[53] According to Nelson,
Marshall implemented this understanding by distinguishing "between political

matters, to be resolved by the legislative and executive branches in the new de-mocratic, majoritarian style, and legal matters, to be resolved by the judiciary in the government-by-consensus style that had prevailed in most eighteenth-century American courts."[54] The Court would attempt to refrain from entering the political fray by focusing on values, such as protecting property rights, on which there was widespread agreement.[55]

None of these understandings of the law-politics distinction survives today in any meaningful fashion. The Court does not avoid issues just because they might be politically controversial.[56] Indeed, one favorite modern argument for judicial review is that the Court can act to solve significant social problems when the political branches are paralyzed. Further, although some defend the distinction between law and politics by emphasizing the differences between how the legislative and judicial branches make decisions, no one defends the eighteenth-century view that judges do not change the law, but simply declare it. To put the point another way, the sharp distinction that the founding gener-ation drew between reason and will no longer holds.

Scholars have been slow to appreciate the significance for constitutional the-ory of the reality that judicial review in the early republic had elements that no longer exist. They have long noted the absence of any controversy over the power of judicial review after the Supreme Court rendered judgment in *Mar-bury*.[57] They have also cited statements made in support of judicial review dur-ing the founding period.[58] But scholars have not emphasized the idea that judi-cial review in the early republic was subject to limiting conditions. The evidence from the founding period supports the conclusion that judicial review in the early republic was very different from the contemporary institution of judicial review, due to these conditions on the exercise of judicial power. It fol-lows that the contemporary institution of judicial review cannot be justified through the arguments that Marshall used in *Marbury*.

3. The new elements of judicial review

The final category is those elements of the contemporary institution of ju-dicial review that have been created since the early republic. A likely candidate is the doctrine of judicial supremacy, the idea that the Supreme Court is the fi-nal authority in matters of constitutional interpretation, especially with respect to the legislative and executive branches of the federal government. As has so often been noted, Marshall never claimed supremacy for the Court in *Mar-*

bury.[59] The opinion ends, after all, with Marshall saying that courts have an *equal* right to the other departments in interpreting the Constitution.[60] The Court committed itself explicitly to judicial supremacy only relatively recently. In *Cooper v. Aaron*,[61] for example, the Court stated that the "federal judiciary is supreme in the exposition of the law of the Constitution."[62]

A less obvious candidate for an important element of contemporary judicial review is the near-total control the Supreme Court has over its own docket. The Court achieved substantial control over its docket only in the twentieth century following passage of the Judiciary Act of 1925. This control contributed to the sense of the justices that the Court has a special mission that differentiates it from other courts. Chief Justice Fred Vinson stated that "[t]he Supreme Court is not, and never has been, primarily concerned with the correction of errors in lower court decisions. . . . To remain effective, the Supreme Court must continue to decide only those cases which present questions whose resolution will have immediate importance far beyond the particular facts and parties involved."[63] In effect, Vinson was saying that the Court did not exist to provide justice to individuals (as many Americans believe), but to decide broad matters of legal policy.

Combined with the expansion of the Court's jurisdiction in the decades following the Civil War, the result has been to transform the Court into a roving commission seeking out important constitutional questions. The Court can deliberately avoid cases that are poor vehicles for new constitutional rules and seek out cases that are good vehicles. The ability to select cases also means that the Court can respond relatively quickly to a public demand to resolve an important constitutional issue.[64]

It is clear that the Supreme Court did not have this ability in the early republic. Chief Justice Marshall's Court was a common law court. The Court had control over its docket only in the sense that there were not that many cases to decide. More important, it would have never occurred to Marshall to use the Court as a policymaking body in the way described by Vinson. Among other points, this would have undermined the law-politics distinction that Marshall strove to maintain. Vinson's Court was one confident of its status as a truly coequal branch of government and comfortable with the idea that its decisions would have significant policy consequences and might be politically controversial. Marshall's Court had none of these characteristics.

In many respects, the agenda of contemporary constitutional theory has been formed out of the acknowledgment that judicial review in the twentieth century has been a more controversial institution than was true in the era of Chief Justice Marshall. This is due partly to the abandonment of the doubtful case rule, but has much more to do with the very different understandings of the distinctions between law and politics that came to prevail in the twentieth century and still prevail in our own time. The questions raised about the legitimacy of the contemporary institution of judicial review therefore cannot be answered by looking to the arguments that prevailed in *Marbury*.

B. *From the Marshall Era to the Twentieth Century*

In the Marshall era, there was arguably no need for a theory of judicial review. In Lawrence Sager's phrase, the conception of judicial review in *Marbury* was the "Little Old Judge"[65]—"don't mind us, we're just doing what little old judges always do." In Marshall's time, it went without saying that common law courts were legitimate government institutions. If in carrying out judicial review the Supreme Court followed the method of the common law, then there was no special need to justify what courts did all the time.

This means that Marshall's justification for judicial review was critically dependent on the distinction he drew between law and politics. In order to act as a standard common law court, the Supreme Court had to stay on the law side of the line and avoid "political questions." As I have argued previously, the Court had to legalize the Constitution in order to make it enforceable by the judiciary.[66] As we have seen, however, this legalization was made possible by a set of understandings about how the law/politics distinction could be maintained.

In the twentieth century, the legal community has abandoned these understandings. No one believes that judges find the law by appealing to general reason, argues that the judiciary should not decide cases that are politically controversial, or advocates the doubtful case rule. Alexander Bickel captured this change when he criticized *Marbury* by saying "that a statute's repugnancy to the Constitution is in most instances not self-evident; it is, rather, an issue of policy that someone must decide."[67] The very fact that a mainstream constitutional scholar such as Bickel could understand constitutional law issues as matters of "policy" captures the great conceptual gulf that lies between Marshall's understanding of law and our own.

Contemporary judicial review is thus not the institution that Marshall helped make secure in *Marbury*. The contemporary Court is more a creation of the circumstances of the twentieth century than a direct descendant of Marshall's Court. As elaborated above, the near-total control the Court has over its docket is a highly significant difference between it and Marshall's common law court. Moreover, the justices have been aware for quite a while that the Court has a unique role as a judicial institution that makes public policy. Before Robert Jackson became a justice, Justice Benjamin Cardozo told him that the New York Court of Appeals was an example of "a lawyer's court. Those are the kind of problems you'll enjoy. Over on [the Supreme Court] there are two kinds of questions—statutory construction, which no one can make interesting, and politics." After he had served on the Court, Jackson reflected, "Of course [Cardozo] didn't mean politics in the sense of party politics, but in the sense of public policy. There's a great deal of truth in that observation. Many of our cases really turn on your views of political policy, governmental policy."[68]

These changes to the institution of judicial review are good examples of how constitutional change occurs outside both Article V and judicial interpretation of the Constitution.[69] No amendment to the Constitution ever confirmed either the decline of the doubtful case rule or the twentieth-century view of the Court as a policymaking body. Nevertheless, these changes in legal consciousness and the power that such changes as docket control entail have altered the Court and its relation to American law, politics, and society. These circumstances have also created the rationale for theories of judicial review.

Theories of judicial review concern the legitimacy and institutional competence of the Supreme Court to make constitutional decisions.[70] These theories typically focus on Court decisions that have significant policy consequences and situate the Court and those decisions in the context of democratic government. Inevitably, theories of judicial review involve comparative judgments about the ability of the judiciary to make decisions relative to the other branches and levels of government. The account of the Court's role embodied in the famous *Carolene Products* footnote[71] is an example of such a theory. Here the Court argued essentially that judicial review was justified when the legislation in question (1) clearly infringed a specific right named in the Constitution; (2) had the effect of excluding citizens from the political process; or (3) was the result of prejudice against discrete and insular minorities.[72] Theories of judicial review have typically at least bowed in the direction of providing a realistic understanding of our political institutions and the Court's role within our constitutional and political arrangements.

While I will elaborate my theory of judicial review below, the point I wish to emphasize here is that the need for such theories does not arise exclusively from the countermajoritarian difficulty. The "difficulty" with judicial review flows not only from a perceived conflict between majority rule and individual rights,[73] but also from doubts about whether Marshall's common law judicial method, understood in the light of legal realism, is adequate to the challenge posed by abstract constitutional provisions such as the Due Process and Equal Protection clauses of the Fourteenth Amendment.[74] Judicial reasoning, no matter how well it is elaborated, will be little different from the policy reasoning used by the political branches if such clauses cannot be interpreted in a satisfactory legalistic way. This places in jeopardy the supposed comparative advantage the judiciary has over the political branches in matters of rights. As I will try to show, the politicization of constitutional issues and the creation of a democracy of rights have substantially undermined, if not eliminated, any comparative advantage the judiciary had in the past.

II. A Democratic Theory of Judicial Review

I will set out my theory of judicial review in four stages. Initially, I undertake an excursus into Alexander Bickel's constitutional theory in order to make the point that a theory of judicial review should be based on a realistic appraisal of contemporary politics. One point I wish to emphasize concerning Bickel is that there are two aspects of his theory that have been widely influential—not just the well-known countermajoritarian difficulty, but also his emphasis on the comparative advantage the judiciary has in matters of principle. Second, I describe the political context in which contemporary judicial review takes place. Third, I justify the value of democracy through the concept of a "democracy of rights," rather than a commitment to majoritarianism. Finally, I draw conclusions from the descriptive and normative arguments offered for the institution of judicial review.

A. Learning from Bickel

Achieving a balanced perspective on Bickel's "countermajoritarian difficulty"[75] has itself been difficult. In understanding why the conflict between majoritarian democracy and an antimajoritarian Supreme Court might have seemed salient to Bickel, it is worth keeping in mind that *The Least Dangerous Branch* was published just four years after one of the worst periods of Court-curbing in the twentieth century, probably second only to the 1937 "Court packing" crisis. In 1958, a toxic combination of southern segregationists and fervent anti-communists nearly enacted significant restrictions on the Court's jurisdiction.[76]

I suggest that we neither accept nor reject Bickel's theory out of hand. Instead, we should learn from Bickel in order to improve our understanding of theories of judicial review. After all, he did set the terms for the debate in ensuing years, even if that debate tended to remain somewhat static.[77] Bickel asserted that the central characteristic of American democracy was popular representation through election and that judicial review ran counter to this characteristic. While he was aware that American government was one of checks and balances and that judicial review can be understood as a check, he argued that judicial review was unique because it was final. Bickel argued, in effect, that there was no other national government institution that made decisions that could not be overturned by the President acting with the support of an ordinary legislative majority. Presumably even the decisions of the Federal Reserve Board can be altered by a legislative majority, but not the rulings of the Supreme Court. To further heighten the insult to democratic institutions, justices have life terms and are not subject to any periodic review, or, of course, to elections.[78]

This argument that defined the countermajoritarian difficulty was only Bickel's starting point. Bickel was not interested in abolishing judicial review or even significantly restricting its scope. His concern was ultimately to specify the proper function of the Court in American democracy.[79] After his discussion of the difficulty, Bickel moved rapidly to give his countermajoritarian Court a positive role as conservator of society's "enduring values."[80] As summarized ably by Anthony Kronman, Bickel saw the Court as "the 'shaper and prophet' of a system of enduring values, one that does not merely reflect an existing national consensus but articulates a moral vision to which we may legitimately aspire. . .

. . the Court is an educator whose mission is to instruct and elevate, to bring out the best in us and show us where our own convictions lead."[81]

A theory of judicial review is a theory of institutional role and must necessarily situate the Supreme Court within the tangled web of American politics. How did Bickel do this? Bickel emphasized two points: the necessarily antimajoritarian character of the Court's decisions and the fact that those decisions can be overturned only through the elaborate process of amendment under Article V. While these points have some force, there is reason to doubt that his somewhat legalistic analysis was really attuned to the realities of political life.[82] Scholars have noted with some wonderment[83] how he could overlook Robert Dahl's influential analysis that the Court is rarely out of step with lawmaking majorities in Congress.[84]

A closer look reveals some similarities in perspective between Dahl and Bickel. Dahl shared Bickel's hard-headed sense that there was no escaping the conflict between democratic principles and judicial review.[85] And Dahl's conclusion that except for short periods, "the Supreme Court is inevitably a part of the dominant national alliance"[86] was consonant with Bickel's desire that the Court protect and advance society's fundamental values. Dahl emphasized, after all, that justices were selected inevitably from the nation's "political elite,"[87] the people most likely to be familiar with such verities.

Dahl's argument that as part of the political alliance that ruled the country, the Court was "almost powerless to affect the course of national policy"[88] did seem to demonstrate that it was an error to focus on those relatively few instances (such as the Court's opposition to child labor legislation) in which it had truly operated as a countermajoritarian block to national policy. The Court could not consistently "counter" the majority if the justices were part of that majority. Bickel missed the empirical evidence that Dahl found compelling by not examining closely the instances in which the Court had struck down national legislation. Bickel's scholarly critics thought it was obvious that he had failed to give an accurate picture of the Court's role in American government.[89]

It would be more useful, however, to direct our attention to how the analyses of Bickel and Dahl were both products of their time. Despite the manifest problems with Bickel's analysis, I suggest he and other scholars of like mind long had the advantage in the debate over judicial review because of the overwhelming impact of the battle between the New Deal and the Supreme Court.[90]

The New Deal experience appeared to show the folly of the Court trying to stand against the considered judgment of a massive, persistent electoral majority and the wisdom of judicial self-restraint. This was the lesson Justice Felix Frankfurter and his clerk Bickel drew from the New Deal. Bickel said famously that "judicial review is a deviant institution in the American democracy."[91] This struck later scholars as an extreme statement,[92] but only because they did not appreciate fully the impact of the New Deal experience (and the 1958 Court-curbing period) on Bickel and his contemporaries.[93] American constitutionalism had undergone an important regime change,[94] and in the new order the political branches had enhanced power and legitimacy derived from their effort to alleviate the Great Depression and prevail in World War II.[95]

The response that could be drawn from Dahl's analysis was that if the Court could not stand against a lawmaking majority, there was no point in making its countermajoritarian character the centerpiece of a theory of judicial review. Fair enough, although someone who lived through the New Deal might have reasonably believed that the cost of forcing the Court to change its mind justified some initial focus on the conflict between democratic majorities and a lagging Court. Moreover, Dahl's analysis itself suggested a problem for his more sanguine account of the Court's role. Dahl relied on theories of partisan realignment in describing the Court as part of the dominant national alliance. He stated that national politics is "dominated by relatively cohesive alliances that endure for long periods of time."[96] The idea was that it was typical in American history for one party, such as the Jeffersonians, Jacksonians, Republicans, or Democrats, to control all three branches of the national government (although control of the Court might lag behind the political branches).[97]

When Dahl wrote, the last partisan realignment in view was that of President Franklin Roosevelt's New Deal, in which a single party (the Democrats) controlled all three branches of the national government. Dahl did not consider what would happen under a prolonged period of divided government.[98] At least by the terms of partisan realignment theory, there would be no dominant national alliance and the Court would face the difficult task of navigating between parties that were closely competitive. Further, Dahl assumed on the basis of past experience that Presidents would normally receive the benefit of a Court appointment every two years.[99] Without steady reappointment, the Court would lag further and further behind trends in national politics.[100]

There is one further lesson to be drawn from the juxtaposition of Dahl and Bickel. Both were theorists of consensus in distinctive but related ways. Dahl believed that the Court's tendency to follow the political consensus produced by the dominant party alliance meant that it could not serve as a bulwark against the tyranny of the majority.[101] Bickel thought that the insulation provided by life tenure suited the justices to articulating fundamental values and principles.[102] I suggest that the example of *Brown v. Board of Education*[103] was an important inspiration here. The Court managed to decide that controversial case as well as subsequent segregation cases unanimously; that total agreement implied by itself that there was something permanent about the principles the justices applied. But Bickel's projected role for the Court would have had far less plausibility if the justices had sharply and consistently disagreed across wide areas of constitutional doctrine. Persistent disagreement would have discredited the proposition that the five justices who prevailed were enforcing fundamental values. How could decisions be based on truly "enduring values"[104] if a single Court appointment could result in the overturning of important lines of precedent? The conclusions drawn by Dahl and Bickel would have been quite different had they not been able to assume the existence of a national consensus on politics and values.

All of this is not to endorse the countermajoritarian difficulty. Like many scholars, I think the difficulty fails to describe the Court's place in our political system.[105] Although American government could not work without the use of majority rule in elections and the lawmaking process, it also clearly includes significant values, rules, and institutions that work against majority rule.[106] From a descriptive point of view, a focus on majoritarianism is too narrow a way of understanding American democracy, let alone American constitutionalism. From a normative point of view, the situation is worse. Bickel's work and that of his successors provided little if any critical reflection on the nature of democratic ideals and principles. He appeared to be saying that the Court had to respect majority rule because the majority demanded it.[107] Bickel failed to offer a robust justification of the value of democracy.

Bickel's insistence on the special capacity of courts to provide for "the creative establishment and renewal of a coherent body of principled rules"[108] was arguably just as influential and certainly less criticized than his insistence that judicial review was countermajoritarian.[109] He contended that the judiciary had a comparative advantage over the political branches in dealing with "matters of principle."[110] The picture Bickel drew was one of simultaneous isolation and engagement. Judges were isolated enough to pursue "the ways of the scholar"[111] in sorting through society's fundamental values.[112] But they were also engaged by particular facts, "the flesh and blood of an actual case."[113] Finally, compared to the political branches, the judiciary was better able to educate the public as to their constitutional responsibilities, those principles to which we all hold allegiance, but may be forgotten "in the moment's hue and cry."[114]

This was an idealistic portrayal of the federal judiciary.[115] Ironically, it was not one endorsed by Bickel himself in other moods. Like other scholars identified with the "legal process" movement, Bickel could be quite critical of the justices and the quality of their reasoning.[116] But praising the judiciary's comparative institutional advantage in matters of principle was a theme that resonated deeply among constitutional scholars over the next forty years.[117] Its resonance had the effect of obscuring the somewhat enervating effect it had on constitutional theory. It tended to encourage an uncritical "deductive institutionalism"[118] that maintained that the judiciary was the forum of principle because it had to be. Following Bickel, scholars compared an ideal Court to a nonideal Congress and concluded, not surprisingly, that the Court was a more attractive institution.[119] Without institutional comparisons grounded in empirical evidence, the insistence on the federal judiciary's devotion to principle began to appear ideological, something legal scholars believed because their arguments would not make sense otherwise.

If we are to learn from Bickel and understand the relationship between judicial review and democracy, we will have to engage in a realistic appraisal of the institutional capabilities of the judiciary to promote constitutional principles while employing a critical, rather than simply conventional, justification of American democracy. At the same time, we cannot use studies such as Dahl's to satisfy ourselves that the Supreme Court will always be in step with public opinion, given that such studies are always dependent on a particular historical and political context. The theory of judicial review I develop below argues that there is a democratic problem with judicial review that is not dependent on any commitment to majoritarianism. But I also hope to show that such a theory cannot be advanced without establishing the historical and political context for contemporary judicial review.

B. The Political Context of Judicial Review

There are two political and institutional realities that must inform any credible theory of judicial review: the persistence of divided government over the past three decades and the politicization of constitutional issues and the federal judicial appointment process.[120] Since Richard Nixon became President in 1969, the President's party has controlled Congress for only eight and a half years (as of 2004). Divided government has arguably increased the Court's power by making it more difficult for an aggrieved political party to strike back. But it has also deprived government of the political consensus that was assumed by modern theories of judicial review such as Bickel's.[121] In a period of divided government, there is no "dominant national alliance"[122] and no persistent lawmaking majority. By the logic of these theories, the risk that the Court could make countermajoritarian decisions (by striking down laws passed under unified government) without fear of being checked by the elected branches has increased significantly.

Divided government has also certainly not assuaged the phenomenon of politicization. Believe it or not, there was a time when issues of affirmative action, school prayer, abortion, and gay rights were not salient in American politics. In this earlier political universe, Supreme Court nominations were not given much attention by the Senate. No one conceived of televising nomination hearings and sometimes not even a transcript was preserved. Nominations to the lower federal courts were approved routinely. It took some time for politicians (other than Southern segregationists) to adjust to the new activism of the Warren Court, but once they did, the appointment process became permanently politicized. Senators now perceived the federal judiciary to be a powerful institution, capable of setting the national political agenda.[123]

The politicization of the appointment process was just one instance of a more general politicization of constitutional issues.[124] Such issues, once rare in presidential elections, became relevant in 1964 when the Republicans nominated Barry Goldwater for president[125] and again in 1968 as Republican candidate Nixon proclaimed the importance of the "law and order" issue.[126] Although President Nixon was able to make four Court appointments, activist decisions like *Roe v. Wade*[127] resulted in another wave of politicization.[128]

During the 1970s, both moderate liberals and moderate conservatives, essentially creatures of the political center, became increasingly polarized around the uncertain course charted by the Burger Court. To provide some fine-grained context, I would like to focus on a few straws in the wind that became the "Reagan revolution." Consider the experience of Charles Cooper, later a figure of some importance in the Reagan administration's Department of Justice.[129] Cooper served as a clerk to then Associate Justice Rehnquist during the term the Court decided a controversial affirmative action case, *United Steel-workers v. Weber*.[130] Rehnquist and Cooper carefully researched the law at issue, the Civil Rights Act of 1964,[131] and found strong evidence that the Act prohibited affirmative action plans like the one at issue. But Justice William Brennan showed his great skill in assembling a majority to uphold the plan and Rehnquist had to write a biting dissent. As a consequence, Cooper lost his belief in an impartial, apolitical Court. Cooper and many Republican legal activists like him drew the lesson from decisions like *Weber* and *Roe* that the only reliable way to affect the path of the Court was through the appointment of jurists who were as reliably conservative as Rehnquist.[132]

Another sign of changing times came in April 1982 with the first national event of the Federalist Society.[133] As might be anticipated, the subject of the first symposium was federalism (a topic still of current interest). The symposium organizers set themselves against the "statist agenda"[134] which they saw advanced relentlessly by the legal profession and legal academics. Describing themselves as "a national organization devoted to the study of legal issues from a conservative and libertarian perspective,"[135] the symposium featured well-known scholars such as Charles Fried, Judge Richard Posner, Lino Graglia, Paul Bator, Walter Berns, and John Noonan, along with newer (and soon to be well-known) conservatives such as Theodore Olson (now Solicitor General), Antonin Scalia (now Associate Justice), and Michael McConnell (now Judge on the U.S. Court of Appeals for the Tenth Circuit).

Charles Fried, the lead author of the symposium, would not long after join the Reagan administration as Solicitor General.[136] Fried believed that the Solicitor General's office had become infected with a "political bias . . . because since the 1930s the prerogatives of the federal government had been overwhelmingly invoked in furtherance of a liberal, regulatory agenda."[137] For Fried, then, what did the "Reagan revolution" mean for the legal system? In terms of the Constitution, "courts should be more disciplined, less adventurous and political in interpreting the law";[138] "the President must be allowed a strong hand in governing the nation";[139] and justice and racial equality should be achieved "without distorting the system of opportunity and reward for merit on which the morale of a free-enterprise system depends."[140] Fried was correct to think that these were new themes for American constitutional law.

Unlike previous presidents, Ronald Reagan was willing to expend significant political capital and staff time to translate these themes into constitutional doctrine through judicial appointments.[141] As Sheldon Goldman, Mark Silverstein, and David Yalof have demonstrated in their comprehensive studies,[142] the Reagan administration made appointments to the federal bench an important part of its overall political strategy. As Silverstein describes, "before the Reagan presidency executive scrutiny of potential nominees to lower federal courts was haphazard at best and limited by respect for senatorial patronage. Under Reagan, however, the President's Committee on Federal Judicial Selection, consisting of key members of the White House staff and the Justice Department, was formed to screen judicial appointments and allow the administration to apply a consistent ideological measure."[143]

Yalof expands on Silverstein's account by describing the Reagan administration's effort to anticipate vacancies on the Supreme Court. When Edwin Meese became Attorney General at the beginning of Reagan's second term, he created a task force to find potential nominees to the Court should a vacancy open up.[144] The task force identified twelve factors to be taken into account in assessing nominees. Among them were such items as: " 'awareness of the importance of strict justiciability and procedural requirements' "; " 'refusal to create new constitutional rights for the individual' "; " 'deference to states in their spheres' "; " 'recognition that the federal government is one of enumerated powers' "; and " 'respect for traditional values.' "[145] The task force looked for federal judges who met the requirements and produced a report for each judge reviewing their opinions. Yalof notes, "[n]ever before in history had there been such an excruciatingly detailed examination of judicial rulings by the Justice Department in anticipation of a Supreme Court nomination."[146]

It is evident that we are no longer in a world in which racial and other minorities can count on the Court when a presidential administration goes looking for Supreme Court nominees who believe that it is unwise to create new constitutional rights. To exaggerate somewhat, once majorities realized that certain Court decisions were contrary to their interests, they resolved to put their own representatives on the Court. This created a new Supreme Court appointment process, one that has been politicized and democratized. Silverstein concludes: "[t]he current [Supreme Court confirmation] process is disorderly, contentious, and unpredictable. In short, it is now a thoroughly democratic process, and the increased public participation in the selection of federal judges and Supreme Court justices is a consequence of profound changes in American politics and institutions. The most important development is the heightened activism of the modern federal judiciary."[147]

It is important to understand that I am not referring to partisanship or what might be called "ordinary politics"[148] when I refer to the federal judicial appointment process as politicized. Even if the appointment process becomes less contentious in the future, it will remain politicized. Politicization is a function of the degree to which rival political groups regard control of the Supreme Court and the federal judiciary as important. Ever since the Warren Court, politicians have perceived the Court as an institution that can affect their goals and political agenda. This guarantees the politicization I describe, regardless of how contentious the nomination process is or becomes.[149]

It was no longer possible for the Supreme Court to achieve the independence from politics required to maintain a consistent posture with respect to the protection of individual rights once the appointment process was politicized.[150] The appointment process might well produce a Court that was fairly cohesive if one political party dominated the presidency and the Senate. As noted, however, divided government (or a government in which neither party can achieve sixty votes in the Senate) seems to be our fate.[151] The contemporary Court has thus become another forum in which political battles over individual rights are played out. It is closely balanced between the contending sides and each presidential election and possible vacancy is monitored for its potential impact on constitutional issues.[152] As Sidney Milkis observes, "the federal courts now [rival] elections as the primary institutional focus of partisan politics."[153]

The politicization of constitutional issues and the appointment process have important implications for theories of judicial review. First, politicization undermines theories that assert that the Supreme Court has a comparative advantage over the elected branches in matters of principle. Politicization means that political divisions over constitutional questions are reproduced in the judicial realm. Bickel, for example, held that the Court was uniquely situated to develop a coherent body of constitutional principles and conserve fundamental values. Coherence and conservation are unlikely, however, when political disagreements are transferred to the judiciary. A continual war of bitter 5 to 4 decisions is more probable, making it implausible that the Court can perform a special function in educating the citizenry or assuming a vanguard role to promote a national dialogue on rights.[154] Rather, the Court is ensnared in the same contentious politics of rights that occupies the elected branches.

To sharpen this point, let's look at Bickel's specific claim that Supreme Court justices have the freedom to follow the ways of the scholar. Few scholars would advance this claim today in the way Bickel did.[155] It seems clear that Bickel's conception of the Court depended on a background value consensus that no longer exists. I have already noted the likely influence of the unanimity achieved by the Court in its decisions dismantling segregation during the 1950s and 1960s. For Bickel and his contemporaries, these unanimous decisions were perfect examples of how reflection could convince the justices that allowing constitutional values like equal protection to trump a previously sanctioned institution was in everyone's enlightened self-interest.

Such unanimity was possible when the justices supported democratic values like political equality in a constitutional regime that was far from being fully democratic. In such a world, the *Carolene Products* footnote worked its magic of guaranteeing the legitimacy of judicial activism that created more democracy.[156] Once claims of outright exclusion and blatant racial prejudice declined, however, the Court ceased speaking with a unanimous voice in decisions affecting African Americans. The judiciary could no longer be insulated from the full force of democratic politics once there was no dominant national alliance leading the way and constitutional issues (such as racial equality) had become politicized. Constitutional disagreements in the political sphere were reproduced in the judicial sphere. Over time, the politicization of constitutional issues has in this way greatly reduced, if not eliminated, any comparative advantage the judiciary once had in matters of principle.

Suppose it is granted that the judiciary does not have a comparative advantage in matters of principle. Various scholars have risen to the challenge of justifying judicial review in its absence by arguing that the judiciary achieves legitimacy as a representative body, although representing public opinion in a different way than the political branches.[157] To see what is wrong with this argument, we need to remember that there is no dominant national alliance. In a world without a partisan realignment and ruled by a closely divided government, political coalitions are reassembled every two years, as the entire House of Representatives and one-third of the Senate stand for reelection. The only way to guarantee that each two-year coalition has representation on the Court is to require justices to serve eighteen-year terms, replacing one justice every two years. Since the current period of divided government began in 1969, turnover on the Court has not come close to matching this criterion. President Jimmy Carter did not have the opportunity to nominate any justices, meaning those two coalitions have no representation on the Court. The same is true for President Reagan's first term (only one appointment), President Bill Clinton's second term (no appointments), and President George W. Bush's first term from 2001–2005 (no appointments).

This lack of effective representation for two-year political coalitions has been reflected in a reversal of the previous general correspondence between the Court's rulings and public opinion. One study shows that since 1981, "the Court appears as an even more ideologically driven but politically isolated institution. Its decisions have been independent of, if not antagonistic to, recent trends in the public mood and have been out of alignment with the dominant coalition in Congress."[158] This has occurred because there has been no dominant political alliance with consensus values that the Court can mirror.[159] Combined with more appointments by Republican presidents than Democratic presidents, this has meant a Court that is presently ideologically imbalanced with respect to public opinion and democratic debate.[160] The case for a politically representative Court therefore cannot be made without a major institutional change in the way justices are appointed.[161]

Our experience since the Reagan revolution shows that having a Supreme Court that is *politicized* does not necessarily lead to a Court that is *representative*, at least in the sense of being centrist with respect to policy outcomes.[162] Many experienced observers of American politics believe that the ultimate consequence of a fragmented constitutional system dominated by coalition politics is policy outcomes that fall roughly in the median of public opinion. *Bush v. Gore* by itself is powerful evidence that the same logic does not work for the Court. Legislative politics in the aftermath of the disputed 2000 presidential election produced a number of cautious reforms. But the politicization of the Court led to a breakdown in legal process and one of the worst opinions in recent decades,[163] one that liberals revile just as much as conservatives revile *Roe v. Wade.*

The problems posed by a politicized judiciary suggest the wisdom of moving at least some of these contentious issues back to the electoral arena. This would not be done out of a concern for the Court's legitimacy—various scholars have argued convincingly that this is not a problem.[164] Rather, this would be justified through a straightforward application of the theory of institutional competence—issues of political principle are best handled by what might be termed fully political institutions.

C. The Value of Democracy

Over the last two decades, a number of prominent scholars have launched wide-ranging attacks on Bickel's countermajoritarian difficulty.[165] One theme common to these attacks is that the value of democracy should not be the normative standard used to evaluate judicial review. Instead, these scholars urge that the Constitution itself should be the baseline for evaluation.[166] Further, these scholars make clear that the Constitution they have in mind is the Constitution as originally adopted in 1787.[167]

I believe these scholars have been led astray in their zeal to show why the difficulty is mistaken. One cannot understand the value of democracy in the contemporary United States by studying the political order brought into being by the 1787 Constitution. As I will show below, not only was that political order deeply undemocratic by our standards, but it violated many of our most basic political values. Using the 1787 Constitution as a baseline to evaluate aspects of our present constitutional order, including judicial review, is reactionary. American constitutionalism and democracy can be understood only from a developmental perspective, one that emphasizes the importance of constitutional change inside and outside Article V.[168] Theories of judicial review should acknowledge that American government has experienced a number of distinct political/constitutional regimes, or governing institutional orders.[169] The nature of government institutions and the politics to which they respond has undergone important changes over time, changes that are captured very imperfectly by the text of the Constitution.

What is important to understand about our contemporary democracy in the first instance is that it allows *ordinary people* to run the state.[170] Democracy might be thought of as the system of government that is the ineluctable consequence of allowing ordinary people to pursue primary political values such as freedom, equality, and justice. Democracy maximizes the amount of information available concerning principles, values, interests, and tastes by giving the great mass of ordinary persons some voice in government.[171] Further, the relatively decentralized democracy prevailing in the United States serves to increase by another order of magnitude the information policymakers have on hand. This information is critical to understanding differing points of view and issues as they arise, anticipating the consequences of various paths of action, and creating solutions to possible problems.

As I have argued elsewhere,[172] our contemporary democracy is based on an ideal of citizenship that includes an effective national guarantee of civil rights, including the right to vote. This ideal of citizenship is largely a twentieth-century phenomenon and is one of the main achievements of the civil rights movement. Americans truly won the democracy they enjoy today only through the struggle of African Americans for meaningful citizenship. In the 1930s, African American leader A. Philip Randolph declared: "'Freedom is never given; it is won. And the Negro people must win their freedom. They must achieve justice. This involves struggle, continuous struggle.'"[173] As one African American journalist put it during World War II: "'Our war is not to defend democracy, but to get a democracy we never had.'"[174]

The idea that our contemporary democracy has its origins in the African American struggle for freedom and political equality guides my theory of judicial review. Our contemporary democracy is something that we have achieved, not something granted to us by the Constitution of 1787 or even the Constitution as modified by the Reconstruction Amendments. The principles of democratic government that are widely accepted today are themselves the outcome of the historical process by which ordinary people came to have a fully effective voice in American government. The appropriate baseline for judging practices such as judicial review is therefore contemporary democratic principles, not eighteenth-century principles and beliefs.

The republican political theory with which the revolutionary generation was familiar did not provide any prominent role for ordinary people in government.[175] Perhaps yeoman farmers had sufficient independence to be citizens, but those involved in the marketplace and dependent on others for their jobs "could scarcely possess the enlightenment and disinterestedness to resist the temptations of power"[176] and competently hold office. The generation that wrote and ratified the Constitution largely retained these pre-Revolutionary republican beliefs. Governmental power had to be exercised by leisured gentlemen possessing landed wealth that gave them the independence to make virtuous judgments on matters of state.[177]

This republican conception of politics did not include political parties, interest groups, universal white male suffrage, or, as noted, a place for ordinary (white) men as public officials. Yet this was precisely the direction in which American politics moved during the first few decades of the republic.[178] As Gordon Wood argues, the Constitution attempted to "temper popular majoritarianism, but no constitution . . . could have restrained the popular social forces unleashed by the Revolution. . . . By the early nineteenth century, America had already emerged as the most egalitarian, most materialistic, most individualistic—and most evangelical Christian—society in Western history. In many respects this new democratic society was the very opposite of the one the revolutionary leaders had envisaged."[179]

Many famous members of the founding generation were shocked by what had occurred.[180] But why? Their surprise is hard to explain if you believe, as many scholars do, that the founding generation established American democracy. Although it is not entirely inaccurate to use the term "democracy" to describe the political order of the early nineteenth century, reflection on the surprise of the founding generation helps establish an important point. Our contemporary democracy in which ordinary people of all races, colors, sexes, religions, classes, and ethnic groups participate is largely a product of the twentieth century, not the eighteenth. Democracy in America is something we have earned over time, not inherited from the beginning.

I will focus on the examples of race and voting rights to illustrate the differences between the "democracy" of the founding generation and our own. Members of the founding generation such as James Madison and Thomas Jefferson reasoned that a republican, liberal, and democratic constitutional order was not possible unless the American population was white. Racial prejudice made it impossible to accept slaves as equals, as required by the premises of the constitutional order.[181]Historian George Fredrickson has called attention to the resulting *Herrenvolk* character of antebellum American democracy.[182] Whites in both the South and North appealed to the presumed biological differences between the races to justify the departure from egalitarian norms. Democracy in antebellum America meant equal citizenship for whites and an inferior status for blacks. In his comprehensive history of the law of New York, William Nelson has updated this *Herrenvolk* understanding to the early decades of the twentieth century.[183] The white citizens of New York believed in local government based in homogenous communities and that they were best suited to run the political system.[184] As Nelson describes: "Inasmuch as American democracy was conceptualized in terms of local self-rule, and homogeneity was deemed essential to that self-rule ... racially exclusionary policies and the preservation of democracy appeared to go hand in hand."[185] This pernicious understanding of what it meant to be a "democracy" had to be overcome before our contemporary democracy could be created.

The case of voting rights can be traced in detail thanks to Alexander Keyssar's valuable study.[186] Keyssar finds that an initial period, lasting until 1850, in which the franchise was expanded was checked by a long period until World War I, which was "characterized both by a narrowing of voting rights and by a mushrooming upper- and middle-class antagonism to universal suffrage."[187] One reason behind the contraction of the right to vote was the limited rationale that had supported its earlier expansion. Those arguing for universal white manhood suffrage in the early republic believed that the country would remain agrarian, a nation of farmers rather than factory laborers.[188] The United States was thus unique among Western countries "in experiencing a prolonged period during which the laws governing the right to vote became more, rather than less, restrictive. . . . the United States was one of the last countries in the developed world to attain universal suffrage."[189]

I have focused on race and voting rights because they are among the clearest examples of how the democratic principles we often take for granted are *recent* accomplishments. The kind of democracy in which we live is indeed different not only from that of the founding generation, but also from that of the Progressive reformers only a century ago. First, we recognize the importance of a national guarantee of civil rights, backed by effective enforcement agencies. These civil rights are truly universal in that they apply to all citizens and include political rights, including the right to vote and to run for office. There are no property, class, race, or sex-based restrictions on the exercise of any civil rights. Second, unlike the Founders, we accept the institutions of political parties and interest groups as legitimate means of organizing citizens for politics. Third, we accept (to a certain extent) a "populist" form of democracy[190] in which all of the elected branches are understood as directly elected by the people (the Electoral College notwithstanding), and there is a more direct role for public opinion in the form of polls, initiatives, and referenda. Fourth, unlike both the Founders and Progressives, we reject slavery, white supremacy, and racial discrimination and the supporting belief of states' rights that supported that system of oppression. Neither the Founders nor Progressives would have accepted the kind of multiracial, multiethnic society and government that we take for granted.

These developments have been in the service of fundamental political values such as political equality, political participation, and having a government that looks after common interests. If it were possible to reduce these values to a single idea, I think Frank Michelman's invocation of Justice Brennan's devotion to "the inestimable value of the ever-redeemable dignity of the individual human being"[191] hits the mark. As Amy Gutmann and Dennis Thompson elaborate, democracy "is a conception of government that accords equal respect to the moral claims of each citizen, and is therefore morally justifiable from the perspective of each citizen."[192] Robert Dahl,[193] Thomas Christiano,[194] and Rex Martin[195] have also made some form of this argument. These theorists all stress that the value of democracy lies not in majority rule, but rather in a commitment to treat citizens equally and ensure that the actual operation of government works to advance the interests of everyone.

A good way to understand our system of government is through the concept of a "democracy of rights."[196] The idea of a democracy of rights helps clarify that in the contemporary world, the *point* of having a democracy is that it does tend to successfully create and enforce basic human rights. There are many examples of this in recent American history, including the Civil Rights Act of 1964,[197] the Voting Rights Act of 1965[198] and its subsequent amendments, and the Americans with Disabilities Act of 1990.[199] As William Forbath has shown, these democratic achievements were the ultimate product of the struggles to gain inclusion by disenfranchised social groups invoking traditions of equal citizenship grounded in the Reconstruction amendments.[200] That is, ordinary

people seeking political recognition and representation helped create our contemporary democratic order. As summarized by Nelson, these groups together
created "a divided, multifarious culture, in which groups with distinctive and
even irreconcilable backgrounds and lifestyles competed for their share of public space and the public good."[201]

This way of understanding the value of our contemporary democracy leads
naturally to a critique of any governmental institution or practice (including
judicial review) that tends to operate against the protection of democratically
created rights.

D. Constructing a Democratic Theory of Judicial Review

The idea of a democracy of rights appears to lead in a straightforward way
to a justification for judicial review.[202] Because rights are valuable political
goods, it would be useful to have a government agency responsible for enforcing rights when the more overtly political branches lose sight of their importance.[203] This justification cuts the other way, however, if the judiciary refuses to
defer to legislatively created rights that implement constitutional values such as
equal protection.[204] In these circumstances, the exercise of judicial review to *destroy* valuable statutory rights would run counter to the principles and values of
contemporary democracy. To the extent that the judiciary has done this in areas such as affirmative action, racial redistricting, and the enforcement of the
Equal Protection Clause, its exercise of judicial review cannot be justified.[205]

One might reasonably ask how significant these examples are.[206] Even if we
concede the arguments about the Supreme Court destroying valuable rights
under the Equal Protection Clause, that is only one area of constitutional doctrine. What are the implications of this critique for constitutional law generally?

I propose to answer this question by reviewing a little known debate between Michael McConnell and Ronald Dworkin.[207] The debate occurred in 1997
as the nation waited for the Court's decision on the asserted right to assisted
suicide in the important substantive due process case, *Washington v. Glucksberg*.[208] Both McConnell and Dworkin had filed amicus briefs in the case, Mc-
Connell opposing the recognition of a right to assisted suicide and Dworkin
writing in support.[209] What was remarkable about this debate was how it introduced themes of comparative institutional competence common to theories of

judicial review into an area of doctrine that had been dominated by theories of constitutional interpretation.

The debate was truly joined when Dworkin made the argument, familiar to readers of his work, that McConnell could defend his position against the right to assisted suicide only by defending a controversial political principle about "the character of a genuine democracy."[210] Dworkin asserted that abstract clauses such as the due process clause were drafted in "moral language"[211] and "[e]verything therefore depends on how that abstract language is to be interpreted."[212] The correct way to proceed, Dworkin believed, was to understand these clauses "as incorporating certain fundamental principles of individual freedom and equality."[213] This was consistent with the way the Supreme Court had interpreted the equal protection and due process clauses. Dworkin admitted that McConnell's historicist theory of interpretation did have some support in the cases and thus the debate should occur over "which of these strategies is appropriate for judges in a democracy."[214] Dworkin viewed his strategy as superior ultimately because it was more faithful to the nature of American constitutionalism. That is, it was "a conception of democracy according to which the powers of the majority are limited by principle even when it is controversial what that principle requires."[215]

Dworkin thus posed the question: What does the Constitution mean? McConnell's response was exemplary: Who decides?[216] McConnell agreed that there was an interpretive disagreement over the principle at issue, although he contended that it would be a mistake to ignore the substantial policy questions involved in recognizing a right to assisted suicide. But he shifted the focus of the debate by contending that this was "a question of constitutional structure."[217] McConnell referred here to the kind of institutional inquiry characteristic of theories of judicial review. In a democracy, the standard way to resolve disagreements over both principle and policy was through public debate and representative institutions. Searching for the answer using Dworkin's methodology might produce attractive principles, but not necessarily ones bearing any relation to the Constitution.[218] According to McConnell, many state legislatures had debated the issue of assisted suicide in the 1990s and only one—Oregon— had voted to approve the practice. Medical associations and official multidisciplinary task forces had recommended against a right to assisted suicide.[219] In light of this extensive societal deliberation, McConnell wondered what right the judiciary had to intervene.[220]

The force of Dworkin's argument for a right to assisted suicide derived from the undoubted past instances in which the Court had interpreted abstract clauses to protect the rights of minorities. On that basis, Dworkin could justifiably ask how McConnell could give "simple political majorities the final power to interpret the abstract rights of minorities."[221] For McConnell, recognition of a new unenumerated right was not out of the question, although he believed Dworkin had not come close to justifying a new right in this case. Fundamentally, said McConnell, "[t]his is not a question of moral philosophy but of institutional legitimacy: not of what is the right answer but of who has the right to decide."[222] The policy justification for laws against assisted suicide, founded on reasonable public deliberation, could not be ignored. Dworkin gave no recognition or deference to this democratic deliberation,[223] whereas for McConnell, it was central.

Of course, this brief editorial-style debate could not resolve any fundamental theoretical issues. Scholars familiar with debates over theories of interpretation and judicial review might find the arguments rather standard. I submit, however, that McConnell's institutional arguments have a great deal of force even for those who accept the legitimacy of *Roe* and the substantive due process doctrine in general. There was an important shift in context between *Roe* and *Glucksberg*. In *Roe*, the Court faced a statute unchanged since the nineteenth century,[224] a failure by many states to reconsider the risks of abortion as a medical procedure, and a divided public. By contrast, in the 1990s many states had recently reconsidered and updated their statutes prohibiting assisted suicide. The states generally rejected a right to assisted suicide, a judgment amply supported by expert opinion.

In addition, the right to assisted suicide was a fundamentally different kind of issue. Dworkin referred to the right as involving "minorities," presumably thinking of those relatively few individuals seeking a physician's help to end their lives. But here there was no danger of stereotyping or a failure of sympathy on the part of legislators. In the era of *Roe*, men dominated state legislatures. In the era of *Glucksberg*, not only were legislatures more diverse but also every legislator could well imagine a close relative, friend, or even themselves in the same position as the plaintiffs. There was no danger of the majority rejecting a claimed right because of prejudice against a reviled minority. Dworkin could not show any deficiency in the democratic process that had produced the ban on assisted suicide.

The McConnell-Dworkin debate thus suggested the weakness of interpretive arguments in support of new unenumerated rights in an era characterized simultaneously by the recognition of the importance of individual constitutional rights and the political nature of those rights. Dworkin tended to argue as if nothing had changed since the time of *Brown*, *Griswold*, and *Roe*, but clearly there had been vast changes in American politics and institutions. As I have argued previously, once the United States became a democracy of rights in the 1960s, the elected branches of government began regularly producing rights that were in many ways more effective than the constitutional rights created by the federal judiciary.[225] In the era of *Glucksberg*, it was taken for granted that rights were valuable political and social goods worthy of protection by legislatures. The right to assisted suicide had therefore already been debated thoroughly in democratic fora before the plaintiffs ever received a hearing in the Supreme Court. This was not a situation like *Brown* and *Griswold* in which the channels of democratic communication were closed for all practical purposes.[226]

The McConnell-Dworkin debate also suggested the implausibility of arguing that the judiciary has a generic comparative advantage in matters of principle. Is it really plausible to believe that the judiciary had a comparative advantage in reasoning about the right to assisted suicide? As McConnell argued, the judiciary could not match the deliberative depth and information on values brought to bear by ordinary citizens, professional organizations, and expert task forces working within democratic institutions. As Cass Sunstein has argued, "[w]hen we are dealing with judicial protection of non-democratic rights, the risks of error—its likelihood and cost—are very high, and the potential benefits are highly speculative."[227]

The logic of the argument I have been constructing from the McConnell-Dworkin debate would seem to hold for judicial protection of abstract constitutional values generally. I would like to illustrate this through the device of comparing what theories of judicial review would have been appropriate at three thirty-year intervals in the Court's jurisprudence: 1938, 1968, and 1998. This device will also help make the important point that my theory of judicial review is one designed for our contemporary circumstances and is not intended to prescribe a role for the Court that would have been appropriate at any point in its history.[228]

In 1938 *Carolene Products*[229] was decided and as its famous footnote[230] suggested, the Court had its work cut out for it if it wanted to expand the sphere of democratic rights and deliberation. State legislation restricted the political process by denying the right to vote and the important freedoms of the press, association, and assembly.[231] In addition, religious and racial discrimination pervaded the political process, in effect excluding minority groups from defending their rights through democratic means.[232] In short, the United States was not a democracy of rights. It did not adhere to many of the democratic norms that we now take for granted and use to criticize the political process in other countries. In fact, if we encountered a country today that had as much Jim Crow–era oppression, anti-Semitism, and lack of basic protection for political rights as 1930s America, we would probably not regard it as a democracy at all.

Given the absence of a democracy of rights, it was desirable for the judiciary to assume a vanguard role to protect and affirmatively defend the value of political rights, including rights against discrimination, for all Americans. The judiciary was assisted by the unitary control the Democratic Party had over the elected branches in undertaking this rather massive task. This ensured a constant stream of justices who would generally support the cause of defending civil rights and liberties, as well as guaranteeing a relatively uncontroversial and nonideological appointment process.

In 1968, the era of unitary government was waning and statutes such as the Civil Rights Act of 1964[233] and the Voting Rights Act of 1965,[234] along with a seemingly relentless stream of activist Court decisions had established the preconditions for an effective democracy of rights. The appropriate judicial role now was one of watchful maintenance and attention to continuous effective enforcement with respect to democratic rights. The steady stream of justices supportive of an activist democratic agenda could no longer be guaranteed, given the more obvious political divisions over the Court's role. In addition, the bitter hearings held over President Lyndon Johnson's nomination of Justice Abe Fortas to replace Chief Justice Earl Warren foreshadowed the era of a permanent politicization of federal judicial appointments.[235]

In 1998, the era of divided government and pervasive politicization was in full flower, and a polity divided on various constitutional questions was matched by a Court persistently divided by 5 to 4 votes. At the same time, a democracy of rights had not only been achieved, but had been institutionalized through reauthorizations of the Voting Rights Act,[236] increased statutory protections for civil rights and civil liberties,[237] and by the permanent presence of interest groups whose object was to increase the range of constitutional values such as privacy, private property, nondiscrimination, and religious freedom.[238] Significant laws such as the Americans with Disabilities Act[239] had been passed that extended constitutional values like nondiscrimination beyond the scope of Supreme Court decisions.[240]

In this fully effective democracy of rights, the appropriate judicial role was to support democratic deliberation about rights by ensuring the success of the new statutory protections for civil rights and civil liberties. The judiciary could not hope to match the amount of information about values and the multilevel debate and deliberation generated by ordinary people with effective access to the political process once a democracy of rights became operational after the 1960s. The judiciary's role was a supporting one because there were no significant barriers to political participation that the judiciary could dismantle. Moreover, the politicization of rights created in part by the Supreme Court itself had undermined any comparative advantage the judiciary once had in matters of principle.

Of course, this is not a description of the role the Rehnquist Court has actually assumed. To the contrary, on too many occasions the Court has reversed the promise of *Carolene Products* by denigrating the political process[241] and refusing to protect racial minorities from the effects of prejudice.[242] In this anti-*Carolene* world, the footnote-four rationale that once supported vigorous review of legislative classifications now runs in the opposite direction. If the judiciary is harming the political process and racial minorities, this counsels that the judiciary apply minimal scrutiny to government actions in these areas.

From this point of view, judicial review has a difficulty with democracy, not with being countermajoritarian. To be more precise, some aspects of the contemporary institution of judicial review are inconsistent with the role the judiciary should have in a democracy of rights.[243] For example, the Court limited the effectiveness of the Voting Rights Act of 1965[244] in *City of Mobile v. Bolden*,[245] set back the effort against race and sex discrimination in *Grove City College v. Bell*[246] and *Wards Cove Packing Co. v. Atonio*,[247] struck down the Religious Freedom Restoration Act[248] (RFRA) in *City of Boerne v. Flores*,[249] hurt the effectiveness of the law against age discrimination in *Kimel v. Florida Board of Regents*,[250] damaged the ability of the legal system to fight gender-motivated violence in *United States v. Morrison*,[251] and dented the Americans with Disabilities Act[252] in *Board of Trustees v. Garrett*.[253]

To summarize, the role of the federal judiciary in the contemporary United States should be structured by the concept of a democracy of rights. In such a democracy, constitutional rights are guaranteed primarily through a dense network of statutory rights protections enacted at all levels of government at the behest of a rights-conscious citizenry. The judiciary should support this network by means of ordinary statutory interpretation guided by an informed appreciation that the ultimate purpose of the network is to ensure the existence of a political order that respects the equal dignity of all citizens. This limited judicial role (relative to, say, the Warren Court) is justified by the contemporary judiciary's lack of a comparative advantage in matters of constitutional principle and the superior information on matters of rights available to ordinary citizens in a fully effective democracy.

I will close this section by considering an important objection from Barry Friedman.[254] He argues that we should test theories of judicial review by asking whether we would adhere to them under different political circumstances.[255] Suppose it turns out, for example, that the Supreme Court allows affirmative action in higher education to continue, while Congress takes action against it.[256] Friedman asks, in effect, whether I care more about democratic rule or racial minorities. Of course, I care about both and that is the dilemma. The point I have tried to make, however, is that in a constitutional world that is sharply politicized, there is no such thing as a safe haven from the stresses of democratic conflict.[257] A Supreme Court suddenly more favorable to the rights of racial minorities would be simply that much more of a bigger target for those conservatives who see such rights as special preferences.[258] The world I prefer is not one in which racial minorities either win all the time or lose all the time, but in which the Court is depoliticized and we spend our time arguing with our fellow citizens rather than our fellow judges. In this politicized age, it no longer makes sense to craft arguments designed only for the attention of the judiciary. Advocates of new rights and defenders of old rights must make them to all branches of government, or risk losing them altogether.

III. Implications and Contrasts

One useful way to explore the implications of the theory presented in section II is to contrast it with some recent arguments in support of judicial review. In this section I contrast my theory with Daniel Farber and Suzanna Sherry's defense of judicial review[259] and Christopher Eisgruber's defense of the idea that the judiciary does indeed have a comparative advantage in matters of rights.[260]

A. Is Judicial Review the Status Quo?

The main targets of Farber and Sherry in their recent clear-headed book are "grand" constitutional theory (global theories of constitutional interpretation) and the unfortunate influence of the countermajoritarian difficulty.[261] I have no quarrel with a quest against grand theory or, indeed, against the countermajoritarian difficulty, as I indicated above. Farber and Sherry make many sound arguments against both that deserve the close attention of scholars.

I have a difficulty, however, with a certain complacency that I detect in their arguments in support of judicial review. Farber and Sherry agree that majoritarianism is important "and thus that judges should never overturn legislation lightly or without persuasive grounds."[262] They accuse their grand scholars, however, of an "obsession with judicial legitimacy."[263] They find this odd given that "judicial review is now an established aspect of democratic regimes."[264] Democracies around the world have adopted judicial review and it should not be regarded as an institution that is hard to justify.[265]

From my perspective, the problem here is that Farber and Sherry do not regard judicial review as a complex institutional practice and do not make clear whether they are using a critical or conventional understanding of what democracy is. At the outset, they say that the "key question"[266] is "whether the system as a whole fits our concept of democracy."[267] Unfortunately, they never define democracy beyond making clear that it is exemplified by the status quo. This lack of attention to the meaning of democracy creates the impression that they believe the United States has always been a democracy, and the fact that judicial review has lasted at least two centuries indicates that it should be "an unquestioned aspect of our system."[268]

The methodology behind this defense of judicial review is a good example of what I have been trying to move away from in my own analysis. First, judicial review has a number of key constituent elements. These elements have changed over time, and thus the task of justifying judicial review has presented different challenges at different periods of American history. For example, I have argued that Marshall's justifications for judicial review would make no sense in our own time (if their assumptions were fully spelled out) because they were based on different understandings of the law/politics distinction. Yet, like many scholars, Farber and Sherry continue to employ Marshall's defenses of judicial review.[269] They contend that critiques of judicial review are "anachronistic,"[270] but this better describes their own analysis.

Second, only a critical theory of democracy can explain and describe the contemporary American polity. If we encountered the government of Marshall's time, for example, in the contemporary guise of the political system of another country, we would not regard that political system as a democracy. The meaning of democracy has changed over time, and our achievement of the particular form I have called a democracy of rights is a very recent one. Further, we cannot justify judicial review by simply noting that it is part of the status quo because this begs the question of whether the status quo can be justified. To do this, we need the cutting edge provided by a critical normative theory of democracy. Even if we think that democracy should be about nothing more than the protection of important individual rights, that would still provide a critical perspective on the exercise of contemporary judicial review, given the Supreme Court's recent destruction of specific rights.

To put these points another way, my theory of judicial review is based on a contextualized, historicist conception of constitutional theory,[271] while Farber and Sherry offer a static defense. Their justification of judicial review as the status quo is not responsive to an anti-*Carolene* world in which judicial review is used as a sword against individual rights and racial minorities. In addition, they ignore the politicization of constitutional issues and the consequent effects on the judiciary. All of these contemporary realities must be confronted before Farber and Sherry can successfully defend judicial review.

B. Are Judges Disinterested Enough to Serve Democracy?

In one of the best recent works of constitutional theory, Christopher Eisgruber argues that "the Supreme Court can be regarded as a representative institution which is well constituted to speak on the people's behalf about matters of principle."[272] As such the Court serves democratic values rather than opposes them. Eisgruber advances a conception of democracy similar to the one I argued for above. A democracy should be "impartial,"[273] which means it "should respond to the interests and opinions of all the people, rather than merely serving the majority, or some other fraction of the people."[274] Eisgruber is concerned to defend the democratic legitimacy of judicial review and in doing so develops a sophisticated version of the argument that the judiciary has a comparative advantage over the elected branches in matters of constitutional principle. That makes his project a challenge to my theory of judicial review.

Eisgruber is a pragmatist and thus does not contend that judges are "more virtuous or insightful than the average American."[275] Further, he urges us to be comfortable with the fact that federal judges are "political appointees, nominated and confirmed by elected officials."[276] This ensures their "conformity to mainstream conceptions of political justice."[277] But judges also have institutional advantages over politicians and ordinary citizens. They have life tenure and jobs at the peak of their profession. They know their choices have consequences and hence are inclined to take their responsibilities seriously. Finally, they are required to issue public justifications for their rulings.[278] These institutional advantages make judges "disinterested"[279] and well matched to the requirements of impartial democracy.

Eisgruber has identified some clear institutional *differences* between judges and ordinary officials and citizens. But are these differences *advantages* and, if so, with respect to what? Eisgruber denies that he needs to justify judicial supremacy in all matters of principle.[280] The Court must work in partnership with other institutions, sometimes deferring to their judgment.[281] Judges are therefore not the only officials who can address matters of principle.[282] Eisgruber defines his task this way: "The power of judicial review presupposes only that judges can usefully speak on behalf of the people with respect to some important issues of political principle, not that judges alone can do so, or that judges can speak on behalf of the people with regard to all such matters."[283]

Nevertheless, for Eisgruber's argument to be relevant to judicial review as it exists today, he has to defend a sphere of judicial supremacy. This defense does indeed emerge as he considers the details of the judiciary's institutional position relative to ordinary officials and citizens. Without the insulation from political, social, and economic pressure guaranteed by life tenure, politicians and citizens "mistake self-interest for moral principle."[284] By contrast, judges are more likely to "decide on the basis of a principled judgment—a judgment, in other words, about what is good from a moral perspective, rather than a judgment about what is good for their careers or their pocketbooks."[285] So judges do indeed have a comparative advantage in reasoning about moral principles compared to elected officials.[286] When Eisgruber discusses the controversy over the constitutionality of RFRA, for example, he says "[t]here is no reason for the justices to defer to Congress on questions about what religious liberty requires,"[287] because "the Court is likely to represent the people better than Congress on questions of moral principle."[288]

Eisgruber's defense of judicial review is designed to meet objections from majoritarian democrats,[289] not a theory based on the concept of a democracy of rights. Eisgruber wants to show that the judiciary is not undemocratic, not that it is perfectly democratic. Even within the boundaries he has set for himself, it is telling that he takes no account of the frequent instances where politicians and ordinary citizens have acted on the basis of principle and protected constitutional values and legal rights. Eisgruber's discussion of the comparative advantage of the judiciary gives no hint of the existence of fundamental rights statutes such as the Civil Rights Act of 1964,[290] the Voting Rights Act of 1965,[291] and the Americans with Disabilities Act.[292] He asserts without argument that the Court represented the people better than Congress by striking down RFRA. It is more likely that the American people believed that they had a fundamental right to the free exercise of their religion, a right Congress was trying, however imperfectly, to protect through RFRA.[293]

To see what is questionable about Eisgruber's argument, we must keep in mind the lessons of the McConnell-Dworkin debate. Important constitutional issues always have a policy dimension. In a fully effective democracy of rights, policymakers have a flood of information at their disposal concerning the interests of the people and the likely consequences of various courses of action. Further, there is a constant flow of principled argument directed at and among policymakers concerning these constitutional issues. There is no basis on which the judiciary can compete meaningfully with the polity as a whole on either of these dimensions.

Moreover, the judiciary cannot contribute an independent voice of principle to a democracy of rights once it has been politicized. In the current age of ideological polarization, principled debate on the Supreme Court tracks principled debates in politics and society generally. The only difference is that the Court operates with an informational disadvantage. To the extent that the Court engages in the old-fashioned adjudication of individual claims, it is likely that the judicial process has a significant advantage over the political process with respect to the litigants. But major constitutional issues of the kind that concern Eisgruber and myself do not involve straightforward adjudication. These cases concern the entire nation, not just the litigants.

In summarizing his case in favor of the democratic legitimacy of judicial review, Eisgruber contends that few would claim "that the United States would have been better off during the last fifty years without judicial review."[294] The experience of the last half century shows that judges have stood up for "values that Americans care about—such as racial equality and free speech and the rule of law—when voters and ordinary politicians lacked the will to do so."[295] Certainly judges have done so and in so acting they helped create both our present democracy of rights and the age of supercharged ideological constitutional debate. Both are products of the activist decisions like *Brown v. Board of Education*[296] and *Reynolds v. Sims*[297] that Eisgruber justly celebrates. But Eisgruber's most persuasive examples all come before the United States achieved the status of a democracy of rights. The idea that activist judicial review was justified by the lack of democratic rights in the past does not justify in the present. Indeed today's activist decisions place democratic rights in jeopardy and so threaten the ultimate legacy of decisions like *Brown* and *Reynolds*—a politicized democracy that can resolve complex questions of rights and principles on its own.[298]

Conclusion

A reader who has made it this far will notice that I have not issued a clarion call to abolish judicial review. Given a minimal pragmatic concern with unforeseen consequences, I see no reason to advocate such a radical change in our institutions. From my point of view, judicial review has to be available for cases that are truly matters of adjudication in that they concern only the litigants. Further, it is consistent with the idea of a democracy of rights that judicial review be available for those now somewhat rare cases where it can be shown that the avenues of political change are closed.[299]

Suppose, however, that the avenues of political change are open, but there is a reasonable case that legislative outcomes have been affected by passion or prejudice. It is at this point that I would part company with many liberals and others concerned about the unreasoning self-interest that seems to play so much of a role in our politics. The politicization of the judiciary ensures that if passions or prejudices are widespread in society, then they will also be present on the federal bench. While it is obviously a mistake to compare an idealized judiciary with a presumptively debased political process, my point goes deeper. The history of public discussion of issues like racial equality shows that what is a matter of passion against principle or prejudice against rights is deeply contested. When what seems to be passion is claimed to be principle, we are past the point where we could summon the spirit of *Marbury* and use the eighteenth-century distinction between law and politics to settle our most fundamental political questions.

A Democracy of Rights: The Dark Side?

A Comment on Stephen M. Griffin

VICKI C. JACKSON

Professor Griffin's illuminating chapter raises important challenges for constitutional law and constitutional theory. Professor Griffin offers insightful, deeply informed descriptions of shifts in the institution of judicial review in the Court and in the broader intellectual terrain of its adjudicatory work, placing significant weight on a dynamic understanding of what the Constitution has become and on the means for its development. He makes a valuable argument that it is in important measure due to the civil rights movement of the 1950s and 1960s that we have come to understand ourselves as a democracy founded on equality of rights of all. That we are such a democracy today is not due to something bestowed on us in 1789, or the aftermath of the Civil War, but rather to ongoing struggles—of African Americans, of women, of immigrants and their families, of religious minorities, of gays and lesbians—to expand our understandings of equality and rights.[1]

Professor Griffin seeks to link this understanding of the dynamics of change in our conceptions of equal citizenship with a new understanding of the role of judicial review and the politicized dynamics of judicial appointments. His call to attend to changes in politics and in the institution of judicial review could not be more timely, though I am not entirely sure I agree with his optimism about democratic politics and thus with some of his conclusions. In an effort constructively to engage with his project, I comment on five aspects of his chapter: his narrative of a change in the practice of judicial review; how we came to be a "democracy of rights"; his conception of the value of legislatively created rights; his conception of judicial independence; and the traction of a theory of judicial review based on a historicized understanding of the polity.

I. Continuity and Discontinuity:
Narratives of Judicial Review

Professor Griffin places considerable weight on the significance of the "doubtful case" rule at the dawn of judicial review (and hence of early defenses of judicial review) and its subsequent disappearance. But his account seems (at least to this federal courts teacher) to overstate discontinuities in the practice of judicial review. *Marbury* is itself a classic paradigm of a "doubtful case." Certainly the inconsistency of the jurisdictional statute with the Constitution was not patently clear, as generations of law professors have spent valuable class time pointing out to students.[2] Whatever lip service may have been paid to the idea of the "doubtful case," it is hard to say that the doctrine could have played that central a role in justifying judicial review in the face of *Marbury* itself. Nor has the idea behind the doubtful case rule entirely disappeared from constitutional law. Even today the Court episodically, though faint-heartedly, mentions the presumption of constitutionality, a latter-day version of the "doubtful case" rule.[3] Consider here also the idea of deferential review of equal protection challenges in economic cases and Justice Stephen Breyer's willingness to defer to Congress in the regulation of complex new technologies even where constitutional rights may be at stake.[4] On the other hand, the pace of the Court's invalidation of federal statutes certainly seems to have increased in recent years,[5] so Professor Griffin may be on to something important that has shifted in whether the Court feels any sense of constraint in translating its disagreements with other branches into constitutional law.

Second, Professor Griffin is correct to emphasize the importance of the shift in legal consciousness from a sense that law exists independently and must be found to an understanding that law is made. Although it is surely harder to insist on the distinction between "judgment" and "will" in a post-realist world, yet, I believe, most judges continue to see this difference as essential to the legitimacy of their judgments.[6] The post-realist consciousness that law is made may be pervasive, yet it coexists with an important sense that many cases can be decided by finding the appropriate law. Moreover, where the Court is self-aware that it is "making law" it seeks to do so through a distinctive, and more constrained, set of processes than other lawmakers.[7] Any modern theory of judicial review, and of constitutional interpretation, surely must grapple with *both* of these realities of contemporary legal consciousness.

Professor Griffin's emphasis on the importance of the Court's agenda control through certiorari marks an important shift in institutional roles. But how does the Court's capacity to select the cases it hears affect theories of judicial review and interpretation? Professor Griffin argues that the Court's power to set its own agenda helps undermine the distinction between law and politics, by allowing the Court to seek out only the most "important" of cases, those that are likely to press the boundaries of law and politics. I agree that the Court's control over its own agenda, and, more important, its use of that power in recent years to halve its docket, does undermine an important feature of the institution of judicial review that helped assimilate its exercise to "law," rather than "will." If a court can "will" which cases and issues come before it, it may be that much harder to decide (or to appear to decide) the issues based on legal judgment.

Moreover, here to reinforce Professor Griffin's point, judicial review of the constitutionality of legislation was not the only important task contemplated for the Article III courts. For example, Alexander Hamilton clearly contemplated that the federal courts would mitigate statutory errors, not necessarily rising to the level of constitutional violations, through ameliorative construction.[8] Whether the Supreme Court's latter-day reluctance to decide statutory issues absent a conflict is consistent with this vision is unclear, given the availability of lower federal courts.[9] Whether theories of judicial review and constitutional interpretation should be reconfigured to take account of the increased specialization of the Supreme Court on major issues of federal law, or whether instead legislative attention should be directed to reconsidering the entirely discretionary nature of the Court's certiorari jurisdiction, are important questions.

On balance, however, Professor Griffin's account, both in its reliance on the doubtful case rule and its failure to acknowledge the degree of juridical commitment to the distinction between law and policy, overstates the discontinuities between the past and the present, leaving more room to think that justifications of judicial review from the founding era may continue to have some relevance today.

II. Discontinuity or Continuity in a Democracy of Rights?

On the question of what kind of democracy we now have, while I think Professor Griffin basically is quite right in his emphasis on change and struggle in defining what it is we now have, he may overstate the degree of discontinuity on the ideal of political equality and underestimate the continued role of courts in sustaining a good "democracy of rights." Professor Griffin asserts that the Constitution did not contemplate a role in governance even for "ordinary white men," much less for women and minorities. Yet for its time, the Constitution leaned in the direction of equality in significant ways, including by providing very limited qualifications for federal public offices and a prohibition on religious tests for public office.[10] The inalienable rights of men, articulated by that generation, never entirely left the rhetoric of constitutional meaning.[11] I would suggest that over time the minor theme of political equality, subordinated to many other interests in the original Constitution, came to be understood as central as different groups struggled to expand the reach of political and civil equality.[12]

Next, I wonder whether it is appropriate to treat the "democracy of rights" as independent of activist judicial review of rights. If it is the case that similar concerns tend to motivate both courts and legislatures, one might speculate that there is a mutually reinforcing dialogue that occurs, among courts, legislative bodies, and broader publics, over the scope and nature of rights.[13] Taking the courts out of this dialogue may have unintended effects on legislative commitments to rights; judicial decisions may well provide the foundations for legislative courage or inspiration in protecting rights. Professor Griffin, I think, recognizes the possibility that the 1964 Civil Rights Act and the 1965 Voting Rights Act may in some respects be the progeny of *Brown*, but his view seems to be that now that Congress has become more committed to the idea of rights, the Court will primarily just get in the way. Maybe yes, maybe no. The Court has thus far been more aggressive than many legislatures in protecting women's reproductive rights, and less so in protecting disabled people from discrimination; but it has been very much engaged in the business of defining constitutional rights. If the Court removes itself, as per Professor Griffin's reformulation of the role of judicial review (i.e., to halt vigorous judicial review), the ripple effects on our broader understandings of rights are hard to calculate.

I also wonder how firmly we are situated in a benign democracy of rights. Professor Griffin writes, "It is evident that we are no longer in a world in which racial and other minorities can count on the Court when a presidential administration goes looking for Supreme Court nominees who believe that it is unwise to create new constitutional rights." His comment provokes another: If we are in a world where a presidential administration goes looking for such a Supreme Court nominee, can it be said that we are now in a "democracy of rights"? Is it likely that such a presidential administration wants to avoid justices favorably inclined to new rights in order to have more freedom in promoting such rights in the legislature? And if not, how does the election of such a president square with Professor Griffin's optimistic notion about our living in a democracy of rights? How in a democracy of rights would such a president be elected, or decide to nominate such persons to the Court, and how would the Senate confirm them? So I wonder (and worry) whether Professor Griffin may both idealize the deliberative capacities of "our contemporary democracy"[14] and manifest undue optimism about whether we are firmly and discontinuously planted in a democracy of rights.

The degree of continuity and discontinuity with the past is an important question, as Professor Griffin's argument so wisely recognizes. If our democracy of rights still remains something to be struggled over, it is not clear to me that we should put the Court entirely on the sidelines and rely entirely on the more political branches. I say a bit more about why below.

III. Legislatures and Rights:
Are Rights Always a Good Thing?

Professor Griffin's basic claim is that courts in a democracy should not undo rights that the people themselves have created: "The exercise of judicial review to *destroy* valuable statutory rights would run counter to the principles and values of contemporary democracy." One difficulty with this position is that "rights" often exist on both sides of a legislative position. There are, at least potentially, dark sides to many stories of rights, both constitutional and statutory—consider the asserted right of individual gun ownership and its possible effects on the right to domestic security and freedom from violence; the "rights" of victims of crime to seek harsher punishment for wrongdoers and the right not to be subject to "cruel and unusual" punishment; or proposed statutory "rights" of manufacturers of products or services not to be sued for injuries to consumers. Even rights fundamentally connected to representative government have dark sides; consider here the free speech right to make defamatory nonmalicious statements about public officials, and the injury to reputation that may ensue. There may be conflicts in rights as well: Do the rights of religious institutions under the Religious Freedom Restoration Act (RFRA) impinge on the rights of majorities in small towns to enact zoning ordinances? Do the "rights" of criminal defendants interfere with the rights of citizen-victims? And, given the role of money in politics, consider the "rights" that major corporate interests have been able to procure—recently, the "rights" of the public domain lost out, in both Congress and the Court, to the statutory "rights" of copyright holders seeking extension of the term of existing copyrights.[15] By contrast, the "rights" of aliens, or convicted criminals, have not done so well in the legislative arena.

If we can conceive of the legislature as creating "bad" rights (just as some believe the Court created "bad" rights in *Lochner*), or of the legislature creating "good" rights that undermine other "good" rights, than I think we need criteria other than "rights" alone to govern. Who should decide on those criteria? We might want courts to articulate and enforce those normative criteria because courts are less subject to capture by temporarily self-interested majorities or by highly organized minority interests. Congressional efforts to extend "rights" should thus remain subject to review for consistency with basic normative values of the Fourteenth Amendment, such as respect for human dignity, a proposition that does not require the strong versions of judicial exclusivity and autonomy in judgment manifest by some recent decisions.[16]

An alternative, critical approach to the cases that Professor Griffin finds problematic might be found in the work of Professor William Cohen.[17] Many of the cases Professor Griffin has identified as inappropriate uses of the power of judicial review are at least nominally cases about federalism.[18] Congressional legislation has been invalidated not because it violated individual rights under the Constitution, nor because it otherwise required primary conduct that the Constitution prohibited, but rather because Congress's action was found to exceed the power it was granted (in contrast to the states) under the federal division of power. Cohen analyzed Justice William Brennan's one-way ratchet theory of congressional power to expand the protection of rights recognized under the Fourteenth Amendment but not to contract them,[19] arguing that a correct understanding of Justice Brennan's claim turned precisely on those issues of institutional competence to which Professor Griffin directs us. Congress, Cohen argued, did not have institutional competence to second-guess courts as to the minimal content of liberty (or equality) guaranteed by the Bill of Rights, but Congress did have better competence to make federalism judgments than liberty judgments: If a law were one a state could enact (in that it did not violate the minimal content of federal constitutional rights), Congress's doing so at the national level should be viewed with considerable deference from the Court. So while I agree with Professor Griffin that the Court has been insufficiently deferential to Congress in the creation of rights in cases like *Morrison*, it does not seem to me that his solution—a general abandonment of vigorous judicial review with a presumption against judicial creation of rights—is necessarily the best fit. Professor Cohen's approach, or others based on it, might provide a more discriminating tool.

Professor Griffin is surely correct that the "democracy of rights" we presently have was neither created nor necessarily envisioned by the framers of our two most important constitutional moments—the 1789 founding and the Reconstruction era amendments. And I share his essential argument that the more democratic quality of public decision-making ought to make for a judicial role that is in many cases more deferential to legislative decisions, reflecting the more democratic quality of our polity. In his emphasis on the role of the African American struggle for civil rights in the legislative arena, Professor Griffin may, however, slight the institutional role of the Court in responding to and assisting in that struggle. Just as the Voting Rights Act of 1965 has played an important role in reconstituting political life, so too did the Court's one-person-one-vote reapportionment decisions.[20] The Court's equal protection decisions and its emphasis on the fundamental character of the right to vote seem to me to have importantly contributed to the subsequent decades' development of "rights responsive" legislatures. Judicial review in the past had an important role in attempting to ensure that the process of politics stays fair. The challenges today are different—good democratic rule can be undermined not only by malapportionment but by other destabilizing phenomena that make elections matter less. Whether in an era of divided government or single party domination, it is not clear to me that judicial review in support of minority rights is unnecessary or inappropriate to exercise on behalf of democracy.[21]

Lawrence v. Texas may be an example.[22] Professor Griffin treats *Lawrence* as essentially insignificant because it mirrors the moves already made in many states.[23] This approach, I think, understates *Lawrence*'s importance in two respects. First, *Lawrence* was issued at a time when federal statutory law—recently enacted federal statutory law—discriminated against gays and lesbians in the military (through the "don't ask don't tell policy") and with respect to federal benefits laws (Defense of Marriage Act—DOMA).[24] The Court has thus taken a position of principle in some tension with that of the national government. Second, *Lawrence* did not merely grudgingly decide to strike down the state sodomy law, but offered compelling reasons for why adult, consensual, private homosexual relationships merited protection under the Constitution.[25] Professor Griffin underestimates the value of the Court's decision in a case like *Lawrence*, in which a substantial majority joins in an eloquent judicial disquisition on the nature of human liberty, dignity, and autonomy, a decision that can both reflect emerging (but not necessarily ascendant) public opinion and crystallize or encourage the accretion of opinion in the direction of its decision through its invocation of the language of constitutional principle. *Lawrence* suggests that putting all our eggs in any one basket of the national government—Congress as opposed to the courts—would cut off an important source of fostering our sense of the principled bases for the recognition of rights.[26]

IV. Politicization and the Political Judiciary?

Professor Griffin argues that the politicization of constitutional issues, and of the federal appointments process, has "permanently undermined the judiciary's comparative advantage in matters of constitutional principle." Indeed, he suggests, "It was no longer possible for the Supreme Court to achieve the independence from politics required to maintain a consistent posture with respect to the protection of individual rights once the appointment process was politicized." Here, I think, he falls into a confusion between the politicization of the appointment process and that of the adjudicatory process.

He is no doubt correct that there has been a significant change in the nominating process, compounded by thirty years of divided government; and he may be right that the Court today is seen as far more important than it was perhaps in the past, though even in Alexis de Tocqueville's time the American propensity to turn every issue into a legal issue was noted. But Professor Griffin errs in assuming that a politicized appointment necessarily entails a politicized judiciary and in ignoring the comparative institutional value of a structurally independent judiciary.

Any observer must agree that there has been a politicization of judicial appointments. Although Professor Griffin attributes this to divided government, it seems that there is a connection between his "democracy of rights" and the politicization of both constitutional law and judicial appointments. A short way to tell this story is to say that Congress, now dependent on a wider swath of the people as a constituency, has realized that what people want are rights, and it has given them rights. Once "rights" become the province of the political process—a phenomenon related as well to the demystification of the common law—the politicization of rights seems naturally to follow. Congress has an interest in defending rights it has helped to protect or secure from judicial challenge.

I agree that the politics of the appointment process may undermine the Court's claim to superiority in deciding deeply contested questions. But it is a far cry from acknowledging that point to the conclusion that the Court has no comparative advantage at all.

Professor Griffin's argument essentially dismisses the significance, for understanding the constitutional role of judicial review, of the independence of the judiciary after appointment. This is a mistake. Even people chosen for their views on particular subjects have a freedom to shift their thinking in a life-tenured position that does not compare to the mental freedom those who must stand for election or reappointment enjoy.[27] Moreover, as members of the judiciary, judges take on an institutional role of protecting the courts as an institution which brings with it interpretive traditions, including stare decisis, that help protect existing right (as they may obstruct new ones).

As Professor Eisgruber and many others have recognized,[28] the indepen-dence of judges who do not have to account back to those who appointed them for their decisions introduces a possibility for long-term public-interestedness to a greater extent than exists for those who hold electoral positions and have to run for reelection. As Eisgruber argues, federal judges, even those chosen through a highly political process of nomination and confirmation, nonethe-less occupy a position, once confirmed, in which there is a greater possibility for unself-interested decision making than is institutionally possible from most elected representatives. The guarantee of life tenure and salary enables judges to make decisions about cases, including cases involving deeply contested ques-tions of great import for human dignity, not only free from concern that their own future livelihood or position will turn on the decision but from a perspec-tive that encourages distinguishing between personal preference and valid gov-ernmental conduct.[29] This does not, of course, rule out ideological or even par-tisan decision making but it does remove one significant set of incentives for such self-interested decision-making that exists in other constitutional settings.

The possibility for disinterested decision-making, that can take a longer term view than the next election cycle, and that appreciates the benefits of link-ages to the past as well as the future, figures nowhere in Professor Griffin's scheme. Professor Griffin's argument also ignores other process values of adju-dication—the value in letting parties be heard and in focusing on real parties with real facts as a prod to engaged judgment. To the extent Congress does not pretermit such decision-making through fast-tracking litigation to the Court, a judicial "sober second look" can sometimes happen and offer real value in pro-viding reflection and decision-making after the initial political momentum has passed.[30]

Professor Griffin asserts that the courts "cannot contribute an independent voice on principle to a democracy of rights once it has been politicized," be-cause any debate in the Court simply mirrors debates in politics but at an in-formational disadvantage. I am not sure how this is different than at any other time in the Court's history; and the fact that the themes being discussed are those in society at large elides the point that the Court may be able to act in a more consistent and thus principled way. Professor Griffin's more basic point appears to be that, even if nothing has changed about the effects of the Court's independence on the Justices' capacity for decision-making, we can now count on Congress to provide for rights.

I think we can count on Congress more than in the past—but again, I would hesitate to depend on it entirely. Look not only at congressional treatment of gays and lesbians but at the civil liberties restricting provisions of the USA Patriot Act.[31] True, the Court has not and may not correct all these excesses, but it is unlikely to make them worse. And although the Court has stood in the way of effectuating some of the statutory rights Congress has prescribed—and thus in some sense has made "worse" the situation of the beneficiaries of such legislation—it has done so for the most part as a remedial or federalism matter, leaving it open to other governmental institutions to step in and provide equivalent relief.[32] The idea of the judiciary as a forum for development of principles or the articulation and application of enduring values and aspirations may, in other words, be no more idealized than Professor Griffin's ideal of deliberative democracy outside of the Court.[33]

V. Constitutional Theory and History?

Underlying his critique of the current Court's decisions may be that a majority of the Justices are committed to what Professor Griffin regards as bad principles. I share his concerns that the Supreme Court, in a series of cases in the last decade, seemed to have embarked on an unjustified destruction of valuable statutory rights designed to implement the equal protection clause. And I share his view that constitutional theory must account for real changes in constitutional structure that have occurred since *Marbury*—here I mean particularly the Fourteenth Amendment and later amendments which entail commitments to equality for citizens and people as foundational norms, which ought to play an important role in constitutional interpretation and incline the Court to be deferential to good faith congressional efforts to implement these values. But I am, I suppose, puzzled at the claim that changes in our politics imply a more subordinate position for judicial review more generally. I am particularly puzzled at the conception of the function of or audience for the kind of historicized constitutional theory Professor Griffin presents here. There are questions to be raised about any general theory of judicial review, or constitutional interpretation, but I wonder if so historically contingent a theory is not subject to some peculiar difficulties.

First, constitutional theory under a conventional approach is expected to explain or condemn cases that ought to be explained or condemned. It envisions not only forward guidance but also a kind of backwards testing. It is harder to do this persuasively with a theory that is good for this time and place only, as a theory premised on the actual condition of divided government may be. Moreover, to the extent that the theory rests on the political presence of divided government (rather than on the constitutional arrangements that may produce divided government through the tri-partite bodies, with their different election cycles, that must be involved in approving legislation), I am unclear why the Court should take a back seat. One might think it more important for the Court to play a role in a polity with single party dominance, because of the greater possibility for trampling rights and views held by persistent minorities. But that rule is politically divided in a society that generally values rights does not require a change in the theory of judicial review as intended to protect individual rights, though it might diminish the occasions on which it will need to be used.[34] And it is unclear whether Professor Griffin means to argue only that courts should defer to legislation that is consistent with protecting constitutional rights (even if it goes beyond what the Court believes is necessary) and the more general claim that "vigorous judicial review can no longer be justified." For anything? To the extent that he argues the former, I think there is much to be said for that as a matter of constitutional interpretation, for reasons having less to do with patterns of divided government and more to do with the consistency of the direction of legislation with basic constitutional values.

Second, I wonder who it is that would be persuaded by a highly historicized theory like Professor Griffin's. If you are a judge on a court opposed to new statutory rights, is there something in this argument to persuade you to change your mind? If you already believe that congressional creation of new rights is normatively a good thing, you will be comfortable with taking a back seat. But what reason does this approach offer to a judge who is troubled by what she sees as an unwarranted accrual of legislative power in the guise of extending rights?

On the other hand—*Who are you to take away rights?*—is a very powerful question when directed to courts. It is Professor Griffin's question. If we conceive in very old-fashioned terms the question, "What is the Court there for?," and answer that it is there for the protection of the legal rights of individuals, then this new turn is very troubling. So let me suggest that it is, in a sense, a very old-fashioned, *Marbury*-ish view—of the role of courts in protecting individual legal rights—that lies at the base of Professor Griffin's argument. If courts are designed to protect individual rights from overreaching government, and if the power of judicial review is derived at least in part from that "emphatically" judicial role, then when individuals do not need this protection, the Court should generally be silent. The power of at least this aspect of *Marbury*'s reasoning, then, despite its older provenance, may still be at work here.

Marbury and the Authoritarian Straddle

A Comment on Stephen M. Griffin

LOUIS MICHAEL SEIDMAN

Stephen Griffin's perceptive and learned ruminations on judicial review serve to remind us that normative constitutional theories come in two types and that each type comes with one problem.

In Type A theories, the theorist starts with a set of reasonable, but contestable, substantive political or ethical preferences. She then argues for a particular constitutional arrangement on the ground that this arrangement is most likely to vindicate these substantive preferences. For example, a generation ago, Jesse Choper argued for judicial abstention regarding federalism and separation of powers questions on the ground that the political process tended to produce the "right" outcome to these disputes.[1] In our own time, Akhil Amar has argued that we should privilege constitutional text over constitutional doctrine because "[w]hat the American People have said and done in the Constitution is often more edifying, inspiring, and sensible than what the Justices have said and done in the case law."[2]

The problem with Type A theories is that they will have no appeal at all to people who do not share the posited substantive preferences. If one has the standard view of constitutional law—that it is a method of resolving disputes between people within a community who do not share substantive preferences[3]—then this is a large problem indeed.

This problem leads people to become Type B theorists. Type B theories start with a set of constitutional arrangements rather than a set of substantive preferences. Theories of this sort insist that principled people must give up on their substantive preferences when they conflict with these constitutional arrangements. Indeed, these theories do work only in circumstances where our obligation to constitutionalism causes us to reject what would otherwise be our substantive preferences. For example, Herbert Wechsler insisted that constitutional adjudication could be "principled" only when judges were prepared to apply a constitutional rule in a way that would defeat a cause they favored.[4] Similarly, Ronald Dworkin argues that the requirement of "fit" takes certain constitutional results off the table even if those results comport with the substantive demands of justice.[5]

The problem for Type B theorists is to explain what exactly is "principled" about giving up on what may be our most fundamental ethical and political principles for the sake of one among many possible sets of constitutional arrangements. For people who take their ethical and political principles seriously, this, too, is a very large problem.

I believe that all normative constitutional theory is either of Type A or Type B and that all such theory (including the theory I have argued for) therefore necessarily suffers from one or the other of the problems I have described. It follows that it is unfair to criticize a theorist for having one or the other of these problems. On the contrary, most of the interesting action in constitutional theory revolves around figuring out how to finesse or obfuscate these problems. In this sense, thinking about constitutional theory is a little like doing psychoanalysis: The analyst's main focus is not on what the analysand says, but on the evasive maneuvers the analysand uses to avoid getting to the heart of things.

I want to focus on one particular evasive maneuver both because it is, I think, quite important, and because it goes to the heart of Professor Griffin's chapter. We might call this maneuver the Authoritarian Straddle. When a theorist engages in the Authoritarian Straddle, she presents herself as a Type B theorist even though she is really a Type A theorist. She does so by pretending that policy positions that are fairly contestable are really constitutionally mandatory. When this maneuver is successful, the theorist can present herself as bound by constitutional principle without giving up on any of her substantive preferences because these preferences are treated as if they are, themselves, required by principled constitutional theory.

The Authoritarian Straddle has an old and distinguished pedigree. Indeed, it goes back to the beginning of American constitutional theory—that is to *Marbury v. Madison*[6] itself. To switch from psychoanalysis to theology (not a big switch, I suppose) it might therefore be said that constitutional theory was born in sin and that all theory since *Marbury* is irretrievably fallen.

In this respect, I have a mild quarrel with Professor Griffin's treatment of *Marbury*. I think that he has been suckered in by John Marshall's Authoritarian Straddle. Professor Griffin argues that judicial review as it existed in the early nineteenth century was different from modern judicial review because, among other things, Marshall's generation adhered to the doubtful case rule, stayed clear of political questions, and was not corrupted by the politicization of the appointment process.

Of course, this was the self-presentation of Marshall's generation. John Marshall wanted us to believe these things because he wanted us to think of him as a Type B theorist. Marshall therefore pretended that his own substantive reading of the Constitution was uncontroversial and that he was steering clear of political questions. But in fact, as many others have pointed out,[7] Marshall's reading of Article III was far from uncontroversial. Moreover, anyone who knows anything about the background of the *Marbury* dispute knows that it was steeped in political controversy. And it is deeply ironic to point to the modern politicization of the appointment process as a difference between the *Marbury* generation and our own when *Marbury* itself grew out of a vicious and partisan struggle over judicial appointments.

That so perceptive a scholar as Professor Griffin has been taken in by the Authoritarian Straddle suggests just how dangerous the maneuver can be. Perhaps the more significant question, though, is whether, no doubt without realizing it, Professor Griffin himself engaged in the straddle. In this respect, there is an odd disjunction in Professor Griffin's analysis. Griffin rightly points out that previous theorists like Alexander Bickel relied implicitly upon the assumption that there was a consensus about what our fundamental values were, whereas today, to quote Griffin, "Persistent disagreement [discredits] the proposition that the five justices who prevailed were enforcing fundamental values."

This observation rightly emphasizes the central role that legitimate disagreement must play in any constitutional theory. Yet elsewhere Griffin himself seems to implicitly accept the very kind of consensus theory that he also rejects.

He does so, I think, because insistence on a supposed consensus is required for the Authoritarian Straddle to work.

For example, Professor Griffin thinks that the key question for constitutional theorists is whether, under contemporary political conditions, judicial enforcement of constitutional rights has a comparative advantage over other institutional arrangements. Professor Griffin is exactly right to focus on how judicial review actually functions under modern conditions. Moreover, his observations about the ways in which it intersects with divided government and the politicization of the appointments process are very perceptive. Unfortunately, however, his focus on comparative advantage is more problematic. Whether or not the Supreme Court has a comparative advantage in matters of principle depends on which principles we are talking about. If we were all in agreement about what our principles should be, there would be no problem. But we are not in agreement.

Sometimes it is possible to obfuscate this disagreement by stating our principles on a very high level of generality. Thus, Professor Griffin says that democracy requires that we "treat citizens equally and ensure that the actual operation of government works to advance the interests of everyone." Who could disagree with that? But precisely because no one can disagree, principles stated on this level of generality tell us nothing about which institution has a comparative advantage in enforcing them.

As soon as Professor Griffin descends to the level of specificity that makes the principles useful, he falls into the Authoritarian Straddle. Thus, for Professor Griffin the modern Supreme Court has demonstrated its incompetence by its decisions in areas like affirmative action, racial redistricting, and the enforcement of the equal protection clause. He claims that decisions like *City of Mobile v. Bolden*,[8] *Grove City College v. Bell*,[9] *Wards Cove Packing Co. v. Atonio*,[10] *City of Borene v. Flores*,[11] and *Kimel v. Florida Board of Regents*[12] demonstrate that modern judicial review "run[s] counter to the principles and values of contemporary democracy."

I happen to share Professor Griffin's substantive views about these cases, but I also think that we need to recognize that there are some people who are acting in good faith and are not outside our moral universe yet have different views. Like it or not, there are people out there who think that decisions such as these have protected the country against factional, special interest, racist, and unconstitutional legislation. They think that the decisions are rights protecting, rather than rights destroying.

The same point can be made more generally. An important feature of American constitutional law (at least in the form enforced by courts) is its libertarian bias. Judicial review operates as a one-way ratchet. The Supreme Court at least sometimes holds that the Constitution limits the power of government to invade a private sphere, but it virtually never holds that the Constitution mandates government intervention into private arrangements. In contrast, the political branches sometimes operate to check government intervention (as when, for example, Congress puts limits on the power of police officers to search news organizations),[13] but the political branches also on occasion adopt programs regulating the private sphere (as, for example, when Congress passed the 1964 Civil Rights Act[14] or the Americans with Disabilities Act[15]).

Professor Griffin thinks that human freedom will best flourish in a "democracy of rights" under which the government sometimes regulates private power. It follows logically from this posture that one would favor constitutional arrangements that gave the political branches the space to enact such programs.

Suppose though that one were a person who believes that human freedom is best achieved by allowing people to make decisions within a private sphere. As David Bernstein, among others, has effectively argued, government regulation has sometimes entrenched rather than dismantled racial and other hierarchies.[16] On this view, it is private markets, rather than government intervention, that best protect individual rights. If one held this view, then judicial review's one-way ratchet would give judges a systematic, institutional advantage in promoting human freedom.

Although I deeply respect Professor Bernstein's work, in the end, I think, I am prepared to throw my lot in with Professor Griffin. Like him, I think that government control of a private sphere at least sometimes maximizes human freedom. But it hardly follows that the people we disagree with are unreasonable, evil, or stupid. If their views are within the bounds of reasonable constitutionalism, then a particular constitutional arrangement cannot be rejected just because the arrangement favors those views.

Perhaps I am misunderstanding Professor Griffin. Perhaps he is in fact a Type A theorist. If he is indeed beginning with a set of contestable value judgments and limiting his audience to people who share those judgments, there is nothing wrong with suggesting to them what kinds of institutional arrangements best serve their interests. The trouble is that Professor Griffin's chapter does not read this way. I understand him (maybe misunderstand him) to be a Type B theorist. He wants to claim, I think, that his view of judicial review in a democracy of rights is transsubstantive—that all people of goodwill can come together to support this version of constitutionalism. Unfortunately, this claim can only be made plausible by resorting to the Authoritarian Straddle—by an implicit claim that matters that are and should be contestable are instead permanently resolved by deep constitutional principles.

The pity is that Professor Griffin intermittently seems to understand just this point. In the penultimate sentence of his chapter, he writes the following: "The history of public discussion of issues like racial equality shows that what is a matter of passion against principle or prejudice against rights is deeply contested." He is absolutely right about that, and it is to his great credit that he recognizes this truth. But we are not yet at the end of history and for as long as history continues, this contest will not be resolved by Professor Griffin's constitutional theory or, for that matter, by mine or anyone else's.

Since we are not yet at the end of history, perhaps it is appropriate to go back to the beginning. Chief Justice Marshall inaugurated American constitutional law with the Authoritarian Straddle by insisting that only he had a good faith, legitimate, and disinterested understanding of Article III. His opinion goes on for pages, but the guts of it can be summarized in four words, written over a century later by that great constitutional scholar Ring Lardner: "Shut up, he explained."[17] The Authoritarian Straddle amounts to a purported explanation—whether offered by judges or constitutional theorists—for why we should shut up. The best version of our constitutional tradition is that for the last two hundred years, we have rejected this explanation. We have stubbornly refused to shut up. Yes, the political setting of judicial review has changed; yes, we are (or at least I hope we will be again soon) in an era of divided government; yes, the appointments process has become politicized; yes, there are a bunch of people on the Supreme Court now who, I wish, were not there—but none of these reasons provides a good explanation for why we should stop talking now.

Notes

Sherry: The Intellectual Background of *Marbury v. Madison*

I thank Lisa Bressman and Paul Edelman for comments on earlier drafts of this chapter. Excellent research assistance was provided by Charles Canter (Vanderbilt class of 2005) and Vanderbilt reference librarian Steve Jordan.

1. By suggesting that *Marbury* "worked," I do not mean to imply that it established the practice of judicial review but rather that it successfully helped preserve the practice and weather the Court's first major crisis.

2. William Van Alstyne, *A Critical Guide to* Marbury v. Madison, 1969 Duke L. J. 1, 2 (1969) ("fragile"); on the early Court, see generally William Casto, *The Supreme Court in the Early Republic: The Chief Justiceships of John Jay and Oliver Ellsworth* (1995); Scott Douglas Gerber, ed., *Seriatim: The Supreme Court Before John Marshall* (1998).

3. On the weakness of the early Supreme Court generally, see, e.g., Michael J. Klarman, *How Great Were the "Great" Marshall Court Decisions*, 87 Va. L. Rev. 1111, 1123–25 (2001); Van Alstyne, supra note 2; on the lack of a courtroom, see Charles Warren, *The Supreme Court in United States History*, vol. 1, 168–71 (1923); George L. Haskins and Herbert A. Johnson, *History of the Supreme Court of the United States: Foundations of Power: John Marshall, 1801–15* (Vol. II of the Holmes Devise), 79–81 (1981); on Chase impeachment, see, e.g., William H. Rehnquist, *Grand Inquests: The Historic Impeachments of Justice Samuel Chase and President Andrew Johnson* (1992); Warren at 269–99.

4. On Marshall generally, see, e.g., R. Kent Newmyer, *John Marshall and the Heroic Age of the Supreme Court* (2001); Charles F. Hobson, *The Great Chief Justice: John Marshall and the Rule of Law* 58–64 (1996); on Marshall and Jefferson, see, e.g., Donald O. Dewey, *Marshall Versus Jefferson: The Political Background of* Marbury v. Madison (1970); on the Court's difficulties with Congress, see, e.g., Van Alstyne, supra note 2, at 1–6; James M. O'Fallon, *Marbury*, 44 Stan. L. Rev. 219, 221–27 (1992); Dean Alfange, Jr., Marbury v. Madison *and Original Understandings of Judicial Review: In Defense of Traditional Wisdom*, 1993 Sup. Ct. Rev. 329, 349–56 (1993); L. A. Powe, Jr., *The Politics of Amer-*

ican Judicial Review: Reflections on the Marshall, Warren, and Rehnquist Courts, 38 Wake Forest L. Rev. 697, 699–703 (2002); on the adoption of the Eleventh Amendment, overruling *Chisholm v. Georgia,* 2 U.S. 419 (1793), see, e.g., Casto, supra note 2; John Orth, *The Judicial Power of the United States: The Eleventh Amendment in American History* (1987).

5. *Stuart v. Laird,* 5 U.S. 299 (1803).

6. For these and other critiques of *Marbury,* see, e.g., Haskins and Johnson, supra note 3, at 185; Lief Carter, *Think Things, Not Words,* 43 J. Pol. 317, 318 (1981); Henry P. Monaghan, Marbury *and the Administrative State,* 83 Colum. L. Rev. 1, 7–13 (1983); Akhil Amar, Marbury, *Section 13, and the Original Jurisdiction of the Supreme Court,* 56 U. Chi. L. Rev. 443 (1989); Alfange, supra note 4, at 393–400; Christopher L. Eisgruber, *John Marshall's Judicial Rhetoric,* 1996 Sup. Ct. Rev. 439, 454 (1996); Klarman, supra note 3, at 1117–22 (and sources cited therein); Sanford Levinson, *Why I Do Not Teach Marbury (Except to Eastern Europeans) and Why You Shouldn't Either,* 38 Wake Forest L. Rev. 553 (2002); and sources cited (and refuted) in William E. Nelson, Marbury v. Madison: *The Origins and Legacy of Judicial Review* 2, 127 (2000). For a defense of Marshall's legal analysis, see James E. Pfander, Marbury, *Original Jurisdiction, and the Supreme Court's Supervisory Powers,* 101 Colum. L. Rev. 1515 (2001).

7. For accounts of the lack of criticism, see, e.g., Warren, supra note 3, at 248; Robert Lowry Clinton, *Marbury v. Madison* and Judicial Review 102 (1989); Nelson, supra note 6, at 72; on the spread of judicial review to states, see, e.g., Nelson at 75; on global spread, see, e.g., Ran Hirschl, "Beyond the American Experience: The Global Expansion of Judicial Review" in Marbury Versus Madison: *Documents and Commentary* 129 (Mark A. Graber and Michael Perhac, eds., 2002); the cases are *Martin v. Hunter's Lessee,* 14 U.S. 304 (1816) and *McCulloch v. Maryland,* 17 U.S. 316 (1819).

8. Robert G. McCloskey, *The American Supreme Court* 40 (1960).

9. The cases are *Plessy v. Ferguson,* 163 U.S. 537 (1896); *Brown v. Board of Education,* 347 U.S. 438 (1954); *Bowers v. Hardwick,* 478 U.S. 186 (1986); and *Lawrence v. Texas,* 539 U.S. 558 (2003).

10. See, e.g., Marvin I. Urofsky and Paul Finkelman, *A March of Liberty: A Constitutional History of the United States,* vol. 1, 1–7 (2002).

11. William Blackstone, *Commentaries on the Laws of England,* vol. 1, 267 (W. Morrison, ed. 2001); Edward Coke, *Institutes of the Laws of England,* vol. 1, 11 (J. H. Thomas, American ed., 1827); *Dr. Bonham's Case,* 8 Coke Rep. 107, 118a (1610).

12. See Julius Goebel, Jr., *History of the Supreme Court: Antecedents and Beginnings to 1801* (Vol. 1, Holmes Devise) 1–6 (1971); Robert Lowry Clinton, *God and Man in the Law: The Foundations of Anglo-American Constitutionalism* 91–92 (1997); Nelson, supra note 6, at 24–26 (2000); William E. Nelson, Marbury v. Madison *and the Establishment of Judicial Autonomy,* 27 J. Sup. Ct. Hist. 240, 241 (2002); David Thomas Konig, "Legal Fictions and the Rule(s) of Law: The Jeffersonian Critique of Common-Law Adjudica-

tion," in *The Many Legalities of Early America* 97, 101–3 (Christopher L. Tomlins and Bruce H. Mann, eds., 2001). See also Gordon S. Wood, *The Radicalism of the American Revolution* 323–24 (1992) (judges in colonies and early republic appointed because of social and political rank, not legal expertise).

13. See generally Urofsky and Finkelman, supra note 10, at 74–75.

14. *Marbury* quotation, 5 U.S. at 177; for Marshall's innovations, see generally Sylvia Snowiss, *Judicial Review and the Law of the Constitution* (1990); Alfange, supra note 4.

15. For confirmation that judicial review was practiced and accepted before *Marbury*, see, e.g., Charles Warren, *Congress, the Constitution, and the Supreme Court* 43–47 (1925); Charles Grove Haines, *The American Doctrine of Judicial Supremacy* 105–12 (1959); Casto, supra note 2, at 175–78; Hobson, supra note 4, at 58–64; Suzanna Sherry, *The Founders' Unwritten Constitution*, 54 U. Chi. L. Rev. 1127, 1134–46 (1987); Alfange, supra note 4, at 329, 366–67; William Treanor, *The Case of the Prisoners and the Origins of Judicial Review*, 143 U. Pa. L. Rev. 491, 569–70 (1994); Mark A. Graber, "The Problematic Establishment of Judicial Review," in *The Supreme Court in American Politics: New Institutional Interpretations* 28, 34 (Howard Gillman and Cornell W. Clayton, eds., 1999); Klarman, supra note 3, at 1113–17; Saikrishna B. Prakash and John C. Yoo, *The Origins of Judicial Review*, 70 U. Chi. L. Rev. 887 (2003).

16. For similar arguments about what Marshall accomplished in *Marbury*, see Paul W. Kahn, *The Reign of Law: Marbury v. Madison and the Construction of America* (1997); Snowiss, supra note 14; for a discussion of how the "legalization" of the Constitution contributed to the triumph of judicial supremacy, see Larry Kramer, *Foreword: We the Court*, 115 Harv. L. Rev. 5 (2000).

17. On inalienable rights generally, see, e.g., Bernard Bailyn, *The Ideological Origins of the American Revolution* 175–98 (1967); Gordon S. Wood, *The Creation of the American Republic 1776–1787*, at 292–94 (1969); Goebel, supra note 12, at 92; Jack N. Rakove, *Original Meanings: Politics and Ideas in the Making of the Constitution* 290–93 (1996); for sources for quoted language, see Sherry, supra note 15, at 1128–34; Nelson, supra note 6, at 36; for discussion of Madison's speech on the Ninth Amendment, see Sherry, supra note 15, at 1163 and nn. 154 and 155; on state constitutional provisions, see Suzanna Sherry, *Natural Law in the States*, 61 Cincinnati L. Rev. 171, 181 and n. 58 (1992); John Choon Yoo, *Our Declaratory Ninth Amendment*, 42 Emory L. J. 967 (1993).

18. See generally Snowiss, supra note 14, at 36–37, 65–89 (1990); Sherry, supra note 15; Sherry, supra note 17.

19. The cases are *McCulloch v. Maryland*, 17 U.S. 316 (1819) and *Fletcher v. Peck*, 10 U.S. 87 (1810); the *Marbury* quotations are found at 5 U.S. at 162, 163.

20. On prior views of natural law, see sources cited in notes 17 and 18, supra; on changing views of government, see, e.g., Nelson, supra note 6, at 28–40.

21. John Hart Ely, *Democracy and Distrust: A Theory of Judicial Review* 39 (1980);

Lochner v. New York, 198 U.S. 45 (1905); *Planned Parenthood of Southeastern Pennsylvania v. Casey*, 505 U.S. 833 (1992) (privacy).

22. For Rush quotation, see Benjamin Rush, *Address to the People of the United States* (1787), reprinted in *The Documentary History of the Ratification of the Constitution*, vol. 13, 45, 47 (1981); on Madison's course of study, see Rakove, supra note 17, at 42–43; on the new science of politics, see generally, Wood, supra note 17, at 3–45; Forrest McDonald, *Novus Ordo Seclorum: The Intellectual Origins of the Constitution* (1985).

23. On Marshall generally, see, e.g., Newmyer, supra note 4; Hobson, supra note 4, at 58–64; for some of Marshall's defense of the Constitution, see excerpts from the Virginia ratifying convention reprinted in Daniel A. Farber and Suzanna Sherry, *A History of the American Constitution* 297–98 (1990); see generally Goebel, supra note 12, at 387–89; on Marshall's use of deductive logic, see, e.g., Alfange, supra note 4, at 420–37 and sources cited therein.

24 On *Chisholm* and the Eleventh Amendment, see, e.g., Casto, supra note 2; Orth, supra note 4; the cases are *Martin v. Hunter's Lessee*, 14 U.S. 304 (1816) and *McCulloch v. Maryland*, 17 U.S. 316 (1819); on the relationship between judicial review and states' rights see, e.g., Daniel A. Farber, *Judicial Review and Its Alternatives: An American Tale*, 38 Wake Forest L. Rev. 415 (2003).

Bloch: *Marbury* Redux

1. Susan Low Bloch, *The* Marbury *Mystery: Why Did William Marbury Sue in the Supreme Court?*, 18 Const. Comment. 607 (2001).

2. Judiciary Act of Feb. 27, 1801, ch. 14, 2 Stat. 103 (1801). The Court was originally named the Court of Appeals of the District of Columbia. Susan Low Bloch and Ruth Bader Ginsburg, *Celebrating the 200th Anniversary of the Federal Courts of the District of Columbia*, 90 Geo. L. J. 549, 559 (2002). It became officially named the Court of Appeals for the District of Columbia Circuit in 1948. Act of June 25, 1948, ch. 646, §§ 41, 45, 62 Stat. 869, 870, 871.

3. *United States ex rel. Stokes v. Kendall*, 26 F. Cas. 702 (D.C. Cir. 1837), *aff'd*, 37 U.S. 524 (1838). While *Kendall* was decided thirty years after *Marbury*, the jurisdictional statutes had not changed during that period.

4. Bloch, supra note 1, at 613.

5. Bloch, supra note 1.

6. Conversation with Professor Terry Sandalow (April 2003).

7. See affidavit of James Marshall in *Marbury v. Madison*, 5 U.S. 137 (1 Cranch) 137, 146 (1803).

8. Letter from Professor Alvin Goldman (on file with author).

9. John Marshall had been the Secretary of State under President Adams when Mar-

bury and the other justices of the peace were appointed. He was the one who sealed the commissions but failed to deliver all forty-two. Bloch, supra note 1, at 608.

10. "The early English common law of disqualification had the advantage of simplicity: A direct financial interest disqualified a judge from presiding; bias, or any other type of conflict, merited no concern. The guiding axiom of the day was Lord Coke's famous admonition, with reference to cases impacting a judge's pocketbook, that 'no man shall be a judge in his own case. . . . Under this approach, a judge might be disqualified because he stood to pocket the fine which he had to impose; or to evict a tenant from a property in which he had an interest; or even, for a time, to gain or lose by the decision as a taxpayer.' While American civil law incorporated the bar against presiding with a financial conflict of interest, it greatly, if gradually, expanded the concept of financial interest, thereby broadening the grounds available for disqualifying a judge. Congress enacted the first disqualification statute in 1792. The law required recusal 'when the judge had a financial interest in the litigation or [had] represented either party as counsel.' " Ziona Hochbaum, *Taking Stock: The Need to Amend 28 U.S.C. 455 to Achieve Clarity and Sensibility in Disqualification Rules for Judges' Financial Holdings,* 71 Fordham L. Rev. 1669, 1676 (2003) (footnotes omitted). See also John P. Frank, *Disqualification of Judges,* 56 Yale L. J. 605, 608 (1947); Cody W. Smith, Jr., *Judges—Disqualification to Act Because of Stock Interest,* 22 S.C. L. Rev. 261, 262 (1970).

11. *Martin v. Hunter's Lessee,* 14 U.S. 304 (1816).

12. Waxman made this suggestion in the course of preparing for a reenactment of *Marbury* before the Ninth Circuit Judicial Conference in June 2003. Moot Court preparation at Wilmer, Cutler, and Pickering (June 2003).

13. Lee started by contending that the Court had jurisdiction to issue the requested writ. Lee pointed out that in Section 13 of the Judiciary Act of 1789, "a law passed at the very first session after the adoption of the constitution," and Congress had specifically given the Supreme Court the authority to issue writs of mandamus to persons holding office under the authority of the United States. *Marbury* (1 Cranch) 148. This statute, said Lee, was constitutional under Article III either because a writ of mandamus was within the Court's appellate jurisdiction "in its largest sense," id., at 147, or because Congress can permissibly enlarge the Court's original jurisdiction. Id., at 148. Lee said nothing about the Secretary of State being a "public minister."

Parenthetically, one has to ask why Marshall paid virtually no attention to Lee's arguments or his ordering of the issues. Of course, had Marshall done either—adopt Lee's order and start with the question of jurisdiction and/or adopt the merits of Lee's jurisdictional argument—Marshall could not have achieved all he achieved in *Marbury.*

14. As a policy matter, it would make sense for the Constitution to specify that, at a minimum, the Supreme Court's original jurisdiction would include particularly sensi-

tive cases such as those controversies between states and those involving foreign ministers. Admittedly, suits against the Secretary of State could also be controversial and sensitive—as Marbury's suit against Madison clearly was—but there is nothing in the history of the drafting of the Constitution that suggests the framers of Article III were worrying about such suits when they were specifying the Supreme Court's original jurisdiction. On the contrary, in *The Federalist 81*, it seems reasonably clear that only suits against *foreign* ministers were contemplated for the original jurisdiction of the Supreme Court:

> The Supreme Court is to be invested with original jurisdiction, only "in cases affecting ambassadors, other public ministers, and consuls, and those in which A STATE shall be a party." Public ministers of every class are the immediate representatives of their sovereigns. All questions in which they are concerned are so directly connected with the public peace, that, as well for the preservation of this, as out of respect to the sovereignties they represent, it is both expedient and proper that such questions should be submitted in the first instance to the highest judiciary of the nation. Though consuls have not in strictness a diplomatic character, yet as they are the public agents of the nations to which they belong, the same observation is in a great measure applicable to them. In cases in which a State might happen to be a party, it would ill suit its dignity to be turned over to an inferior tribunal.

The Federalist 81, at 487 (Alexander Hamilton) (Clinton Rossiter ed. 1961).

15. *Ex Parte Gruber*, 269 U.S. 302, 303 (1925) ("Article III, § 2, cl. 2, of the Constitution provides that this court shall have original jurisdiction 'in all cases affecting Ambassadors, other public Ministers and Counsuls.' Manifestly, this refers to diplomatic and consular representatives accredited to the United States by foreign powers, not to those representing this country abroad."). *Gruber* cites *Milward v. McSaul*, 17 F. Cas. 425, 426 (S.D.N.Y. 1846), which says "a consul has no official character in his own country. He is no more a private citizen in view of the laws of his own government, and is clothed with a privilege only in respect to the foreign nations where he represents his government and exercises his consular functions."

16. Professor Richard Fallon, in an interesting article written before publication of my *Marbury Mystery* article, points out that Marbury, despite having a vested legal right, may have had no remedy. Richard Fallon, *Marbury and the Constitutional Mind: A Bicentennial Essay on the Wages of Doctrinal Tension*, 91 Calif. L. Rev. 1 (2003). Acknowledging that the Supreme Court in *Kendall* upheld the D.C. Circuit's power to issue a writ of mandamus against federal officials, Professor Fallon doubts that the Supreme Court, "in the politically charged atmosphere of 1803, would have upheld the authority of the D.C. Court to order mandamus relief for William Marbury against James Madison." Id.

at 47, n. 271. To support his skepticism, Professor Fallon cites Richard Ellis who noted that Marshall had "serious doubts about the political expediency of hearing the motion [in *Marbury*] in the first place . . . [and wanted] to avoid a direct confrontation with the executive department." Id. (quoting Richard E. Ellis, *The Jeffersonian Crisis: Courts and Politics in the Young Republic* [1971] at 67). Professor Fallon goes on to observe that Marbury "appears to have abandoned efforts to secure his commission following the Supreme Court's decision: . . . [B]y the time of the Supreme Court's ruling, the 'term had almost half expired for which Marbury and his associates had been appointed,' and 'these appointees must have lost all interest in the contest for offices of such slight dignity and insignificant emoluments.' " Id. (quoting Albert J. Beveridge, *The Life of John Marshall: Conflict and Construction, 1800–1815* [1919] at 125).

Professor Fallon does not ask why Marbury sued initially in the Supreme Court and thus his article does not address that question. But his observations are not at all inconsistent with my theory that Marbury sued in the Supreme Court because it was the only forum in which the judiciary could avoid a confrontation with the executive and still assert several important conclusions irrelevant to the ultimate decision that the Court lacked jurisdiction to vindicate William Marbury's claim to relief. Beveridge's suggestion that Marbury and the other appointees "lost all interest" in these offices assumes they previously *had* an interest when they first sued. But the appointed term, five years, was always short, the dignity just as "slight," and the emoluments just as "insignificant," when they initiated their suit in December 1801. Moreover, more than half the term still remained when the Supreme Court issued its decision in February 1803. Little had changed. I believe the reason Marbury and his colleagues did not follow up by suing in the D.C. Circuit was not that they had lost interest in the office, but that they had achieved what they wanted when they received the Supreme Court's pronouncement; they had neither need nor interest in continuing the battle with the Jefferson administration. Marbury and his Federalist colleagues had won and knew better than to continue forward and risk taking points off the scoreboard.

Friedman, The Myths of *Marbury*

I thank Vanessa Baird, Michael Collins, Mike Gerhardt, Mark Graber, Teri Peretti, Mark Ramseyer, Fred Schauer, Mike Seidman, Jeff Staton, and Mark Tushnet, as well as my anonymous reviewers, for their useful comments on a draft of this piece, and Melissa Aoyagi, Harlan Cohen, and Jane O'Brien for excellent research assistance.

1. A similar take on the three stories told here can be found in Richard H. Fallon, Jr., Marbury *and the Constitutional Mind: A Bicentennial Essay on the Wages of Doctrinal Tension*, 91 Cal. L. Rev. 1 (2003). William Nelson provides a pithy account of the case and its role in the origins of judicial review. William E. Nelson, Marbury v. Madison*: The Origins and Legacy of Judicial Review* (2000).

2. 5 U.S. (1 Cranch) 137 (1803).

3. See, e.g., Paul W. Kahn, *The Reign of Law:* Marbury v. Madison *and the Construction of America* 9 (1997) (" 'The government of the United States has been emphatically termed a government of laws and not of men.' So the Supreme Court declared in 1803, in one of the earliest and still the greatest of constitutional law cases: *Marbury v. Madison.*" [citation omitted]).

4. See *Marbury*, 5 U.S. (1 Cranch) at 173–80 (invalidating Section 13 of the Judiciary Act of 1789, which authorized the issuance of writs of mandamus to public officers).

5. See Mark A. Graber, "The Problematic Establishment of Judicial Review," in *The Supreme Court in American Politics: New Institutional Interpretations* 28, 34 (Howard Gillman and Cornell W. Clayton, eds., 1999) (noting that had *Marbury* required executive action, compliance would have been highly unlikely); Fallon, supra note 1, at 10–11 ("*Marbury*'s suit against Madison threatened to elicit a knockout blow. If the Supreme Court headed by the newly confirmed Federalist Chief Justice John Marshall ruled for Marbury, it was widely expected that Madison, at Jefferson's direction, would ignore the decision."). This understanding of Marshall's impotence in *Marbury* led Balkin and Levinson to question what exactly the facts of the case are: Are they the "legal" facts related in the decision to explain the legal rules offered there, or the political ones that contextualize the case? Once contextualized, they argue, the reading of the case changes in important ways. See Jack Balkin and Sanford Levinson, *What are the Facts of* Marbury v. Madison?, 20 Const. Comment. 255 (2003).

6. See *Federalist 78*, at 465 (Alexander Hamilton) (Clinton Rossiter, ed., 1999) ("The judiciary . . . has no influence over either the sword or the purse; no direction either of the strength or of the wealth of the society, and can take no active resolution whatever.").

7. This alternate story is elaborated upon in Barry Friedman, *Mediated Popular Constitutionalism*, 101 Mich. L. Rev. 2596 (2003).

8. Mark Tushnet, *Taking the Constitution Away from the Courts* 7 (1999).

9. See, e.g., Robert G. McCloskey, *The American Supreme Court* 25 (Sanford Levinson, rev. 3d ed., 2000) ("[Marshall's] preeminence among builders of the American constitutional tradition rests not only on his well-known boldness, his 'tiger instinct for the jugular vein' as an enthusiastic met aphorist once called it, but on his less-noticed sense of self-restraint."); id. at 27 ("[T]he touch of genius is evident when Marshall, not content with having rescued a bad situation, seizes the occasion to set for the doctrine of judicial review. . . . The moment for immortal statement was at hand all right, but only a judge of Marshall's discernment could have recognized it."); see also, e.g., Susan Low Bloch, *The* Marbury *Mystery: Why Did William Marbury Sue in the Supreme Court?*, 18 Const. Comment. 607, 627 (2001) (noting that with this "relatively simple case" Marshall was "able to establish the power of the federal judiciary to review both executive and legislative actions, while 'modestly' declining jurisdiction, ordering no one to do anything,

and thus providing no opportunity for defiance or resistance. It was a remarkable feat for which we are all in his debt.").

10. Alexander Bickel, *The Least Dangerous Branch: The Supreme Court at the Bar of Politics* 1 (1962); see also Erwin Chemerinsky, *Constitutional Law: Principles and Policies* 36–37 (1997) ("*Marbury v. Madison* is the single most important decision in American constitutional law. It established the authority for the judiciary to review the constitutionality of executive and legislative acts. Although the Constitution is silent as to whether federal courts have this authority, the power has existed ever since *Marbury*.").

11. The precursors to *Marbury* are discussed, as is the literature on the subject, in Larry D. Kramer, *The People Themselves: Popular Constitutionalism and Judicial Review* (2004).

12. See, e.g., Barry Friedman, *The History of the Countermajoritarian Difficulty, Part One: The Road to Judicial Supremacy*, 73 N.Y.U. L. Rev. 333, 354 (1998) ("[I]t is necessary to distinguish the power of judicial review (essentially judicial supremacy in a case) from the broader concept of judicial supremacy, meaning that a Supreme Court interpretation binds parties beyond those to the instant case, including other state and national governmental actors.").

13. See, e.g., Robert A. Burt, *The Constitution in Conflict* 199 (1992) ("[T]he claim for judicial supremacy in constitutional interpretation was not widely or definitively accepted in American society until after the Civil War—not simply in temporal sequence but as a direct response and imagined antidote to the War. By the end of the nineteenth century . . . the Supreme Court had become the virtual embodiment of absolute sovereign authority."). The discussion above is a brief restatement of an argument found in Friedman, supra note 12, at 340.

14. 17 U.S. (4 Wheat.) 316 (1819).

15. 5 U.S. (1 Cranch) 299 (1803).

16. See generally Dwight Wiley Jessup, *Reaction and Accommodation: The United States Supreme Court and Political Conflict 1809–1835* (1987); Leslie Friedman Goldstein, *State Resistance to Authority in Federal Unions: The Early United States (1790–1860) and the European Community (1958–1994)*, 11 Stud. Am. Pol. Dev. 149 (1997).

17. In 1831, the State of Georgia hung the Cherokee Corn Tassels in spite of the Supreme Court's issuance of writ of error prohibiting the execution. See *Cherokee Nation v. Georgia*, 30 U.S. (5 Pet.) 1 (1831). During the following year, Georgia imprisoned missionaries working on Cherokee lands, and defied an order of the Court holding the statute under which they were held unconstitutional. See *Worcester v. Georgia*, 31 U.S. (6 Pet.) 515 (1832). For insightful discussion of the Cherokee cases, see generally Jill Norgren, *The Cherokee Cases: The Confrontation of Law and Politics* (1996). Additional examples of Court decisions met with state defiance include: *Green v. Biddle*, 21 U.S. (8 Wheat.) 1 (1823), focusing on Kentucky's claim that federal courts lacked jurisdiction to

rule on the constitutionality of state statutes—in this case, a Kentucky statute making it difficult to remove squatters from private land—resulting in Kentucky's dispatch of diplomatic commissioners to negotiate with the Court for dismissal of the case and *Charles River Bridge v. Warren Bridge*, 36 U.S. (11 Pet.) 420 (1837), concerning the right to charter a free bridge in competition with a previously chartered toll bridge, which prompted a committee at the Massachusetts Democratic Convention to report that " 'in the Warren Bridge case, the Supreme Court at Washington has no more constitutional right to meddle with the question than the Court of King's Bench,' " Charles Warren, 1 *The Supreme Court in United States History* 773 (rev. ed., 1926 [1922]) (quoting United States Telegraph, Jan. 27, 1831).

18. See, e.g., Richard E. Ellis, *The Jeffersonian Crisis* 76–82 (1971) (discussing the Chase impeachment); Keith E. Whittington, *Reconstructing the Federal Judiciary: The Chase Impeachment and the Constitution*, 9 Stud. Am. Pol. Dev. 55, 93 (1995).

19. 17 F. Cas. 144 (C.C.D. Md. 1861) (No. 9487).

20. See Abraham Lincoln, "Message to Congress in Special Session (July 4, 1861)," reprinted in 4 *Collected Works of Abraham Lincoln* 421, 430 (Roy P. Basler ed., 1953) (presenting Lincoln's instructions to ignore the order in *Ex Parte Merryman*).

21. For an extended discussion of court-curbing measures during Reconstruction, see Barry Friedman, *The History of the Countermajoritarian Difficulty, Part II: Reconstruction's Political Court*, 91 Geo. L. J. 1, 25–45 (2002), which outlines congressional measures to strip the Court's jurisdiction and manipulate its size and personnel during the 1860s and 1870s. See also 6 Charles Fairman, *History of the Supreme Court of the United States: Reconstruction and Reunion, 1864–88 Part One* 161 (Stanley N. Katz, ed., 1971) (noting "[t]he authorized membership of the Court, originally fixed at five, had been increased to seven in 1807, to nine in 1837, and to ten by a statute of 1863" and a new bill introduced in 1866 was intended to change the number again, back to nine). Whether the Court's size was changed to influence outcomes during Reconstruction is contested, and there always was another justification offered. See Friedman, supra, at 43 (citing Charles Fairman, *Mr. Justice Bradley's Appointment to the Supreme Court and the Legal Tender Cases*, 54 Harv. L. Rev. 1034, 1128–55 [1941]).

22. Attempts to exert popular control over the courts during this period are discussed extensively in William G. Ross, *A Muted Fury: Populists, Progressives, and Labor Unions Confront the Courts, 1890–1937* (1994).

23. See Steven P. Croley, *The Majoritarian Difficulty: Elective Judiciaries and the Rule of Law*, 62 U. Chi. L. Rev. 689, 714–17 (1995) ("Whereas the first twenty-nine states of the Union adopted nonelective variations of the basic federal constitutional method for selecting most of their judges, states entering the Union during and in the wake of Andrew Jackson's presidency . . . adopted constitutions providing for the election of most of their judges." [citations omitted]).

24. See *Perry v. United States*, 294 U.S. 330, 358 (1935); *Norman v. Baltimore & Ohio R.R. Co.*, 294 U.S. 240, 316 (1935).

25. See Arthur Krock, *Roosevelt Speech Was Ready on Gold*, N.Y. Times, Feb. 21, 1935, at 1 (reporting the existence of a speech drafted for Franklin Roosevelt in which he would "ask the public specifically to choose between the 'legalism' of the courts and the 'facts,' which required legislative and executive action.").

26. For a discussion of Franklin Roosevelt's attempt to "pack" the membership of the Supreme Court, see William E. Leuchtenburg, *The Supreme Court Reborn* (1995) and Joseph Alsop and Turner Catledge, *The 168 Days* (1938).

27. See C. Herman Pritchett, *Congress versus the Supreme Court 1957–60* 5 (1973 [1961]) ("[T]he decisions of June 17, 1957, coming as they did on top of *Nelson*, *Jencks*, and other rulings upholding the rights of persons charged with subversive activities, led to attacks on the Court in Congress which were not limited by any regional lines.").

28. See J. Patrick White, *The Warren Court Under Attack: The Role of the Judiciary in a Democratic Society*, 19 Md. L. Rev. 181, 189 (1959) ("Southern Congressmen, having failed in their initial effort to mobilize anti-court sentiment with desegregation as the issue, were quick to perceive that their basic purpose of discrediting the Supreme Court would be served whether the issue was undue concern for civil liberties or softness to communism or state's rights."); Pritchett, supra note 27, at 120 ("It is paradoxical, but probably true that the segregation issue increased the bitterness of the legislative drive against the Court and at the same time guaranteed the defeat of the attack.").

29. See Anthony Lewis, *41–40 Senate Vote Kills Bills Aimed at Supreme Court*, N.Y. Times, Aug. 22, 1958, at 1 (reporting Senate vote, 41–40, defeating proposed Jenner-Butler bill).

30. See Richard H. Fallon, Jr., Daniel J. Meltzer, and David L. Shapiro, *Hart and Wechsler's The Federal Courts and the Federal System* 321–22 (5th ed., 2003) (describing host of bills introduced in the 1970s to challenge Supreme Court jurisdiction). Quite recently two bills have passed the House of Representatives stripping the Supreme Court of jurisdiction in specific areas, but neither of these has made any progress through the Senate. See Marriage Protection Act of 2004, H.R. 3313, 108th Cong., 2d Sess. (stripping federal courts of jurisdiction to hear or decide any case pertaining to the constitutionality or requiring the interpretation of the Defense of Marriage Act, 28. U.S.C. 1738C [2000]); Constitution Restoration Act of 2004, H.R. 3799 and S. 2082, 108th Cong., 2d Sess. (foreclosing federal court subject-matter jurisdiction where a state entity is sued by reason of its "acknowledgement of God as the sovereign source of law, liberty, or government.").

31. See, e.g., Neal Devins, *Shaping Constitutional Values* 13 (1996) ("John Marshall undoubtedly would be surprised that his declaration, in *Marbury*, that courts "say what the law is" was subsequently understood to mean that the "federal judiciary is supreme"

in expounding the Constitution's meaning."); Neal Devins and Louis Fisher, *Judicial Exclusivity and Political Instability*, 84 Va. L. Rev. 83, 91 n. 58 (1998) ("Marbury, of course, did not rule that the Court's constitutional interpretations were final and definitive; instead, the Court simply declared that it had the power to invalidate unconstitutional Congressional action."); William W. Van Alstyne, *A Critical Guide to* Marbury v. Madison, 1969 Duke L. J. 1, 37 (1969) ("There is, then, no doctrine of national substantive judicial *supremacy* which inexorably flows from *Marbury v. Madison* itself, i.e., no doctrine that the only interpretation of the Constitution which all branches of national government must employ is the interpretation which the Court may provide in the course of litigation."); see also Larry D. Kramer, *The Supreme Court 2000 Term Foreword: We the Court*, 115 Harv. L. Rev. 4, 87 (2001) (noting that "[i]t has recently become fashionable to dismiss *Marbury* as an altogether trivial case. Some such reaction was, perhaps, predictable given the previous generation's hyperventilated celebration of the case."); Jack N. Rakove, *The Origins of Judicial Review: A Plea for New Contexts*, 49 Stan. L. Rev. 1031, 1035–41 (1997) ("If we did not already know that *Marbury* was so momentous a case, we would be hard pressed to explain why it is so celebrated. In many ways, the revisionists' skepticism seems well justified. However intriguing its politics [including Marshall's failure to recuse himself], the fact remains that the decision had little palpable import.").

32. See Jean Edward Smith, *John Marshall: Definer of a Nation* 324 (1996) ("[Marshall] simply stated that the Constitution was law, and that as a judicial matter, it could be interpreted by the Court in cases that came before it."); see also Rachel E. Barkow, *More Supreme than Court? The Fall of the Political Question Doctrine and the Rise of Judicial Supremacy*, 102 Colum. L. Rev. 237, 239 (2002) ("The duty 'to say what the law is' does not necessarily imply a court monopoly on interpretation."); Orrin G. Hatch, *Modern* Marbury *Myths*, 57 U. Cin. L. Rev. 891, 893 (1989) ("Marshall did not lay claim to any special power to enforce the Constitution or to police the other agencies of government. [He] merely reasoned that the Supreme Court must resolve disputes over which it has jurisdiction according to the law.").

33. See, e.g., Barkow, supra note 32, at 301–2 ("In the past few decades . . . the Supreme Court has become increasingly blind to its limitations as an institution—and, concomitantly, to the strengths of the political branches—and has focused on *Marbury*'s grand proclamation of its power without taking that statement in context." [citations omitted]); Charles A. Beard, *The Supreme Court—Usurper or Grantee*, 28 Pol. Sci. Q. 1 (1912), reprinted in *Judicial Review in American History* 24, 34 (Kermit L. Hall, ed., 1987) ("[I]t is difficult to understand the temerity of those who speak of the power asserted by Marshall in *Marbury v. Madison* as 'usurpation.'"); Raoul Berger, *Government by Judiciary: The Transformation of the Fourteenth Amendment* 362 (1977) ("Were the evidence that judicial review was contemplated and provided for by the Framers far less weighty, it should yet be preferred to a theory which rests judicial review on no evidence at all, for

that represents a naked usurpation of power nowhere granted."); Charles Grove Haines, *The American Doctrine of Judicial Supremacy* 334–46 (1914) (discussing the "usurpation theory," one of the "chief lines of attack upon the American practice of judicial supremacy."); William Trickett, *The Great Usurpation*, 40 Am. L. Rev. 356 (1906); Kramer, supra note 31, at 128–29.

34. But see William E. Nelson, Marbury v. Madison *and Massachusetts* 7 ("John Marshall had no propensity to turn *Marbury* and *Stuart* into instance of judicial review of the sort which the Jeffersonians feared. . . . [He] appreciated the need to steer clear of partisan controversy and not to challenge unnecessarily legislation enacted by democratic majorities.").

35. 5 U.S. (1 Cranch) 137, 177 (1803).

36. See, e.g., *United States v. Morrison*, 529 U.S. 598, 616 n.7 (2000) ("No doubt the political branches have a role in interpreting and applying the Constitution, but ever since *Marbury* this Court has remained the ultimate expositor of the constitutional text."); *United States v. Nixon*, 418 U.S. 683, 703–5 (1974) (citing *Marbury*, in reaffirming that "it is the province and duty of this Court 'to say what the law is' with respect to the claim of privilege presented in this case."); *Cooper v. Aaron*, 358 U.S. 1, 18 (1958) (quoting Marshall in support of the statement that *Marbury* "declared the basic principle that the federal judiciary is supreme in the exposition of the law of the Constitution."); see also Van Alstyne, supra note 31, at 38 ("If . . . it should be thought surprising that *Marbury v. Madison* could sensibly be considered by anyone as authoritatively establishing the doctrine of federal substantive judicial supremacy, however, one need look no further than the Supreme Court [in *Cooper v. Aaron*] itself to find an example of such a view!").

37. See, e.g., Herbert Jacob, et al., *Courts, Law, and Politics in Comparative Perspective* 82 (1996) ("England lacks a written, 'basic law,' and the traditional governing principle is parliamentary supremacy: Parliament has the final say on what it can do, and it can change any law that it so chooses."). But see Human Rights Act, 1998, c. 42 (Eng.) (creating quasi-constitutional law in England by incorporating European Convention on Human Rights into British domestic law and requiring common law and primary and secondary legislation to be read to comply with the Act or amended).

38. See Van Alstyne, supra note 31.

39. See Barkow, supra note 32, at 241 ("The current Supreme Court has taken the one-sided supremacy rhetoric from *Marbury* and *Cooper* to another level: the coordinate branches of the federal government. The Rehnquist Court's view of the relationship among the three branches of the federal government is decidedly more hierarchical than coordinate. And at the top of that hierarchy sits the Court itself."); Kramer, supra note 31, at 128 ("In a manner not unlike the Court of the Gilded Age, the current Supreme Court has, by slow degrees, begun systematically to extend the reach of judicial review.").

40. The discussion that follows does not claim to be comprehensive in its treatment

of positive theories about why those in power tolerate (or welcome) judicial review. There is scholarship discussing additional theories not dealt with above. See e.g., Charles L. Black, Jr., *The People and the Court: Judicial Review in a Democracy* (1960) (arguing that judicial review serves a legitimating function for acts of government); Mark A. Graber, *Federalist or Friends of Adams: The Marshall Court and Party Politics*, 12 Stud. Am. Pol. Dev. 229 (1998) (developing same thesis in specific historical context); Mark A. Graber, *The Nonmajoritarian Difficulty: Legislative Deference to the Judiciary*, 7 Stud. Am. Pol. Dev. 35 (1993) (arguing national elites utilize judicial review as a way of dealing with problems that divide the ruling coalition); James R. Rogers, *Information and Judicial Review: A Signaling Game of Legislative-Judicial Interaction*, 45 Am. J. Pol. Sci. 84 (2001) (arguing that judicial review provides post hoc information to legislature about laws it has enacted); see also George I. Lovell, *Legislative Deferrals: Statutory Ambiguity, Judicial Power, and American Democracy* (2003) (examining case studies of legislative action empowering judicial authority). Howard Gillman and Keith Whittington both have excellent essays about the political foundations of judicial review. See Howard Gillman, *How Political Parties Can Use The Courts To Advance Their Agendas: Federal Courts in the United States, 1875–1891*, 96 Am. Pol. Sci. Rev. 511 (2002); Keith E. Whittington, *Legislative Sanctions and the Strategic Environment of Judicial Review*, 1 ICON 446 (2003). In an extended comparative study, Ran Hirschl concludes that the move to "juristocracy" is a hegemonic move by elites to "insulate their policy preferences against the changing fortunes of democratic politics." Ran Hirschl, *Towards Juristocracy: The Origins and Consequences of the New Constitutionalism* 49 (2004).

41. See Mark A. Graber, *Naked Land Transfers and American Constitutional Development*, 53 Vand. L. Rev. 73, 75 (2000).

42. *Dred Scott v. Sandford*, 60 U.S. (19 How.) 393 (1856).

43. Akhil Reed Amar, Architexture, 77 Ind. L. J. 671, 678 (2002) ("In the almost eighty years between the Founding and the Reconstruction, the Supreme Court invalidated acts of Congress on only two occasions, *Marbury* in 1803 and *Dred Scott* in 1857." [citations omitted]); Barkow, supra note 32, at 321 ("Between *Marbury* in 1803 and *Dred Scott* in 1856, the Supreme Court did not invalidate a single federal act."); see also Graber, supra note 41, at 106 (noting, but disagreeing with, the "near universal claim that the Supreme Court did not declare a federal law unconstitutional between *Marbury* and *Dred Scott*.").

44. See Graber, supra note 41, at 75 (citing Marshall and Taney Court decisions that "imposed clear constitutional limits on federal power even if, in a technical sense, those rules did not strike down a particular federal measure," such as *Polk's Lesee v. Wendal et al.*, *United States v. Percheman*, and *Pollard's Lessee v. Hagan*); see also id. at 107–8 (citing many examples of "statutory misconstruction" from the first sixty-five volumes of the *U.S. Reports*).

45. See id. at 106–13.

46. Id. at 78 (footnote omitted).

47. Id. at 118.

48. Id. at 117.

49. Michael G. Collins, *Before Lochner—Diversity Jurisdiction and the Development of General Constitutional Law*, 74 Tul. L. Rev. 1263, 1310–20 (2000).

50. Id. at 1320 ("[F]ederal courts . . . applied their own nonfederal default rules to give a uniform construction to a variety of ostensibly state constitutional questions.").

51. Graber, supra note 41, at 114 ("The decisions in many [antebellum] land cases are best characterized as correcting legislative mistakes that the legislature would have corrected if given better information and time.").

52. Lee Epstein, Jack Knight, and Olga Shvetsova, *The Role of Constitutional Courts in the Establishment and Maintenance of Democratic Systems of Government*, 35 Law & Soc'y Rev. 117 (2001).

53. See id. at 151–52.

54. 347 U.S. 483 (1954).

55. See Derrick A. Bell, Jr., Brown v. Board of Education *and the Interest-Convergence Dilemma*, 93 Harv. L. Rev. 518, 524 (1980); Mary L. Dudziak, *Cold War Civil Rights: Race and the Image of American Democracy* (2000); Mary L. Dudziak, *Desegregation as a Cold War Imperative*, 41 Stan. L. Rev. 61, 65 (1988); Michael J. Klarman, *Rethinking the Civil Rights and Civil Liberties Revolution*, 82 Va. L. Rev. 1, 7 (1996); Girardeau A. Spann, *Pure Politics*, 88 Mich. L. Rev. 1971, 2015–16 (1990); see also Lucas A. Powe, Jr., *The Warren Court and American Politics* (2000) (explaining Warren Court "activism" generally as furthering of national elite interests against outliers).

56. Of course, one reason to favor judicial review is if the "ins" at the national level are still the "outs" at the state level, as was true for many of the cases Michael Collins discusses. See supra notes 49–50 and accompanying text. This provides a plausible explanation for many notable exercises of national judicial authority.

57. One not discussed here is Mathew D. McCubbins and Thomas Schwartz, *Congressional Oversight Overlooked: Police Patrols Versus Fire Alarms*, 28 Am. J. Pol. Sci. 165 (1984), arguing that judicial review is a type of oversight that permits Congress to monitor the faithfulness of administrative agencies to legislative goals.

58. J. Mark Ramseyer, *The Puzzling (In)dependence of Courts: A Comparative Approach*, 23 J. Legal Stud. 721 (1994).

59. See id. at 746 ("Judicial independence is not primarily a matter of constitutional text. Both the modern Japanese and the modern American constitutions purport to insulate judges from political leaders. Yet modern American politicians do insulate their judges, while Japanese politicians do not.").

60. Ramseyer notes:

[F]or forty years the LDP consistently won [political elections]. . . . By contrast, American parties win erratically at best. As a result, LDP leaders could reasonably expect that they would continue to control the government. No American leader of either party can do so. If rational politicians face significant odds of being in the minority party, however, they will try to reduce the variance to their political returns. In part, they can do this by insulating the judicial system from political control. . . . American political leaders agree to increase their control over the judiciary into the future, by decreasing their control over the judiciary in the present. . . . By politicizing appointments but depoliticizing control . . . they augment their influence during periods when they are out of power. All this they do, of course, at the cost of decreasing their influence over policy while in power: because politicians will have to run the country with independent judges that their predecessors appointed, they will necessarily have less impact over policy while in office.

See id. at 740–42 (citations omitted).

61. See Lee Epstein, Jack Knight, and Olga Shvetsova, *Comparing Judicial Selection Systems*, 10 Wm. & Mary Bill of Rts. J. 7 (2001).

62. See Richard Drew, *Bringing the State Courts Back In: Party Politics and the Antebellum Surge in American Judicial Power* (manuscript on file with author).

63. For example, Ramseyer's story is entirely plausible with respect to Japan.

64. For a description of the election of 1800, see William Nisbet Chambers, *Political Parties in a New Nation: The American Experience 1776–1809*, at 160, 166–68 (1963).

65. William M. Landes and Richard A. Posner, *The Independent Judiciary in an Interest-Group Perspective*, 18 J. L. & Econ. 875 (1975).

66. See id. at 883, 885–87 (discussing the concept of judicial independence and the manner in which an independent judiciary may be anticipated to enforce existing legislation); see also id., app. at 895–901 (presenting data measuring the degree to which courts overturn legislative deals).

67. Id. at 879.

68. Id.

69. Id. at 895.

70. See Nicholas S. Zeppos, *Deference to Political Decisionmakers and the Preferred Scope of Judicial Review*, 88 Nw. U. L. Rev. 296, 309–12 (1993) (suggesting that the data compiled by Landes and Posner should be expanded to include instances in which the Court interpreted a statute, using constitutional norms, deviating from original legislative intent); see also id., app. A at 335–45 (presenting a list covering fifty-five years of Supreme Court invalidations and interpretations using constitutional norms).

71. See id. at 332–34.

72. 486 U.S. 592, 603–5 (1988).

73. 394 U.S. 618, 621–22 (1969).

74. 390 U.S. 39, 60–61 (1968).

75. See William N. Eskridge, Jr., *The Judicial Review Game*, 88 Nw. U. L. Rev. 382, 383 (1993) ("[T]he Constitution's institutional structure creates what I call 'the judicial review game.' Interest groups are pretty much stuck in the game even though it does not appear to benefit them in the aggregate and even though the game is not demonstrably in the public interest.").

76. See, e.g., Lewis A. Kornhauser, *A World Apart? An Essay on the Autonomy of the Law*, 78 B.U. L. Rev. 747, 767 (1998) ("Positive political theory [PPT], by contrast, focuses on the supply of legislation rather than the demand for it. To do this, PPT takes the interests of citizens and the interests of political representatives as given; it then studies how institutional structures affect the legislative outcomes." [citations omitted]); Edward L. Rubin, *Public Choice, Phenomenology, and the Meaning of the Modern State: Keep the Bathwater, but Throw Out that Baby*, 87 Cornell L. Rev. 309, 318 (2002) ("[Positive political theory] assumes that political actors like Congress or the President are motivated by the desire to maximize the implementation of their positions, but it does not depend on any particular assertion about the nature or origin of those positions." [citations omitted]); see also, e.g., Daniel A. Farber and Philip P. Frickey, *Foreword: Positive Political Theory in the Nineties*, 80 Geo. L. J. 457, 458–63 (1992) (defining positive political theory).

77. See Eskridge, supra note 75, at 389 ("[I]t seems doubtful that the existence of judicial review as an extra step in the creation of public policy is advantageous to interest groups. Yet groups or their surrogates aggressively participate in judicial review.").

78. See id. at 389–90.

79. See id. at 389 ("Judicial preferences are probably less susceptible to interest group influence in the short term, both because life-tenured judges have no incentive to cozy up to groups the way bureaucrats and legislators do and because professional pressures induce judges to prefer rule of law values like coherence and nonretroactivity over policy values favored by interest groups.").

80. John Ferejohn, *Independent Judges, Dependent Judiciary: Explaining Judicial Independence*, 72 So. Cal. L. Rev. 353 (1999).

81. See id. at 376.

82. See supra note 30 (discussing recent jurisdiction-stripping legislation).

83. Ferejohn, supra note 80, at 382.

84. Id. at 357 (emphasis added).

85. Id. at 382–83 (emphasis added).

86. Id. at 384.

87. E.g., Joseph P. Kalt and Mark A. Zupan, *The Apparent Ideological Behavior of Leg-*

islators: Testing for Principal-Agent Slack in Political Institutions, 33 J. L. & Econ. 103 (1990).

88. See Alsop and Catledge, supra note 26, at 70–73 (describing negative reaction to the plan); Barry Cushman, *Rethinking the New Deal Court* 13 (1998) ("Polls taken between February and May of 1937 indicate that the first major domestic initiative of Roosevelt's second term was consistently opposed by a majority of the same American people who had so overwhelmingly returned him to office the preceding November."); Leuchtenburg, supra note 26, at 145.

89. Gregory A. Caldeira, *Public Opinion and the U.S. Supreme Court: FDR's Court-Packing Plan*, 81 Am. Pol. Sci. Rev. 1139, 1149 (1987) ("Two crucial events—*Jones and Laughlin Steel* and Justice Van Devanter's resignation—spelled doom for FDR's bill to enlarge the Court and pack it with justices favorable to the New Deal. Between the two decisions, the Supreme Court decreased support for President Roosevelt's proposal by nearly 10%.... Planned or not, the Court's actions played a dramatic role in defeating the president.").

90. This argument is developed in Barry Friedman, *The History of the Countermajoritarian Difficulty, Part Four: Law's Politics*, 148 U. Pa. L. Rev. 971, 981–82 (2000) (observing that "[a]though ... conjecture, there seems a basis for concluding that had the Court not shifted in the eyes of the public, some retributive action would have been possible. Public sentiment against the Court was strong, and Roosevelt's case would have been bolstered by a bad economy and additional unpopular judicial decisions."). For different perspectives on this point, compare Cushman, supra note 88, at 12–13 (noting the "size and vehemence of the opposition to the plan. From the beginning, the press voiced near-unanimous outrage and disdain. Joining the chorus of protest were numerous bar associations across the nation.... The plan was denounced by numerous civic, patriotic, fraternal, professional, political, and religious organizations.") with Leuchtenburg, supra note 26, at 148 (noting that even "prospects for enacting [the] new [compromise] bill appeared very promising.").

91. See, e.g., Barry Friedman, *The History of the Countermajoritarian Difficulty, Part II: Reconstruction's Political Court*, 91 Geo. L. J. 1, 24 (2002) ("The question, of course, was what was to be done about the possibility that the Supreme Court might actually try to rule on Reconstruction.... The answers were varied, but the thrust of them was clear: One way or another, the Court was to be subjected to the will of the people."); id. at 25 ("[T]he District of Columbia's Daily Morning Chronicle, the arm of Senate Republicans, insisted that the people would not stand idly by while the Supreme Court interpreted the Constitution in a way that 'places the rights of the individual before the safety of the whole people, and which would make it a straight waistcoat binding the arms of the nation while its assailants stab it to death.'" [citations omitted]).

92. For a discussion of this, see Barry Friedman, *The History of the Countermajoritarian Difficulty, Part Three: The Lesson of* Lochner, 76 N.Y. U. L. Rev. 1383 (2001).

93. See Barry Friedman, *Dialogue and Judicial Review*, 91 Mich. L. Rev. 577, 621–22 (1993) ("Not only the Constitution has become more majoritarian, however; so has the society that document governs. Indeed, it is sometimes difficult to tell which transformation has caused the other. We have become a society enamored of the accouterments of popular governance. We revel in national polls; every day we devour media reports on what the polls say we think." [citations omitted]). See generally Lewis B. Kaden, *Politics, Money, and State Sovereignty: The Judicial Role*, 79 Colum. L. Rev. 847, 864 (1979) (discussing the role of the media in contemporary politics).

94. See Friedman, supra note 90, at 981–82 ("The New Deal fight provoked tremendous popular engagement. Congress and the President were swamped with mail, much of it from ordinary citizens." [citations omitted]).

95. See Kramer, supra note 31, at 13–14 ("For much of the nineteenth century, an expansive notion of 'political questions' and a sharp law/politics distinction among issues of constitutional law served to reconcile these conflicting principles. This doctrinal framework broke down during the Lochner era, triggering a prolonged struggle that culminated in the New Deal settlement most famously reflected in *Carolene Products*' footnote four."); see also id. at 122–25 (discussing observations relating to the "New Deal settlement"); id. at 128 (noting that the "Rehnquist Court has, quite simply and literally, abandoned the New Deal settlement."); see generally Bruce Ackerman, *We the People* 105–30 (1991) (discussing the New Deal constitutional transformation and the significance of *Carolene Products* footnote four).

96. See Kramer, supra note 31, at 122 ("The basic terms of the New Deal settlement are well known, having been a centerpiece of constitutional law for more than three generations. First, the Court renewed and continued its traditional role as the primary enforcer of constitutional prohibitions on the states. Second, the Court restored to politics questions respecting the definition or scope of the powers delegated by the Constitution to Congress and the Executive, subject only to a very limited rational basis scrutiny. . . . Lastly, the Court reserved room for 'a more exacting judicial inquiry' to protect a broad category of individual rights." [citations omitted]).

97. Friedman, supra note 90, at 1019–28. Barry Cushman provides a wealth of polling data on public opinion during this period, some of it supportive of the claim in text and some more equivocal. See Barry Cushman, *Mr. Dooley and Mr. Gallup: Public Opinion and Constitutional Change in the 1930s*, 50 Buff. L. Rev. 7 (2002). Of course, opinion polls are just one part of the story.

98. Friedman, supra note 90, at 1028.

99. E.g., Jack M. Balkin and Sanford Levinson, *Understanding the Constitutional*

Revolution, 87 Va. L. Rev. 1045 (2001); Christopher H. Schroeder, *Causes of the Recent Turn in Constitutional Interpretation*, 51 Duke L. J. 307 (2001).

100. See *Tennessee v. Lane*, 124 S.Ct. 1978 (2004).

101. *Rasul v. Bush*, 124 S.Ct. 2686 (2004); *Hamdi v. Rumsfeld*, 124 S.Ct. 2633 (2004).

102. See e.g., Jeffrey Rosen, *One Eye on Principle, the Other on the People's Will*, N.Y. Times, July 4, 2004, at 3 (noting that the Supreme Court "appears acutely aware of the broader political climate in its decisions and tends to reflect the will of the majority of Americans rather than challenging it."); Jeffrey Rosen, *Supreme Mistake*, New Republic, Nov. 8, 2004, at 18.("[T]he Rehnquist Court has largely sided with liberals rather than conservatives in . . . culture battles . . . because liberals have won in the court of public opinion.").

103. Sandra Day O'Connor, *The Majesty of the Law: Reflections of a Supreme Court Justice* 166 (2003) ("Rare indeed is the legal victory—in court or legislature—that is not a careful by-product of an emerging social consensus. Courts, in particular, are mainly reactive institutions.").

104. This literature is discussed at length in Barry Friedman, *Mediated Popular Constitutionalism*, 101 Mich. L. Rev. 2596 (2003).

105. This is changing. See, e.g., Robert C. Post and Reva B. Siegal, *Legislative Constitutionalism and Section Five Power: Policentric Interpretation of The Family and Medical Leave Act*, 112 Yale L. J. 1943 (2003) (grounding legislative role in interpreting the Constitution to secure public support for constitutional meaning).

106. See Friedman, supra note 104, at 2600–13; Michel Troper, *The Logic of Justification of Judicial Review*, 1 Int'l J. Const. L. 99, 109 (2003) ("[D]emocracy cannot provide a strong justification for judicial review, because the democratic principle does not imply judicial review. Thus only weak justifications exist, of two sorts. The first presents the same structure as justification by the supremacy of the constitution: review is a tool in the service of democracy. The second is that constitutional review is not necessary to democracy but is necessary to attain other ends compatible with democracy.").

107. E.g., Christopher L. Eisgruber, *Constitutional Self-Government* 210 (2001) ("There is nothing wrong with the fact that unelected justices decide questions about . . . federalism or gay rights or economic justice on the basis of controversial judgments of moral principle. When other political institutions have pandered to the American people's baser selves, this Court has frequently had backbone enough to stand up for the people's values.").

108. See, e.g., John Hart Ely, *Democracy and Distrust* 73–104 (1980).

[S]ome writers in the 1960s argued that judicial review might be understood as a technique of remanding a question for reconsideration by the people: an appeal from John drunk to John sober. In that form, the defense of judicial review was incomplete. Suppose, after the remand, the people decided that they really did want the statute that the Court had held unconstitutional. I can imagine that the Court would say, "Well, if that's what you really want, we'll let you do it. The statute is no longer unconstitutional, even though it was when we first considered the case." But, I suspect that it would respond more often: "We really meant it the first time around." Sober second-thought review, that is, does not look like judicial review as we have come to know it.

Mark V. Tushnet, *Justice Brennan, Equality, and Majority Rule*, 139 U. Pa. L. Rev. 1357, 1369–70 (1991); see also Friedman, supra note 93, at 678 (referring to "appeal from John drunk to John sober.").

109.   All of this is discussed at greater length in Friedman, supra note 104.

Reed: Judicial Review and the Stages of *Marbury*

1.   David R. Mayhew, *Congress: The Electoral Connection* (1974).

2.   Martin Shapiro, *Courts: A Comparative and Political Analysis* (1981).

3.   *Bush v. Gore*, 531 U. S. 1046 (2000) (on application for stay) (Scalia, J., concurring).

4.   Keith E. Whittington, *Constitutional Construction: Divided Powers and Constitutional Meaning* (1999).

5.   Tom R. Tyler, *Why People Obey the Law* (1990).

6.   James Bradley Thayer, *The Origin and Scope of the American Doctrine of Constitutional Law*, 7 Harv. L. Rev. 129 (1893).

7.   Philip A. Klinkner, *Dwarfing the Political Capacity of the People? The Relationship Between Judicial Activism and Voter Turnout, 1840–1988*, 25 Polity 633 (1993).

Griffin: The Age of *Marbury*

Earlier versions of this article were presented at the 2002 American Political Science Association meeting and at a February 2003 conference, "Rearguing *Marbury v. Madison*," at Georgetown University Law Center. I am grateful for the comments I received on those occasions from Rebecca Brown, Mike Seidman, Vicki Jackson, Mark Tushnet, Suzanna Sherry, and Barry Friedman. Email: sgriffin@law.tulane.edu.

1.   See, e.g., Larry D. Kramer, *Foreword: We The Court*, 115 Harv. L. Rev. 4, 6–8 (2001).

2.   531 U.S. 98 (2000).

3.   5 U.S. (1 Cranch) 137 (1803). See the discussions of *Marbury* in *United States v. Lopez*, 514 U.S. 549, 566 (1995) (holding unconstitutional the Gun Free Schools Zone Act) and *City of Boerne v. Flores*, 521 U.S. 507, 529, 536 (1997) (holding unconstitutional the Religious Freedom Restoration Act).

4.   See, e.g., Jesse H. Choper, *Judicial Review and the National Political Process* (1980); John Hart Ely, *Democracy and Distrust: A Theory of Judicial Review* (1980).

5. Mark Tushnet, *Foreword: The New Constitutional Order and the Chastening of Constitutional Aspiration*, 113 Harv. L. Rev. 29, 85 (1999). See also Mark Tushnet, *The New Constitutional Order* 114–15 (2003).

6. See Alexander M. Bickel, *The Least Dangerous Branch: The Supreme Court at the Bar of Politics* (1962).

7. See id. at 16.

8. See id. at 1–14.

9. See, e.g., Daniel A. Farber and Suzanna Sherry, *Desperately Seeking Certainty: The Misguided Quest for Constitutional Foundations* 146 (2002) (citing favorably Marshall's reasoning in *Marbury*).

10. I will say immediately that this is a prediction because there is already one counterexample. See Michael J. Klarman, *How Great Were the "Great" Marshall Court Decisions*, 87 Va. L. Rev. 1111, 1113–26 (2001).

11. See *City of Boerne v. Flores*, 521 U.S. 507 (1997) (holding unconstitutional the Religious Freedom Restoration Act); *Kimel v. Florida Board of Regents*, 528 U.S. 62 (2000) (holding that the Age Discrimination in Employment Act does not apply to the states); *United States v. Morrison*, 529 U.S. 598 (2000) (holding unconstitutional the Violence Against Women Act); and *Board of Trustees of the University of Alabama v. Garrett*, 531 U.S. 356 (2001) (holding that Title I of the Americans with Disabilities Act does not apply to the states).

12. This is the third article in a series I have written exploring the new terrain of the conflict between democracy and judicial review. See Stephen M. Griffin, *Has the Hour of Democracy Come Round at Last? The New Critique of Judicial Review*, 17 Const. Comm. 683 (2000); Stephen M. Griffin, *Judicial Supremacy and Equal Protection in a Democracy of Rights*, 4 U. Pa. J. Const. L. 281 (2002).

13. See Farber and Sherry, supra note 9.

14. See Stephen M. Griffin, *The Idea of Judicial Review in the Marshall Era*, in *Marbury versus Madison: Documents and Commentary* 61 (Mark A. Graber and Michael Perhac, eds., 2002). I draw on this article in Part I.

15. See Robert A. Dahl, *Decision-Making in a Democracy: The Supreme Court as a National Policy-Maker*, 6 J. Pub. Law 279 (1957). For recent essays on the importance of this article, see *Review Essays*, 50 Emory L. J. 583 (2001).

16. See Griffin, *Judicial Supremacy*, supra note 12.

17. See Farber and Sherry, supra note 9.

18. See Christopher L. Eisgruber, *Constitutional Self-Government* (2001).

19. 5 U.S. (1 Cranch) 137 (1803).

20. See generally Larry D. Kramer, *The People Themselves: Popular Constitutionalism and Judicial Review* (2004).

21. See Alexander Hamilton, James Madison, and John Jay, *The Federalist* (Jacob E. Cooke, ed., 1961).

22. Gordon S. Wood, *The Origins of Judicial Review*, 22 Suffolk U. L. Rev. 1293, 1295 (1988).

23. See Bickel, supra note 6; Stephen M. Griffin, *American Constitutionalism: From Theory to Politics* 104–24 (1996).

24. Hamilton, *Federalist 78*, supra note 21, at 524.

25. See Jack N. Rakove, *The Origins of Judicial Review: A Plea for New Contexts*, 49 Stan. L. Rev. 1031, 1060–64 (1997); Gordon S. Wood, "Judicial Review in the Era of the Founding," in *Is the Supreme Court the Guardian of the Constitution?* 156–60 (Robert A. Licht, ed., 1993).

26. See Kramer, supra note 1, at 87.

27. Wood, supra note 25, at 157.

28. Hamilton, supra note 24, at 524.

29. Id.

30. Id.

31. Id.

32. Id. at 525.

33. Id.

34. See Klarman, supra note 10, at 1120–23.

35. See Sylvia Snowiss, *Judicial Review and the Law of the Constitution* (1990).

36. See James B. Thayer, *The Origin and Scope of the American Doctrine of Constitutional Law*, 7 Harv. L. Rev. 129, 140 (1893).

37. Snowiss, supra note 35, at 60.

38. Hamilton, supra note 24, at 524 (emphasis added).

39. 5 U.S. at 177–78.

40. Id. at 179.

41. See Charles F. Hobson, *The Great Chief Justice: John Marshall and the Rule of Law* 67 (1996). The idea that the doubtful case rule was an important element of judicial review in the early republic is not free from difficulty. William Treanor has questioned its importance based on his review of the arguments of Edmund Randolph and St. George Tucker in the 1782 *Case of the Prisoners* in Virginia (better known as *Commonwealth v. Caton*, 8 Va. (4 Call) 5 (1782)). See William Michael Treanor, *The Case of the Prisoners and the Origins of Judicial Review*, 143 U. Pa. L. Rev. 491 (1994). As Treanor himself notes, however, Randolph's argument provides support for the doubtful case rule. See id. at 552–56. Further, Treanor does not contest the substantial evidence produced by Thayer, Snowiss, and others that the doubtful case rule was part of the context in which the institution of judicial review took shape.

42. 10 U.S. (6 Cranch) 87 (1810).

43. 17 U.S. 316 (1819).

44. 17 U.S. (4 Wheat.) 518 (1819).

45. 25 U.S. 419 (1827).

46. See Hobson, supra note 41, at 67–69; Dean Alfange, Jr., Marbury v Madison *and Original Understandings of Judicial Review: In Defense of Traditional Wisdom*, 1993 The Supreme Court Review 342–44 (1994); William R. Casto, *James Iredell and the American Origins of Judicial Review*, 27 Conn. L. Rev. 329, 337–48 (1995); Klarman, supra note 10, at 1120–22; Kramer, supra note 1, at 79–82.

47. See Snowiss, supra note 35, at 190–94.

48. Charles F. Hobson, 4 *The Papers of John Marshall* 95 (1990).

49. See Hobson, supra note 41, at 51–54.

50. See id. at 70; G. Edward White, *The Marshall Court and Cultural Change*, 1815–35 118, 195–200 (1988); Casto, supra note 46, at 336–38. For a general discussion of the differences between the world of the Marshall Court and our own, see G. Edward White, *Recovering the World of the Marshall Court*, 33 John Marshall L. Rev. 781 (2000).

51. William E. Nelson, Marbury v. Madison: *The Origins and Legacy of Judicial Review* 7 (2000).

52. See Casto, supra note 46, at 349.

53. Nelson, supra note 51, at 8.

54. Id. at 59.

55. See id. at 79–83.

56. See Klarman, supra note 10, at 1122–23.

57. See Richard E. Ellis, *The Jeffersonian Crisis: Courts and Politics in the Young Republic* 66 (1971); Charles Warren, 1 *The Supreme Court in United States History* 248–68 (1926).

58. See Casto, supra note 46, at 337–41.

59. See, e.g., Hobson, supra note 41, at 67; R. Kent Newmyer, *John Marshall and the Heroic Age of the Supreme Court* 162 (2001); Jean Edward Smith, *John Marshall: Definer of a Nation* 323–24 (1996).

60. See 5 U.S. at 180.

61. 358 U.S. 1 (1958).

62. Id. at 18.

63. Quoted in H. W. Perry, Jr., *Deciding to Decide: Agenda Setting in the United States Supreme Court* 36 (1991).

64. See id. at 198–215, 253–65.

65. Lawrence G. Sager, *The Incorrigible Constitution*, 65 N.Y. U. L. Rev. 893, 898 (1990).

66. See Griffin, supra note 23, at 11–19.

67. Bickel, supra note 6, at 3.

68. Quoted in Dennis J. Hutchinson, "The Black-Jackson Feud," in *1988 The Supreme Court Review* 239 (Philip B. Kurland et al., eds., 1989).

69. For general discussions of the problem of constitutional change, see Griffin, supra note 23, and Stephen M. Griffin, *Constitutional Theory Transformed*, 108 Yale L. J. 2115 (1999).

70. See, e.g., Bickel, supra note 6; Ely, supra note 4.

71. See *United States v. Carolene Products*, 304 U.S. 144, 152–53 n. 4 (1938).

72. See id.

73. For an example of this view, see Farber and Sherry, supra note 9, at 140–45.

74. For an excellent discussion, see Barry Friedman, *The Birth of an Academic Obsession: The History of the Countermajoritarian Difficulty, Part Five*, 112 Yale L. J. 153, 222–28 (2002).

75. Bickel, supra note 6, at 16.

76. For recent accounts, see Edward A. Purcell, Jr., *Brandeis and the Progressive Constitution: Erie, the Judicial Power, and the Politics of the Federal Courts in Twentieth-Century America* 258–65 (2000); Friedman, supra note 74, at 193–97.

77. See Griffin, supra note 23, at 107.

78. Bickel, supra note 6, at 16–20.

79. Id. at 23–24.

80. Id. at 26.

81. Anthony T. Kronman, *Alexander Bickel's Philosophy of Prudence*, 94 Yale L. J. 1567, 1580–81 (1985) (footnote omitted).

82. Many scholars have made this point. See, e.g., Laura Kalman, *The Strange Career of Legal Liberalism* 38–40 (1996); Erwin Chemerinsky, *The Price of Asking the Wrong Question: An Essay on Constitutional Scholarship and Judicial Review*, 62 Tex. L. Rev. 1207, 1226–33 (1984); Barry Friedman, *Dialogue and Judicial Review*, 91 Mich. L. Rev. 577 (1993).

83. See Edward A. Purcell, Jr., *Alexander M. Bickel and the Post-Realist Constitution*, 11 Harv. Civ. Rights-Civ. Liberties L. Rev. 521, 537 (1976); Friedman, supra note 82, at 220–21.

84. See Dahl, supra note 15.

85. See id. at 283.

86. Id. at 293.

87. Id. at 291.

88. Id. at 293.

89. See sources in note 82.

90. See Griffin, supra note 23, at 104–6. See also Bruce A. Ackerman, *The Storrs Lec-*

tures: Discovering the Constitution, 93 Yale L. J. 1013, 1014–15 (1984); Mark A. Graber, *Constitutional Politics and Constitutional Theory: A Misunderstood and Neglected Relationship*, 27 Law & Soc. Inquiry 309, 319 (2002).

91. Bickel, supra note 6, at 18.

92. See, e.g., Rebecca L. Brown, *Accountability, Liberty, and the Constitution*, 98 Colum. L. Rev. 531, 551 (1998).

93. See Friedman, supra note 82.

94. See Griffin, supra note 69.

95. See Alexander Keyssar, *The Right to Vote: The Contested History of Democracy in the United States* 243–45 (2000).

96. Dahl, supra note 15, at 293.

97. See id.

98. See William Mishler and Reginald S. Sheehan, *The Supreme Court as a Countermajoritarian Institution? The Impact of Public Opinion on Supreme Court Decisions*, 87 Am. Pol. Sci. Rev. 87, 98 (1993).

99. See Dahl, supra note 18, at 284–86.

100. I will discuss the implications of this point in the next section.

101. See Dahl, supra note 15, at 282–83.

102. See Bickel, supra note 6, at 25–26.

103. 347 U.S. 483 (1954).

104. Bickel, supra note 6, at 26.

105. See Griffin, supra note 23, at 109–10; Frank B. Cross, *Institutions and Enforcement of the Bill of Rights*, 85 Cornell L. Rev. 1529, 1550–61 (2000) and sources cited in note 82. For a significant dissent, see Michael J. Klarman, *The Puzzling Resistance to Political Process Theory*, 77 Va. L. Rev. 747, 772–82 (1991).

106. See Choper, supra note 4, at 12–45.

107. See Graber, supra note 90, at 327–28.

108. Bickel, supra note 6, at 25.

109. For example, the 1988 edition of Hart and Wechsler stated: "Both Congress and the President can obviously contribute to the sound interpretation of the Constitution. But clearly neither branch is so organized or staffed as to be able, without aid from the courts, to build up a body of coherent and intelligible constitutional principle, and to carry public conviction that these principles are being observed." Paul M. Bator et al., *Hart and Wechsler's The Federal Courts and the Federal System* 83 (3d ed., 1988).

110. Bickel, supra note 6, at 25.

111. Id.

112. See id. at 26.

113. Id.

114. Id.

115. See Cross, supra note 105, at 1537–45.

116. See Alexander Bickel and Harry Wellington, *Legislative Purpose and the Judicial Process: The Lincoln Mills Case*, 71 Harv. L. Rev. 1 (1957).

117. See, e.g., Laurence H. Tribe, *American Constitutional Law* 27 (3d ed., 2000); Owen Fiss, *Foreword: The Forms of Justice*, 93 Harv. L. Rev. 1 (1979); Ronald Dworkin, *The Forum of Principle*, 56 N.Y. U. L. Rev. 469 (1981). This Bickelian theme remained prominent in important contributions to the judicial review versus democracy debate published in the late 1980s and early 1990s. See Erwin Chemerinsky, *Foreword: The Vanishing Constitution*, 103 Harv. L. Rev. 43, 83–87 (1989); Sager, supra note 65, at 953–59.

118. Amy Gutmann and Dennis Thompson, *Democracy and Disagreement* 45 (1996).

119. See the discussion in Griffin, supra note 26, at 123.

120. See Tushnet, The New Constitutional Order, supra note 5, at 8–19, 102–6.

121. See Sidney M. Milkis, *Political Parties and Constitutional Government: Remaking American Democracy* 137–73 (1999).

122. Dahl, supra note 15, at 293.

123. See Stephen M. Griffin, *Politics and the Supreme Court: The Case of the Bork Nomination*, 5 J. L. & Pol. 551, 582–88 (1989). See also the important study by Nancy Scherer, *Making a Point: The Politicization of the Lower Federal Court Appointment Process in the Modern Political Era* (2001, unpublished dissertation). Scherer argues that "[w]hile once the lower court appointment system was largely (though, certainly, not exclusively) used by the president and senators to confer *patronage* so as to shore up political support among party activists, beginning slowly in the 1960s, we begin to see a shift towards an appointment system largely (though not exclusively) used by the president and senators to confer *policy* benefits for party activists." Nancy Scherer, "Political Uses of Lower Federal Court Appointments: Mobilizing Elites, Mobilizing Masses," paper presented at 2002 Annual Meeting of the American Political Science Association, at 3 (on file with author) (emphasis in original).

124. For a general discussion, see Mark Tushnet, *Taking the Constitution Away from the Courts* 135–53 (1999).

125. See Philip A. Klinkner and Rogers M. Smith, *The Unsteady March: The Rise and Decline of Racial Equality in America* 276 (1999).

126. See Liva Baker, *Miranda: Crime, Law and Politics* 237–60 (1985).

127. 410 U.S. 113 (1973).

128. See generally Thomas M. Keck, *The Most Activist Supreme Court in History: The Road to Modern Judicial Conservatism* 93–97, 110–13 (2004).

129. Cooper worked at the DOJ from 1981–88, serving as Deputy Assistant Attorney General in the Civil Rights Division from 1982–85 and head of the Office of Legal Counsel from 1985–88.

130.   443 U.S. 193 (1979).

131.   Pub. L. No. 88-352, 78 Stat. 241.

132.   See David G. Savage, *Turning Right: The Making of the Rehnquist Supreme Court* 6–8 (1992).

133.   See *Preface*, 6 Harv. J. L. Pub. Policy (1982) (not paginated).

134.   Id.

135.   Id.

136.   See Charles Fried, *Order and Law: Arguing the Reagan Revolution* 30–31 (1991).

137.   Id. at 37.

138.   Id. at 17.

139.   Id. at 17–18.

140.   Id. at 18.

141.   See Milkis, supra note 121, at 154–57.

142.   See Sheldon Goldman, *Picking Federal Judges: Lower Court Selection From Roosevelt through Reagan* 296–307 (1997); Mark Silverstein, *Judicious Choices: The New Politics of Supreme Court Confirmations* (1994); David Alistair Yalof, *Pursuit of Justices: Presidential Politics and the Selection of Supreme Court Nominees* (1999).

143.   Silverstein, supra note 142, at 120–21 (footnotes omitted).

144.   Yalof, supra note 142, at 142–43.

145.   Id. at 143–44.

146.   Id. at 144.

147.   Silverstein, supra note 142, at 6 (footnote omitted).

148.   For example, Michael Gerhardt concludes in his important study that the federal appointment process is political by design. See Michael J. Gerhardt, *The Federal Appointments Process: A Constitutional and Historical Analysis* 258–59 (2001). I would not disagree, but the phenomenon I am calling politicization is new, at least to the federal judicial appointment process.

149.   As Robert Kagan puts it: "By creating a system in which the courts are open to challenges to governmental authority and public interest lawyers' creative arguments, adversarial legalism turns the judiciary into an arena of continuing political struggle. Because judges can and do make policy decisions, the competing political parties each strive to appoint judges who will be ideologically sympathetic." Robert A. Kagan, *Adversarial Legalism: The American Way of Law* 171 (2001).

150.   Mark Graber provides an incisive argument in support of this position in the context of abortion. See Mark A. Graber, *Rethinking Abortion: Equal Choice, the Constitution, and Reproductive Politics* 121–31 (1996).

151.   It is worth keeping in mind that the last president who was able to appoint a five-member majority to the Court was Franklin Delano Roosevelt. Recent presidents have not been as fortunate.

152. See, e.g., Stuart Taylor Jr., *The Tipping Point*, National Journal, June 10, 2000, at 1810; Kirk Victor, *A Ticking Time Bomb in the Senate*, National Journal, Feb. 17, 2001, at 490; Neil A. Lewis, *Expecting a Vacancy, Bush Aides Weigh Supreme Court Contenders*, N.Y. Times, Dec. 27, 2002, at A1; Mike Allen and Charles Lane, *President Set for Confirmation Fight Over High Court Nominee*, Wash. Post, Jan. 19, 2003 at A4; Stuart Taylor Jr., *Courting Trouble*, National Journal, June 14, 2003, at 1832; Neil A. Lewis and Sheryl Gay Stolberg, *Vacancy or Not, Parties Brace for Supreme Court Fight*, N.Y. Times, June 20, 2003, at A21.

Recently, the battle has been extended to nominations to the courts of appeals. See Jeffrey Rosen, *Obstruction of Judges*, N.Y. Times Magazine, Aug. 11, 2002, at 38; Neil A. Lewis, *Democrats Reject Bush Pick in Battle Over Court Balance*, N.Y. Times, Sept. 6, 2002, at A1; Jennifer A. Diouhy, *Parties Use Judicial Standoff to Play to Core Constituents*, Congressional Quarterly Weekly Report, Oct. 19, 2002, at 2722; Neil A. Lewis, *First the Senate, Now the Courts of Appeals*, N.Y. Times, Dec. 1, 2002, sec. 4, at 3; Jennifer A. Diouhy, *A New Level of Acrimony in Parties' War of Procedure*, Congressional Quarterly Weekly Report, May 10, 2003, at 1078.

153. Milkis, supra note 121, at 156.

154. For an argument that the Court can perform these roles, see, e.g., Tribe, supra note 117.

155. See Eisgruber, supra note 18, at 68–71; James E. Fleming, *The Constitution Outside the Courts*, 86 Cornell L. Rev. 215, 228 (2000).

156. See Ely, supra note 4.

157. See, e.g., Friedman, supra note 82, at 674–80.

158. Mishler and Sheehan, supra note 98, at 95.

159. See id.

160. See id. at 97–98.

161. But see Terri Jennings Peretti, *In Defense of a Political Court* 84–132 (1999) for an apparently contrary analysis. Some of Peretti's concerns, such as whether justices accurately represent the views of the presidents who appoint them, are not relevant to the argument I make here. See id. at 111–31. But Peretti appears to ignore the conclusions of the Mishler and Sheehan study for the post-1981 period. See id. at 101, 178.

162. See Mishler and Sheehan, supra note 98.

163. For criticism, see, e.g., Howard Gillman, *The Votes that Counted* (2001); Jack M. Balkin, Bush v. Gore *and the Boundary Between Law and Politics*, 110 Yale L. J. 1407 (2001); Michael Klarman, Bush v. Gore *through the Lens of Constitutional History*, 89 Cal. L. Rev. 1721 (2001); Louis Michael Seidman, *What's So Bad About* Bush v. Gore? *An Essay on Our Unsettled Election*, 47 Wayne L. Rev. 953 (2001).

164. See Chemerinsky, supra note 117, at 86–87 n. 195; Friedman, supra note 82, at 624–25. For a lengthy and interesting discussion, see Peretti, supra note 161, at 161–88.

165.   See Chemerinsky, supra note 82; Chemerinsky, supra note 117; Sager, supra note 68; Friedman, supra note 82; Brown, supra note 92.

166.   See Brown, supra note 92, at 552; Chemerinsky, supra note 82, at 1231–33; Friedman, supra note 82, at 617–20; Sager, supra note 65.

167.   See Brown, supra note 92, at 553–56; Friedman, supra note 82, at 625. For example, while Friedman acknowledges that the Constitution has become more majoritarian over time, see id. at 620–22, he ultimately rejects the relevance of constitutional change, maintaining that although the Constitution has changed in certain respects, the framers' theory "that a constitution must divide and balance power to protect liberty" has endured. Id. at 625 (footnote omitted).

168.   See Griffin, supra note 23; Griffin, supra note 69.

169.   For the idea of governing regimes, see Mark J. Richards and Herbert M. Kritzer, *Jurisprudential Regimes in Supreme Court Decision Making*, 96 Am. Pol. Sci. Rev. 305, 307–8 (2002); Karen Orren and Stephen Skowronek, *Regimes and Regime Building in American Government: A Review of Literature on the 1940s*, 113 Pol. Sci. Q. 689 (1998–99). See also Bruce Ackerman, 1 *We The People: Foundations* (1991); Tushnet, *Foreword*, supra note 5, at 34.

170.   For evidence on the historical commitment to this principle, see Gordon S. Wood, *The Radicalism of the American Revolution* 243 (1992).

171.   Here I follow some suggestive remarks by Brian Barry. See Brian Barry, *Political Argument* 268–74 (1965).

172.   See Griffin, *Judicial Supremacy*, supra note 12, at 289–91.

173.   Quoted in Klinkner and Smith, supra note 125, at 144.

174.   Quoted in id. at 148.

175.   See William E. Forbath, *Caste, Class, and Equal Citizenship*, 98 Mich. L. Rev. 1, 18–19 (1999).

176.   Wood, supra note 170, at 106.

177.   See id. at 196–212.

178.   See id. at 243–70, 287–305.

179.   Id. at 230.

180.   See id. at 365–69.

181.   See William W. Freehling, *The Road to Disunion: Secessionists at Bay, 1776–1854* 122–26 (1990) (views of Jefferson); Drew R. McCoy, *The Last of the Fathers: James Madison and the Republican Legacy* 5 (1989) (views of Madison).

182.   See George M. Fredrickson, *White Supremacy: A Comparative Study in American and South African History* 154–55 (1981).

183.   See William E. Nelson, *The Legalist Reformation: Law, Politics, and Ideology in New York, 1920–1980* 3–4 (2001).

184.   See id. at 3.

185. Id. at 4.

186. See Keyssar, supra note 95.

187. Id. at xxii.

188. See id. at 45–52, 67–76.

189. Id. at xxiii–xxiv.

190. See James Gray Pope, *Republican Moments: The Role of Direct Popular Power in the American Constitutional Order*, 139 U. Pa. L. Rev. 287 (1990).

191. Frank I. Michelman, *Brennan and Democracy* 40 (1999) (footnote omitted).

192. See Gutmann and Thompson, supra note 118, at 26. See also Eisgruber, supra note 18, at 19.

193. See Robert A. Dahl, *Democracy and Its Critics* (1989).

194. See Thomas Christiano, *The Rule of the Many: Fundamental Issues in Democratic Theory* (1996).

195. See Rex Martin, *A System of Rights* (1993).

196. See Griffin, *Judicial Supremacy*, supra note 12, at 296–99.

197. Pub. L. No. 88–352, 78 Stat. 241.

198. Pub. L. No. 89–110, 79 Stat. 437.

199. Pub. L. No. 101–336, 104 Stat. 327. See the discussion in Griffin, *Judicial Supremacy*, supra note 12, at 284–87.

200. See Forbath, supra note 175, at 23–61.

201. Nelson, supra note 183, at 316.

202. See Griffin, *Judicial Supremacy*, supra note 12, at 299.

203. See id.

204. See id. at 299–301.

205. See id. at 301–13.

206. In *Nevada Dept. of Human Resources v. Hibbs*, 123 S. Ct. 1972 (2003), the Court refused to follow Boerne, Kimel, and Garrett in upholding the money damages provision of the Family and Medical Leave Act of 1993. In general terms, the Court was following the institutional role I advocate here by upholding an act of Congress that created rights that serve constitutional values. However, the Court did not signal any retreat from the kind of strict scrutiny of legislation enforcing Section 5 of the Fourteenth Amendment embodied in those three cases. The same is true of the Court's decision in *Tennessee v. Lane*, 124 S. Ct. 1978 (2004), which held that states were liable for money damages under Title II of the Americans with Disabilities Act.

207. The debate occurred in the online journal *Slate*. See *Slate Dialogue: Assisted Suicide*: Michael McConnell vs. Ronald Dworkin, April 9–June 19, 1997(hereinafter cited as Slate Dialogue) (copy on file with author).

208. 521 U.S. 707 (1997).

209. See Slate Dialogue, supra note 207.

210. Id. at Message 4.

211. Id.

212. Id.

213. Id.

214. Id.

215. Id.

216. See id. at Message 5.

217. Id.

218. See id.

219. See id. at Message 1.

220. See id. at Message 3.

221. Id. at Message 6.

222. Id. at Message 7.

223. See Farber and Sherry, supra note 9, at 138.

224. The Texas abortion law was adopted in 1854. See *Roe v. Wade*, 410 U.S. at 119.

225. I have elaborated on this point in Griffin, supra note 23 and Griffin, supra note 69. A clear example is the Voting Rights Act of 1965. See Keyssar, supra note 95.

226. In *Lawrence v. Texas*, 123 S. Ct. 2472 (2003), the Court ruled that the liberty protected by the Due Process Clause of the Fourteenth Amendment extended to private homosexual conduct and rendered unconstitutional laws prohibiting sodomy. I would not conclude from this case that the Court has an advantage over the political branches in deciding rights claims. I agree with Jack Balkin that "*Lawrence* continues a well known tendency of the Court—It follows larger political and cultural trends, and declares a legal prohibition or practice unconstitutional only when most states have already repealed or greatly limited it." Jack Balkin, *Processes of Constitutional Decisionmaking*, 2003 Supplement 261 (2003). Thus, most of the work involved in promoting gay rights and striking down laws prohibiting sodomy occurred in the larger democratic polity and was certainly not led by the Court.

227. Cass R. Sunstein, *Liberal Constitutionalism and Liberal Justice: A Response*, 72 Tex. L. Rev. 305, 311 (1993).

228. These next few paragraphs are also by way of answering Barry Friedman's sensitive essay, *Historicizing Constitutional Theory* (2002) (unpublished article on file with author). Friedman makes the reasonable request that a theory of judicial review "be able to explain in some coherent way why the cases are different." Id. at 13. That is, why was vigorous judicial review justifiable in the past, but not in the present? My answer to this important question relies on the idea that the United States was not always a democracy, or, at least, that it was not always a democracy of rights.

229. See *United States v. Carolene Products Co.*, 304 U.S. 144 (1938).

230. See id. at 153–54 n. 4.

231. See id.

232. See id.

233. Pub. L. No. 88–352, 78 Stat. 241.

234. Pub. L. No. 89–110, 79 Stat. 437.

235. See Silverstein, supra note 142, at 162–63.

236. See Griffin, *Judicial Supremacy*, supra note 12, at 284.

237. See id. at 284–87.

238. See id. at 291–93.

239. Pub. L. No. 101–336, 104 Stat. 327 (1990).

240. See Tushnet, supra note 124, at 168.

241. See *Morrison, Garrett,* and *Bush v. Gore.*

242. See Klinkner and Smith, supra note 125, at 339–43.

243. For discussion and examples, see id. at 286–89.

244. Pub. L. No. 89–110, 79 Stat. 437.

245. 446 U.S. 55 (1980).

246. 465 U.S. 555 (1984).

247. 490 U.S. 642 (1989).

248. Pub. L. No. 103–41, 107 Stat. 1488 (1993).

249. 521 U.S. 507 (1997).

250. 528 U.S. 62 (2000).

251. 120 S. Ct. 1740 (2000).

252. Pub. L. No. 101–336, 104 Stat. 327 (1990).

253. 121 S. Ct. 955 (2001).

254. See Friedman, supra note 228.

255. See id. at 15.

256. See id. at 15–16.

257. See Griffin, *Judicial Supremacy*, supra note 12, at 313.

258. Thus, the recent decision by the Court in *Grutter v. Bollinger*, 123 S. Ct. 2325 (2003), which upheld affirmative action at the University of Michigan Law School, should not be taken to establish a new consensual baseline for this area of policy. Conservatives will continue to work to limit or eliminate affirmative action through state law and judicial appointments.

259. See Farber and Sherry, supra note 9, at 140–60.

260. See Eisgruber, supra note 18.

261. See generally Farber and Sherry, supra note 9.

262. Id. at 145.

263. Id.

264. Id.

265. See id.

266. Id. at 141.

267. Id.

268. Id.

269. See id. at 146.

270. See id. at 145.

271. On the idea of contextualized constitutional theory, see Griffin, supra note 69, at 2156–62.

272. Eisgruber, supra note 18, at 68.

273. Id. at 54.

274. Id.

275. Id. at 58.

276. Id. at 64 (footnote omitted).

277. Id. at 66.

278. See the summary in id. at 71.

279. Id.

280. See id. at 57.

281. See id.

282. See id.

283. Id.

284. Id. at 60.

285. Id. at 59.

286. See id. at 139.

287. Id. at 201.

288. Id.

289. See id. at 49–52.

290. Pub. L. No. 88–352, 78 Stat. 241 (1964).

291. Pub. L. No. 89–110, 79 Stat. 437 (1965).

292. Pub. L. No. 101–336, 104 Stat. 327 (1990).

293. See, e.g., Garrett Epps, *To An Unknown God: Religious Freedom on Trial* 215–41 (2001); John T. Noonan, Jr., *Narrowing the Nation's Power* 15–40 (2002).

294. Eisgruber, supra note 18, at 73 (footnote omitted).

295. Id. at 74 (footnote omitted).

296. 347 U.S. 483 (1954).

297. 377 U.S. 533 (1964).

298. See Griffin, *Judicial Supremacy*, supra note 12.

299. Prison reform litigation might be one example, given that prisoners are barred from voting in some states. See Christopher L. Eisgruber, *Constitutional Self-Government and Judicial Review: A Reply to Five Critics*, 37 U.S.F.L. Rev. 115, 133 (2002).

Jackson: A Democracy of Rights: The Dark Side?

1. Although all of these struggles have contributed to what we have become, I share Professor Griffin's sense that the struggle of African Americans for what he calls "meaningful citizenship" has played a central role in widespread acceptance of equality ideals of contemporary American democracy.

2. For analysis of some of the doubtful components of the Court's analysis, see William W. Van Alstyne, *A Critical Guide to* Marbury v. Madison, 1969 Duke L. J. 1.

3. See, e.g., *United States v. Morrison*, 529 U.S. 598, 607 (2000) ("Due respect for the decisions of a coordinate branch of Government demands that we invalidate a congressional enactment only upon a plain showing that Congress has exceeded its constitutional bounds.").

4. See, e.g., *Lawrence v. Texas*, 539 U.S. 558, 579–80 (2003) (O'Connor, J., concurring in the judgment) (noting that economic legislation or tax laws normally pass constitutional muster because they are scrutinized under rational basis review, and citing, inter alia, *Williamson v. Lee Optical of Okla., Inc*, 348 U.S. 483 (1955); *Denver Area Educ. Telecommunications Consortium v. FCC*, 518 U.S. 727, 740–53 (1996) (emphasizing need for "flexibility necessary to allow government to respond to very serious practical problems" in analyzing First Amendment challenges to cable television regulations and upholding statutory provision permitting cable operators to prohibit broadcast of "patently offensive" or "indecent" material)).

5. Query, though, whether judicial invalidation of statutes has increased when compared to the pace and volume of enactment of federal legislation.

6. I do not agree with Professor Griffin's suggestion that the "law/politics" divide in *Marbury* was ever about the Court itself avoiding decision of politically controversial issues. Chief Justice Marshall was not saying that the Court should avoid politically controversial issues in confining itself to the realm of law. Rather, as Marshall well knew, his decision of the question of Marbury's commission was quite politically controversial; his effort was to define a realm of law within which, no matter how controversial, it was the Court's duty to act.

7. These processes include the felt obligation to offer principled reasons for overruling prior decisions, see, e.g. *Payne v. Tennessee*, 501 U.S. 808, 827–30 (1991); *Lawrence v. Texas*, 539 U.S. at 566–78 (explaining reasons for overruling *Bowers*); see also *Planned Parenthood v. Casey*, 505 U.S. 833, 855–61 (1992) (O'Connor, J., Kennedy, J., and Souter, J.), and establishing categorical doctrinal rules to resolve, and constrain, future decision making. See, e.g., *Employment Division v. Smith*, 494 U.S. 872, 882–90 (1991) (rejecting balancing under compelling governmental interest test and holding that First Amendment does not require accommodation for religiously motivated excuses from compliance with generally applicable, valid neutral statutes). The efficacy of the reason-giving

requirement and of doctrinal limits may reasonably be questioned; yet their existence provides at least a framework for argument that may on occasion constrain judicial decision making.

8. See *The Federalist Papers 81* (referring to the importance of independent judges, faced with "bad laws," to exercise a "disposition to temper and moderate" their application); *The Federalist 78* ("the firmness of the judicial magistracy is of vast importance in mitigating the severity and confining the operation" of "unjust and partial laws" even where there has not been infraction of the Constitution).

9. For James Madison, the availability of any Article III courts to mitigate errors in fact-finding affecting federal rights was also of importance. See Richard H. Fallon, Daniel J. Meltzer, and David L Shapiro, *Hart and Wechsler's Federal Courts and the Federal System* 8 (5th ed., 2003) (summarizing Farrand's description of Madison's position in the Convention). The availability of Article III review has been significantly restricted in recent years, not only through the Court's exercise of its certiorari jurisdiction and its development of limitations on habeas corpus but also through congressional action restricting the opportunity to vindicate federal rights of criminal procedure on state post conviction review. See Anti-Terrorism and Effective Death Penalty Act of 1996, Pub. L 104–132, 110 Stat. 1214, codified in part in 28 U.S.C. §2254 (d), (e). Congress's effort to restrict vindication of rights of criminal procedure ought to give one further pause about any claim that Congress has become more rights oriented than the Courts.

10. See U.S. Const. Art. I, §§2; 3, Art. II, §1; Art. VI.

11. Cf. Gary Jeffrey Jacobsohn, *Apple of Gold: Constitutionalism in Israel and the United States* 3–4 (1993) (arguing for Lincoln's understanding that equality was a constitutional aspiration needing fulfillment).

12. See Vicki C. Jackson, *Holistic Interpretation, Comparative Constitutionalism and Fiss-ian Freedoms*, 58 U. Miami L. Rev. 265, 271–74 (2003)

13. See generally Barry Friedman, Marbury *in the Modern Era: Mediated Popular Constitutionalism*, 101 Mich. L. Rev. 2596 (2003); Barry Friedman, *Dialogue and Judicial Review*, 91 Mich. L. Rev. 577, 607–14 (1993).

14. Notwithstanding the significant impact of democratization on the national and state political processes in the United States, legislative and executive bodies are not well situated to engage in principled decision making over any long-term period. This is not to say that they do not occasionally take principled positions, but it is not the bread and butter of daily life in either of these branches, in contrast to the work of the courts.

15. See *Eldred v. Ashcroft*, 537 U.S. 186 (2002).

16. See Vicki C. Jackson, *Ambivalent Resistance and Comparative Constitutionalism: Opening Up the Conversation About Proportionality, Rights and Federalism*, 1 U. Pa. J. Const. L. 583 (1999); Vicki C. Jackson, *Federalism and the Court: Congress as the Audi-*

ence?, 574 Annals 145 (2001) (suggesting that the Court could and should give more consideration to considered views of Congress while retaining its traditional role as interpreter of the Constitution); cf. Robert C. Post and Reva B. Siegel, *Equal Protection by Law: Federal Antidiscrimination Legislation After* Morrison *and* Kimel, 110 Yale L. J. 441 (2000) (arguing that equal protection guarantees have been best developed when Court acts in some form of institutional partnership with Congress in developing and effectuating meaning of constitutional rights); Robert C. Post and Reva B. Siegel, *Legislative Constitutionalism and Section Five Power: Policentric Interpretation of the Family and Medical Leave Act*, 112 Yale L. J. 1943 (2003) (arguing that it is legitimate for Congress to legislate under Section 5 of the Fourteenth Amendment on different understandings of the Constitution than the Court, but that the Court is not bound by Congress's understanding in evaluating constitutionality of law); Robert C. Post and Reva B. Siegel, *Popular Constitutionalism, Departmentalism, and Judicial Supremacy*, 92 Calif. L. Rev. 1027 (2004) (arguing that judicial supremacy and popular constitutionalism may coexist in ongoing dialogue about relation between constitutional law and the Constitution).

17. See William Cohen, *Congressional Power to Interpret Due Process and Equal Protection*, 27 Stan. L. Rev. 603 (1975).

18. It is possible that Professor Griffin views the federalism issues in the Court's recent decisions (in *Boerne, Morrison, Kimel*, and *Garrett*) to be a red herring, and not a good or correct explanation of what the Court is really about. There is much to be said for the proposition that the Court is not consistently devoted to federalism issues, and that the Court has at times seemed more systematically hostile to the role of courts in protecting certain kinds of individual rights. See, e.g., Jed Rubenfeld, *The Anti- Antidiscrimination Agenda*, 111 Yale L. J. 1141 (2002). But that does not mean that federalism plays no role in the decisions in which the Court discusses it.

19. As Professor Cohen noted, there were two obvious problems with the one-way ratchet: First, if the ratchet is founded on special institutional competence, why could it not work in both directions? Justice Brennan's answer lies, interestingly, in an application of a "doubtful case" rule, under which courts should only invalidate laws if the unconstitutionality is clear, leaving the legislature room to exercise its competence to find a violation where a court would not, but where a Court has found a violation, given the restraint imposed by the presumption of constitutionality, it would be very unusual—though not impossible—for a legislature to enact laws based on additional evidence on which a different conclusion could be reached. See *Oregon v. Mitchell*, 400 U.S. 212, 249 n. 31 (1970) (Brennan, J., concurring and dissenting in part) (implying that if Congress "unearth[ed] new evidence" and enacted its own version of a statute which the Court had found to violate the Fourteenth Amendment, the new act might be upholdable). Second, the ratchet theory does not account for the possibility that rights could be in

conflict, e.g., where a statute provides for gag orders against the press in criminal cases. Cohen, supra note 17, at 606–8, 619.

20. These decisions, such as Reynolds v. Sims, 377 U.S. 533 (1964), resulted in prompt, major change in state legislative apportionment to the benefit of the democratic legitimacy and vigor of state governments. That is not to deny that the apportionment cases have had their own dark side, in the unremitting emphasis on mathematical exactitude to the exclusion of other factors, in the thinness of the concept of democratic participation they represent, and perhaps in legitimizing excessive or unwarranted judicial interventions in elections. It is, though, to claim that the Court's intervention in the 1960s to dislodge severely malapportioned and incumbent-protecting state legislatures toward more democratic forms of participation was a necessary and beneficial one. Professor Griffin does not take issue with such decisions but suggests that (in part due to changes they may have encouraged) vigorous judicial review today is unwarranted. That we have a more inclusive democracy does not, however, mean that there is no role for vigorous judicial protection of rights, especially for unpopular minorities.

21. See, e.g., *Cook v. Gralike*, 531 U.S. 510 (2001) (invalidating state law requiring ballot labels concerning candidate position on term limits); *United States v. Eichman*, 496 U.S. 310 (1990) (invalidating national statute prohibiting flag burning).

22. 539 U.S. 558 (2003).

23. Cf. Jack Balkin, *What* Brown *Teaches Us About Constitutional Theory*, 90 Va. L. Rev. 1537, 1542–44 (2004) (noting that at "the time *Lawrence* was decided, the movement for gay rights had gained more success in winning over popular opinion . . . in favor of decriminalizing gay or lesbian sexual relationships than the corresponding movement for desegregation had achieved when *Brown* was decided.").

24. On "don't ask don't tell," see 10 U.S.C. §654 (b) (2); see also 10 U.S.C. §654(b) (1) (providing for discharge for engaging in homosexual acts). On DOMA, see the Defense of Marriage Act, Pub. L. No. 104–199, 110 Stat. 2419 (1996).

25. Thus, quoting from the joint opinion in Casey, the *Lawrence* Court wrote: " '[M]atters, involving the most intimate and personal choices a person may make in a lifetime, choices central to personal dignity and autonomy, are central to the liberty protected by the Fourteenth Amendment. At the heart of liberty is the right to define one's own concept of existence, of meaning, of the universe, and of the mystery of human life. Beliefs about these matters could not define the attributes of personhood were they formed under compulsion of the State.' Persons in a homosexual relationship may seek autonomy for these purposes, just as heterosexual persons do." 539 U.S. at 574 (quoting *Casey*, 505 U.S. at 851). The *Lawrence* Court went on to find that the continued existence of *Bowers* "demeans the lives of homosexual persons," id. at 575, and overruled the case.

26. The claim here is in part an empirical one, though reinforced by recent litigation

involving detention of suspected terrorists, in which over a close to two-year period the Congress was silent as the administration asserted the power indefinitely to hold, incommunicado and without lawyers, U.S. citizens in the United States. See *Hamdi v. Rumsfeld*, 124 S.Ct. 2633 (2004).

For thoughtful exploration of the complexity of the relationships between popular opinion and judicial decisions, see e.g., Barry Friedman, Marbury *in the Modern Era: Mediated Popular Constitutionalism*, 101 Mich. L. Rev. 2596 (discussing public opinion's influence on the Court and the Court's capacity to influence public opinion). Although as both Friedman and Michael Klarman have shown, court decisions may create popular backlashes, see Michael J. Klarman, *From Jim Crow to Civil Rights: The Supreme Court and the Struggle for Racial Equality* (2004), we must not minimize the ideological impact of *Brown* in crystallizing views outside the South against racial segregation and in encouraging a rights consciousness among African Americans that facilitated the assertion of equality claims. See also William N. Eskridge, Jr., *Some Effects of Identity Based Social Movements on Constitutional Law in the Twentieth Century*, 100 Mich. L. Rev. 2062, 2388-90 (2002) (arguing that Court's most important contributions have been in protecting unpopular minorities from brutalization at a time when members of the particular group are too weak and unpopular to use political processes for their advancement).

27. Cf. Eskridge, supra note 26, at 2406. ("It is fashionable on both the Left and Right to denigrate judges as biased, imperial, or impotent. . . . But judges, especially those on the nation's highest court, bring to identity issues the virtues of intelligence, procedural wisdom, and as much impartiality as life tenure can give a human being. In reading thousands of pages of oral arguments, internal memoranda, and conference notes for the Supreme Court in [identity-based social movement] cases, I was most impressed by all the Justices' seriousness and the ability of most of them to grow beyond the perspectives they brought to the Court.")

28. See Christopher Eisgruber, *Constitutional Self-government and Judicial Review: A Reply to Five Critics*, 37 U.S. F. L. Rev. 115 (2002).

29. See id. at 144-48 (life tenure enhances disinterested decision making); 134-35 (implying that, in contrast to voters, the position of judges encourages distinction between first-order beliefs about behavior and second-order beliefs about government conduct; suggesting that the voting booth "may lead voters to mistake self-interest for moral value or to act on First-Order moral values at the expense of Second-Order ones").

30. See Alexander M. Bickel, *The Least Dangerous Branch* 26 (1962) ("[Courts'] insulation and the marvelous mystery of time give courts the capacity to appeal to men's better natures, to call forth their aspirations, which may have been forgotten in the mo-

ment's hue and cry. This is what Justice Stone called the opportunity for 'the sober second thought.'") (quoting Harlan F. Stone, *The Common Law in the United States*, 50 Harv. L. Rev. 4, 25 (1936)).

31. See 50 U.S.C. §1861 § (b)–(d) (authorizing warrants for books, papers and records "for investigation . . . to protect against international terrorism" and providing that "No person shall disclose to any other person (other than those persons necessary to produce the tangible things under this section) that the Federal Bureau of Investigation has sought or obtained tangible things under this section"); see also American Library Association Resolution on the USA Patriot Act, at http://www.ala.org (accessed October 30, 2004) (expressing opposition to certain provisions of the Patriot Act). Consider also the congressional oversight of the Census Bureau's efforts to improve the way in which it recorded persons in the 2000 census, an oversight seen by some as an attempt to thwart the Census Bureau's quest to avoid undercounting minority residents. See Steven A. Holmes, *New Jersey Is a Battleground as States Inherit Census Fight*, N.Y. Times, June 6, 2000, A1; Steven A. Holmes, *Republicans Keep Pressing Census Bureau*, N.Y. Times, Aug. 30 2000, A16.

32. Many of its most critiqued recent decisions invalidating federal laws have left the statute's substantive application intact but prohibited use of a particularly effective remedy, i.e., suits by private individuals directly against the state for monetary relief. See, e.g., *Kimel v. Fla. Bd. of Regents*, 528 U.S. 62 (2000); *Ala. Board of Trustees of Univ. of Alabama v. Garrett*, 531 U.S. 356 (2001). In more recent cases, moreover, the Court has relaxed the stringency of its review of such provisions and upheld application of private remedies against states under the Family and Medical Leave Act and under Title II of the Americans with Disabilities Act. See *Nev. Dept of Human Resources v. Hibbs*, 538 U.S. 721 (2003); *Tennessee v. Lane*, 124 S. Ct. 1978 (2004). Even *United States v. Morrison*, 529 U.S. 598 (2000) does not suggest any constitutional infirmity with state action to provide victims of gender-motivated assaults with damages through causes of action. See Julie Goldscheid, *Advancing Equality in Domestic Violence Law Reform*, 11 Am. U. J. Gender Soc. Pol'y & L. 417, 421 (2003) (noting that many states have laws that "create or authorize civil remedies for gender-bias crimes" and questioning importance of civil rights remedy compared with other forms of legal and social intervention); see also Julie Goldscheid and Risa E. Kaufman, *Seeking Redress for Gender-Based Bias Crimes—Charting New Ground in Familiar Legal Territory*, 6 Mich. J. Race & L. 265, 270–71 (2001) (describing existing state laws and efforts in light of *Morrison* to enact additional ones, providing civil rights remedies for gender-bias crimes).

33. For elaboration of the idea of judicial review based on just principles or political morality, see, e.g., Ronald Dworkin, *The Forum of Principle*, 56 N.Y. U. L. Rev. 469, 516–18 (1979); see also Bickel, supra note 30, at 58 (judicial review as "the principled

process of enunciating and applying certain enduring values of our society"). For Bickel, when courts adjudicated on the merits they needed to be principled; but, he argued, courts should sometimes exercise the power to not decide.

34. To say that the Court should engage in a different form of review for legislation enacted under conditions of single party dominance than under divided government, which might be an implication of his focus on divided government, would, if carried to its full extent, require a distinctive approach to review of legislation enacted during periods of actual divided government and those enacted during periods of single party dominance. This might be an interesting approach to explore, but one more fine-grained than what I understand Professor Griffin to be proposing.

Seidman, *Marbury* and the Authoritarian Straddle

1. See Jesse H. Choper, *Judicial Review and the National Political Process* 175, 263 (1980) (arguing that political control over federalism and separation of powers questions has not led to centralized autocracy).

2. Akhil Reed Amar, *Foreword: The Document and the Doctrine*, 114 Harv. L. Rev. 26, 27 (2000).

3. For a sophisticated and nuanced statement of the standard view, see John Rawls, *Political Liberalism* 224–25 (1993) (arguing that "[a]s far as possible, the knowledge and ways of reasoning that ground our affirming the principles of justice and their application to constitutional essentials and basic justice are to rest on the plain truths now widely accepted, or available to citizens generally").

4. See Herbert Wechsler, *Towards Neutral Principles of Constitutional Law*, 73 Harv. L. Rev. 1 (1959).

5. See Ronald Dworkin, *Freedom's Law: The Moral Reading of the American Constitution* 10 (1996) (arguing that principled judges may not read their own moral convictions into the Constitution).

6. 5 U.S. (1 Cranch) 137 (1803).

7. See, e.g., Alexander Bickel, *The Least Dangerous Branch: The Supreme Court at the Bar of Politics* 1–14 (2d ed., 1986); William W. Van Alstyne, *A Critical Guide to* Marbury v. Madison, Duke L. Rev. 1 (1969).

8. 446 U.S. 55 (1980).

9. 465 U.S. 555 (1980).

10. 490 U.S. 642 (1989).

11. 521 U.S. 507 (1997).

12. 528 U.S. 62 (2000).

13. See 42 U.S.C. 2000aa.

14. 42 U.S.C. 2000a et seq.

15.   42 U.S.C. 12101 et seq.

16.   See David E. Bernstein, *Only One Place of Redress: African Americans, Labor Regulations, and the Courts: From Reconstruction to the New Deal* (2001).

17.   Ring Lardner, "The Young Immigrants," in *The Ring Lardner Reader* 411, 426 (Maxwell Geismar, ed., 1963). For an explanation by a real constitutional scholar of why we should not shut up, see Mark Tushnet, *"Shut Up He Explained,"* 95 Nw. U. L. Rev. 907 (2001).

Index

The authorized representative in the EU for product safety and compliance is:
Mare Nostrum Group
B.V Doelen 72
4831 GR Breda
The Netherlands

www.ingramcontent.com/pod-product-compliance
Lightning Source LLC
Chambersburg PA
CBHW030922180526
45163CB00002B/437